SOCIAL POLICIES AND SOCIAL CONTROL

New perspectives on the 'not-so-big society'

Edited by Malcolm Harrison and Teela Sanders

First published in Great Britain in 2014 by

Policy Press
University of Bristol
6th Floor
Howard House
Queen's Avenue
Clifton
Bristol BS8 1SD
UK
Tel +44 (0)117 331 5020
Fax +44 (0)117 331 5367
e-mail tpp-info@bristol.ac.uk
www.policypress.co.uk

North American office:
Policy Press
c/o The University of Chicago Press
1427 East 60th Street
Chicago, IL 60637, USA
t: +1 773 702 7700
f: +1 773-702-9756
e:sales@press.uchicago.edu
www.press.uchicago.edu

British Library Cataloguing in Publication Data
A catalogue record for this book is available from the British Library

Library of Congress Cataloging-in-Publication Data
A catalog record for this book has been requested

ISBN 978 1 44731 074 7 hardcover

Cover design by Andrew Corbett
Front cover illustration kindly supplied bt Steve Bell
Printed and bound in Great Britain by CPI Group (UK) Ltd,
Croydon, CR0 4YY
Policy Press uses environmentally responsible print partners

Contents

List of boxes and figures

Boxes

Figures

List of abbreviations

ARC	application registration card
ASBO	Anti-Social Behaviour Order
CCG	clinical commissioning group
DBD	donation after brain death
DCD	donation after circulatory death
DLA	Disability Living Allowance
DRR	Drug Rehabilitation Requirement
DTTO	Drug Treatment and Testing Order
EIA	Equality Impact Assessment
ESA	Employment and Support Allowance
EU	European Union
HLA	human leukocyte antigen
IB	Incapacity Benefit
JSA	Jobseeker's Allowance
LHA	Local Housing Allowance
LINk	Local Involvement Network
NDC	New Deal for Communities
NEW-ADAM	New England and Wales Arrestee Drug Abuse Monitoring
PDU	problematic drug user
PIP	Personal Independence Payment
QCT	quasi-compulsory treatment
RSL	registered social landlord
SAT	standard assessment task
UK	United Kingdom
UKBA	United Kingdom Border Agency
UKDPC	United Kingdom Drug Policy Commission
VAT	Value Added Tax
VBS	Vetting and Barring Scheme
WCA	Work Capability Assessment
WRAG	work-related activity group

Preface and acknowledgements

This book breaks some new ground by discussing social control issues across a variety of social policy domains, against a backdrop of major welfare restructuring under the UK coalition government and its immediate predecessors. There have been considerable challenges for the authors in trying to grasp and interpret coalition plans and programmes that were developing at speed on numerous fronts, and were still being elaborated as chapters were completed. We hope that discussions contain relatively few misunderstandings on details, but if there are limitations then these may reflect the difficulties of hitting what was sometimes a 'moving target', alongside the inevitable implications of compression when describing complex situations. Chapter drafts were being finalised variously from late 2012 through to the early months of 2013, and editing and selective updating then followed.

As authors chose their own conceptual frameworks and lines of argument, there is considerable variety in approaches and foci. While some passages refer to overtly oppressive disciplinary practices, others touch upon milder persuasions such as the responsibilisation inherent in some user participation arrangements. We hope that diversity of styles and scope will help make the book interesting to a range of readers. Authors were invited to create one or more summary boxes within their chapters to give swift impressions of content or themes, but these complement rather than replace the main texts. As editors, we also encouraged contributors to include appropriate sources that supplemented conventional academic ones or their own research findings. Thus, newspaper and website commentaries and reports are sometimes referred to where offering suitable illustrations or highlighting recent situations. Individual authors take responsibility for their own chapters, although we have encouraged reference to some general themes.

We are grateful to the many people who have encouraged this enterprise. Valued support has come from the publishers and the School of Sociology and Social Policy at Leeds. The reviewers appointed by Policy Press provided numerous useful suggestions. On behalf of all the authors, we also want to thank friends, colleagues, partners and other family members who have assisted or made space for the writing. An endnote to Chapter One mentions specific help generously given by Peter Dwyer, John Flint, Judy Nixon and Emma Wincup at an important stage.

We want to thank Steve Bell for permission to reproduce one of his cartoons on the cover of the book. Marx appears there transformed into Cameron, while the well-known aspiration associated with Marxian and socialistic thinking – *from each according to their abilities and to each according to their needs* – is superseded by a statement that neatly challenges the advocates of today's UK public policies. The cartoon is a brilliantly critical image for present times, not least in relation to social policies. Thanks also to Ray Harrison, for reminding us soon after the cartoon first appeared of how outstanding it was.

Malcolm Harrison and Teela Sanders,
August 2013

Notes on contributors

Kate Brown is a Lecturer in Social Policy at the University of York. Her research interests relate to ideas about vulnerability and the governance of vulnerable people's lives. Before returning to university to study for her PhD at the University of Leeds, Kate worked in the voluntary sector for around 10 years, supporting vulnerable groups such as young people and women who sell sex, young drug users and families affected by domestic violence.

Laura Davies is a Research Fellow on the research programme 'Following Young Fathers' at the University of Leeds, funded by the Economic and Social Research Council (ESRC), which aims to develop understandings of the changing lives, relationships and support needs of young fathers. Her PhD thesis was titled *Earning and caring in families that have experienced divorce: A study of family law, social policy and family practices.* This explored experiences of a sample of parents in managing employment and the care of their children after a divorce or separation, in the context of a changing welfare landscape. Key research interests include care ethics, welfare to work, family policy, policy evaluation, intergenerational exchange, sociology of the family, gender and lifecourse transitions.

Malcolm Harrison retired in 2010 from a chair in Housing and Social Policy at the University of Leeds, and is currently an Emeritus Professor there, based in the School of Sociology and Social Policy. He has published and taught in urban studies and planning, social policy, and housing, with particular contributions around ethnic relations and difference. Current writing interests include social control and options for property-based defensible welfare systems.

Laura Hemingway has taught and researched in housing, social policy and disability studies since 2003, and carried out in-depth research on disability, housing, home and access to owner-occupation for her PhD at Leeds University. She has also worked on a major review of university performance in relation to disabled people, covering policies, responses and access issues for England and Wales. Laura's publications include contributions to the *Disability Archive* and the journal *Disability and Society* (2010) and her monograph *Disabled people and housing* (Policy Press, 2011).

Jenny McNeill is a researcher who recently gained her PhD in Social Policy at Nottingham Trent University. Her research interests include housing, homelessness, welfare and social exclusion. Jenny's thesis explored the role of promoting employability in the resettlement of single homeless people. She has worked with homelessness charities as a researcher and as a volunteer, and has published recently in the journal *Social Policy and Society*.

Ana Manzano is a Research Fellow at the University of Leeds, with experience of applying realist evaluation in healthcare, an area in which she has published on standards and principles. She is interested in exploring the relationship between policy and practice, and the role of frontline practitioners in programme implementation.

Doug Martin is Deputy Programme Manager in Child and Family Studies at the University of Leeds' Lifelong Learning Centre. He has worked in the National Health Service, schools and children and young people's services. Doug led local authority Every Child Matters: Change for Children Programmes before moving to work nationally on the development of 'integrated multi-professional working'. His research and consultancy seeks to cut across traditional professional and service 'silos' that too often fail to recognise children, young people and families' needs. Doug's work focuses on contributing towards positive, integrated, holistic child- and family-centred responses, particularly with those recently labelled 'hard to reach' or 'troubled'.

Gabrielle Mastin completed a PhD in the School of Social Policy and Sociology at the University of Leeds in 2013, exploring the involvement of older people with services and support systems in a local case study area. She is currently working as a researcher for an independent training provider. Her ongoing research interests include old age, social care and service user engagement, and she has publications in the fields of ageing, old age and discrimination.

Mark Monaghan is a Lecturer in Sociology, Social Policy and Crime at the University of Leeds. Mark has researched and published on drug policy. His ESRC-funded PhD studentship followed the scientific and political battles through which cannabis classification decisions were made in the UK in the last decade. His recent monograph *Evidence versus politics: Exploiting research in UK drug policy making?* was published in 2011 by Policy Press. Mark is an Associate Editor of the journal *Evidence & Policy*.

Ruth Patrick is a Postgraduate Researcher in the School of Sociology and Social Policy at the University of Leeds. Her doctoral research explores the lived experiences of welfare reform in the UK, and her research interests encompass welfare, disability, citizenship and qualitative longitudinal research methods. She is a columnist for *Disability Now*. Ruth's most recent publications include 'All in it together? Disabled people, the coalition and welfare to work' (*Journal of Poverty and Social Justice*, 2012) and 'Work as the primary "duty" of the responsible citizen: a critique of this work-centric approach' (*People, Place & Policy Online*, 2012).

Teela Sanders is a Reader in Sociology at the University of Leeds. Her research focus has been on intersections between gender, regulation and the sex industry, including exploring hidden economies. Her monographs include *Sex work: A risky business* (Willan, 2005) and *Paying for pleasure: Men who buy sex* (Willan, 2008). She co-wrote *Prostitution: Sex work, policy and politics* (Sage, 2009), along with Jane Pitcher and Maggie O'Neill. With Kate Hardy, Teela recently completed a project funded by the ESRC on the UK striptease industry (see *Flexible workers: Labour, regulation and mobility in lap dancing*, forthcoming). An ESRC Follow on Award enabled work with Rosie Campbell to influence Sex Entertainment Venue policies and produce an accessible resource for dancers, with safety and other information.

Ala Sirriyeh is a Lecturer in Sociology in the School of Sociology and Criminology at Keele University. Her research interests include topics related to migration, refugees, children and young people, home and identity. Some of her research has been published in the monograph: *Inhabiting borders, routes home: Youth, gender, asylum* (Ashgate, 2013).

Andrew Wallace is a Senior Lecturer at the University of Lincoln. His main research interests encompass policies of urban renewal, the sociology of community, and class divisions and the reproduction of marginalised and relegated populations. He is the author of *Remaking community?* (Ashgate, 2010).

Part One
Setting the scene

ONE

Introduction

Malcolm Harrison and Teela Sanders

Introducing the focus and purposes of this book

Politicians frequently claim to support liberty and empowerment. Yet governments and political leaders often advocate policies that restrict citizens or seek to persuade them strongly in specific directions. This occurs not only in relation to criminal justice, environmental protection or safety on the roads (as might be expected), but also in various welfare and social security domains where policies have more traditionally been thought of as meeting needs and responding to social rights claims. This collection addresses the recent and present state of play in a variety of UK policy fields as far as disciplinary approaches, penalties, exclusions or service-user responsibilities are concerned. Although social control strategies and practices have had long histories within social policy, there appears to have been some increase since the early 1980s in their attraction, acceptability and perceived salience for mainstream politicians. The authors in this book explore and interpret recent trends and issues, illuminating developments that have crucial effects on freedoms.

Unsurprisingly, the control exerted by governments over individuals has been an enduring topic within social policy debates. An extensive literature has reported on the regulation of behaviours in numerous settings, providing rich research information on histories and outcomes. Yet publications detailing and interpreting social control practices across a range of UK social policy and 'welfare' domains remain relatively rare. This collection sets out to enhance and update what is available in that regard, bringing together new writings that touch upon aspects of social control and persuasion in a diverse array of social policy territories. Contributors consider features and implications of official policies aimed at inhibiting, shaping, managing, disciplining or penalising the behaviours of various categories of people, and comment on assumptions, justifications or conceptual framings that inform practices and approaches. The book focuses especially on recent policy developments and themes, but also acknowledges historical resonances, and particular legacies of governments from the 1980s onwards. The authors understand that forms of social control may occur within many settings, ranging from households to religious organisations, and from private firms to government agencies. The central preoccupations of this volume, however, are with regulatory strategies instituted by or for government, or in collaboration with it. The present chapter starts to set the scene by referring to the control of behaviours, mentioning drivers, ethics and justifications, indicating the social division of social control, and noting some recent developments against the backcloth of welfare state change. There is then a short introduction to the book as a collaborative enterprise.

Studying the control of behaviour

One important focus within this collection is the theme of behaviourism as a growing element in social policy discourses, environments and practices (although individual chapters do not necessarily always describe disciplinary elements of social policies by using the term 'behaviourist'). The controlling and influencing of behaviour often feature explicitly in contemporary political portfolios (see for instance Osborne and Thaler, 2010; Cabinet Office Behavioural Insights Team, 2011), and sections of the book note behaviourism as a growing element within recent and current social policy developments. It is a phenomenon seen in day-to-day practices, repertoires and routines,[1] as well as at the strategy level. Strategies include a variety of coercions or persuasions, while excluding people from support sometimes becomes in itself a perceived key to behaviour alteration. For researchers, behaviourism serves as one useful descriptor that may be deployed when examining how governments, organisations or practitioners seek preferred outcomes in terms of 'behaviour modification', or justify what they do by claiming that particular behavioural results will follow. Focusing on behaviourism can help when reviewing politicians' ambitions and approaches in a variety of policy territories, and the term complements other useful concepts and words when social control is explored.

It is important to add that this book does not adopt or endorse understandings from behaviourist economics or psychology, or seek to justify methods that governments bring forward to incentivise, discipline or 'nudge' populations. Given the intentions behind the volume, specific ideas for controlling or influencing people tend to be viewed here as parts of a spectrum of intervention concepts that need to be evaluated for their potential effects and detailed implications, rather than as understandable elements of some supposedly desirable moral programme. It may sometimes be appropriate for academics to help design or improve social control practices, but for this book such a role generally has low priority. Certainly, it is not taken for granted that behaviourist strategies focused via 'top-down' ideas about individuals are appropriate adjuncts of modernisation, sensible planning or more effective governance. In some of the domains discussed, contributors may prefer to treat governmental approaches as rooted in structural relationships and political power, while recognising the contested nature of interventions that have tightened selectivity, extended criminalisation and increased obligations for many low-income groups. As this collection indicates, when researchers think about behaviourism they need not invoke images of freestanding 'rational' individual decision makers set outside real social contexts, or take on normative roles alongside politicians in developing methods for 'nudging' or penalising people.

Unfortunately, it may go against the dominant political grain in some policy areas to acknowledge that understanding human agency requires observers to fully position behaviours in relation to structural factors, interpersonal relationships, local contexts, complex household strategies, resources and feasible pathways. Already, writing in the New Labour period, Taylor-Gooby (2008, pp 269, 277-8) indicated potential difficulties for some social policy academics in gaining recognition in environments where policy making was increasingly infused by an 'individual rational actor logic'. This shift seems part of a broader reorientation in preoccupations that sometimes embraces somewhat dismissive outlooks on socioeconomic environmental factors, and may imply substituting rather abstract and individualising models of activity for actual group and household histories and perspectives. By including behaviourism as a target topic, the collection indirectly confronts trends in thinking here that affect academia as well as policy making.

No collection of this type can be comprehensive, and there are important gaps that ideally will be filled by other writers (especially regarding the distinctiveness of Northern Ireland, Scotland and Wales, and comparisons with other countries). Furthermore, while coverage in some chapters connects social control with 'difference', there is clearly scope for complementary work making such links more central. Nonetheless, it is hoped that readers will find material here that proves useful for understanding contemporary social control, together with some challenging lines of argument. For people keen to explore further the relationships between criminal justice, crime and social policy, excellent material is available in Wincup (2013). For some ambitious and intriguing work outside Britain, bringing 'developments on the social welfare and crime control fronts into a single analytic frame', see Wacquant's writings (2009, p xx; also 2008). The present volume does not set out separately a preferred agenda for future research or theory development (although see Chapter Thirteen). Nonetheless, the contributions do point to numerous potential sites for empirical investigation of people's experiences as the clients or foci for policies, alongside the merits of mapping and scrutinising behaviourist strategies, their implementation and their impact. At a broader level, perhaps this collection might be seen as offering some components useful to scholars working on theoretically orientated accounts of welfare systems, given the increased significance of persuasion, coercion and containment.

Realities, fears and legitimation

It would be wrong to deny the very real household experiences that underpin some calls for governments to tackle problematic behaviours. There is a very strong case for constraints over various kinds of transgressions, including interpersonal violence, racist harassment, dangerous driving, corrupt financial activities and serious disruptions of the *quiet enjoyment* people should expect in their homes. The political development of social control, however, has not necessarily responded very systematically to the importance, frequency or detailed character of particular problems, to the impact they have on affected individuals or (crucially) to the causes of persistent disorders and dangers.

Various explanations have been offered for increases in governmental interventions over behaviours in Britain, with popular political debate often attributing growth in social regulation to pressing contemporary needs generated by rising threats from criminality, deviance, deliberate worklessness, community failure or family breakdown. Such factors might be argued by some politicians to account not only for the high levels of incarceration in the UK or the strengthened regulatory frameworks now applied to children, but also the increased conditionality applied to areas of 'welfare' support. Yet the shape and weight of policy developments probably owe more to perceptions and priorities among the powerful (or groups and organisations they are keen to show sympathy with) than to precise household experiences or evidence of positive intervention outcomes at grass roots. Nonetheless, some disciplinary approaches attract quite wide support at the level of principle, and the foundations for this deserve comment.

Drivers of popular support for social control may have included some strengthening of fear and intra-class or intra-group hostilities accompanying socioeconomic fragmentation, employment change, population change and uneven development. People's specific fears may be affected by a wide array of factors (for relevant general analysis see Garland, 2001). Examples might include:

- sensationalised and unbalanced press reporting;
- increased crime opportunities created by access to motor vehicles;
- the disappearance of some local employees who were once a positive factor in life at 'street level';
- the growth of imprisoned populations (and consequent high numbers of ex-prisoners);
- the growing 'night-time economy';
- the widespread impact of alcohol and other substance abuse (with manifest failures of repressive criminal justice systems to resolve challenges from drug addiction and its related private enterprises).

Local demands for punitive actions may also reflect a decline of informal mechanisms for social control at neighbourhood level, itself affected by various changes in individualisation, altered degrees of social dependence on residence localities, household composition and turnover rates, services, local employment, income levels, leisure and so forth. In effect, there is a complex mosaic of activities, events and impressions providing bases for concerns among households, and to which substantial street disorders in the coalition government period have added. In some contexts, ideas about misbehaviour appear to overlap with concepts of the undeserving, and it is difficult to separate hostile perceptions of behavioural 'characteristics' from assumptions linked to intra-class demarcations, ethnicity, gender, disability and other differentiations.

Governments (and parts of the media) may play upon rather than discourage negative perceptions of 'less-deserving' people. Piggott and Grover (2009, p 163) have indicated clearly how attempts can be made to construct 'a popular environment' conducive to a retrenchment that bears harshly on disadvantaged groups. Meanwhile, politicians present some minority ways of living as threats to a broader social order, as with government's view of New Age Traveller lifestyles during the Thatcher years, or the supposedly damaging 'self-segregation' practices attributed to minority ethnic groups during the emergence of New Labour's community cohesion policies (Harrison et al, 2005; Flint and Robinson, 2008). Negative visions of specific places have a long history, and misleading accounts of categories of people such as single parents have sometimes been expressed by political actors against locality backcloths (see for instance Clapham et al, 1996, p 33, on the 'babies on benefit' controversy). Recipes offered by politicians and commentators have included a variety of well-rehearsed ideas for interventions designed to change behaviours at both household and neighbourhood levels. Public concerns about misbehaviours also provide political opportunities to challenge social and workplace rights. Thus, Prime Minister Cameron's 'fightback' after the 2011 English riots was reportedly to include a 'new war' on human rights as manifested in European legislation, or on their 'misrepresentation' (Cameron, 2011a).

In UK national politics there is some tendency to incorporate genuine local safety worries within grander visions. The theme of a 'broken society' recently deployed by some politicians exemplifies the ambiguities, vagueness and problems of limited evidence that can occur. It is a potentially complicated social construction capable of contested interpretations from diverse perspectives. A claim about such brokenness, however, cannot be sustained satisfactorily through individualised accounts of the 'irresponsible poor', the 'failing family' or the deviant perpetrators of riotous acts. Actors and actions need to be seen within specific economic, institutional, social, cultural and spatial environments that help condition choices. It is important to consider:

- how particular groups and individuals make sense of their worlds and options;
- the attempts they may make to live in the most rational ways possible;
- the importance of interdependencies;
- the case for assisting independence in ways that fit people's own understandings about needs (for support for the *right to independent living*, see *The Guardian*, comment and letters, 1 March 2012 and 17 May 2012).

Relevant constraints facing households include child poverty and poor educational prospects, illness, negative practices linked to 'difference' (including discrimination), insecurities, low pay and stressful conditions affecting many lawful employment paths, and predations into everyday life by the alcoholic drinks, illegal drugs, gambling and 'loans' industries.

Many of the larger fractures, inequalities and forces generating brokenness lie beyond the political capacity or will of governments, so that behaviourist targeting of minorities and visible 'transgressors' serves in effect as a 'default option', and perhaps helps to contain or mask the impact of widespread socioeconomic problems. With apparent diminution of the capacities of employment, neighbourhood networks or family relationships to secure a social order perceived as adequate, some selectivist support arrangements for households offer alternative avenues for locating, managing and controlling the potentially 'undeserving'. Low-income and vulnerable groups – facing socioeconomic disadvantage, media condemnations and declining public sector support – can experience a 'downward spiral' of conditions, and processes of what might be called relative dispossession (Harrison, 2009). What is central, however, is that developments in social control discourses primarily reflect political needs and aspirations, and are often inadequately based as far as evidence is concerned. Some campaigns against the 'undeserving' may be part of 'a specific political strategy', with arguments relying on 'emotional rather than factual appeals' (Clarke, 1983, p 255). Interventions may not necessarily provide effective mechanisms for long-term resolution of people's worries, or alter environmental settings in which problems arise and recur.

The social division of welfare and of social control

To move beyond the justificatory claims of mainstream Westminster politicians and their advisors, it is necessary to place social control in the context of general welfare and social policy arrangements. Welfare systems can be delineated in terms of an ensemble of mechanisms through which support and services for consumers have supplemented, substituted for or underpinned income from direct wages and private wealth. Differing welfare and support channels have had implications for household pathways, rights, capital accumulation and the social construction of groups (and their citizenship) in political discourses. Although today's debates on 'welfare' often cast it as something rather narrow (and linked primarily to dependencies among the poor, vulnerable or old), state institutions in reality have brought assistance, support or legitimacy to households' welfare on a much wider front. Historically, there have been many examples of explicit policies helping better-off or 'respectable' groups, such as tax concessions for house-buyers or members of occupational pension schemes, support for farmers[2] or price discounts enabling the better off among council housing tenants to buy their homes. Assistance for relatively successful groups has waxed and waned with the flow of political debate and economic pressures, but the treatment given has often contrasted sharply with approaches to people of lower status.

Links between differentiation in welfare arrangements on the one hand and socioeconomic divisions on the other have been tackled via the social division of welfare thesis (Titmuss, 1958; Sinfield, 1978; Harrison with Davis, 2001). This notes the significance of fiscal and occupational welfare support (given via tax arrangements or with employment), alongside directly provided income assistance and services. As has been long understood, capacities to accumulate capital and plan over lifetimes have been integral to more satisfactory state-sponsored welfare pathways (cf Sinfield, 1978, pp 149-51). It can also be argued that middle- and upper-income groups have proved relatively adept at maximising their use of universalistic provisions, and benefited disproportionately from major infrastructure investment. To some extent, cycles of transmitted intergenerational advantage seem to have operated for privileged groups, underpinned by legal arrangements, tax and occupational welfare systems, access to superior resources and enabling infrastructure (Harrison, 1995, p 20; Orton and Rowlingson, 2007, p 65). Channels to welfare here have been relatively untouched by explicit disciplinary preoccupations among politicians. Indeed, for some middle-class groups and allied 'deserving' categories, persuasions and control practices have been adopted rather carefully. The 'nudge' agenda now embraced explicitly by politicians may appear particularly appropriate today for the better placed, with its implications that the search should ideally be for positive incentivisation rather than coercion.

Beyond fiscal and occupational welfare, crucial roles are played by state institutions through recognition given to property rights, and their defence through law, policing and other interventions. These rights constitute key means through which relations between people over material resources are governed, and help to secure welfare in a variety of forms for their possessors. No comprehensive account of state involvements in household welfare could leave out the institutional power exerted to confirm, underpin and govern resource holdings and their acquisition, use or transfer (where inheritance laws are very important). Any thorough libertarian analysis recognises property rights sustained by governments not only as potential keys to individual liberty, but also as possible bases for state-licensed 'theft', exclusion and disempowerment of the poor. In contrast, economic liberal conceptions of freedom from state intervention under-acknowledge governments' confirmation and enhancement of the resource base of the better off. Indeed, some economic liberals may assert that politicians should further incorporate business interests into policy development, and not disturb the wealthy by substantial taxation or regulation (cf Monbiot, 2011).

When it comes to vulnerable and lower-income groups, however, scenarios shift, with the disadvantaged sometimes subject to behaviourist disciplines and obstructive income support systems. There is no assumption by the present writers here that welfare systems do not benefit low-income households. Some UK public sector organisations and mechanisms have provided key means for meeting needs and protecting social rights of vulnerable clients, while public service motivations among governmental or voluntary sector personnel have often generated supportive practices. The social policy agenda has been very varied, including concerns with social protection and intensive care (especially for children and older people) that are particularly complex in their goals, ethics and politics. There is also ongoing recognition for 'deserving' groups, with support in older age in particular proving relatively hard for competitive politicians to deny. Some universalistic help for travel and heating costs persists here, despite challenging political and media debates around this, while realisation of the economic liberal vision of means-testing state pensions remains distant. Despite complications and variations, however, it could be argued that while governments seem relatively comfortable in supporting the powerful and 'nudging' the middle class, they show persistent tendencies to direct harsher treatment at the poor or disadvantaged. In effect, there seems to be an ongoing *social division of social control*, albeit with considerable complexities.[3] At the very least, therefore, it seems important to ask *why* strategies for social control in social policy fields so often have negative consequences for disadvantaged groups in particular.

One answer may be that forms of provision have implications for the capacity and willingness to discipline populations (see Chapter Two). Selectivist systems designed for vulnerable and low-income groups seem especially prone to disciplinary tendencies, and sometimes inflict stigma or indignity. A current example is that the government apparently intends introducing vouchers or food stamps to replace cash payments for short-term emergency support, enabling tight behaviourist restrictions over how the poorest people spend these meagre resources (*The Guardian*, 27 March 2013, pp 1, 18-19). More locally voiced ideas for controls have recently included making benefits for 'overweight' people conditional on attending exercise classes (see *The Guardian*, 5 and 7 January 2013), while past examples occasionally even involved extreme local proposals such as imposing sterilisation on council housing applicants (Young and Kramer, 1978, pp 202, 291). What might seem surprising, however, is that prominent mainstream UK politicians today so rarely give high priority to strengthening social rights so as to protect poor people from such disciplinary and 'therapeutic' intrusions.

Ethical and normative issues of social control

There is an impressive scholarly literature illuminating standpoints, philosophies and ethical issues relevant to social control (see for example Deacon, 2002; Grant, 2012), and debates about normative claims can relate closely to contemporary social policy themes (including incentivisation, conditionality, nudges and contractarianism). It would go beyond this collection's focus to try to explore the normative arguments systematically in any depth, but it is desirable early in the book to clarify openly the positions held by the present editors. Five points are noted regarding the acceptability of social control strategies in social policy.

First, there is no prior assumption that social control and persuasion are unnecessary or indefensible in principle. Indeed, reference has already been made to the strong case for constraints over various kinds of transgressions. Many forms of aggression, violence, abuse, threat and coercion against individuals require well-developed and thoughtful regulatory responses, whether potential perpetrators are on the street, within domestic contexts, on the internet or actors within businesses or governmental bodies. Going further, a case can sometimes also be made for control or persuasion seeking to shape people's actions in ways seen widely as positive and desirable, but not directly about public safety or protecting potential individual victims from harm. Justification may prove more demanding here, however, especially if control is directed at 'freestanding' individuals rather than at staff operating within institutions such as companies. Close scrutiny of propositions and evidence are needed.

Second, contexts, settings and accompaniments for social control may well be crucial. Arguments in favour of a policy may be invalidated if there is a significant lack of 'fit' between the approach adopted and the complexities of social and economic circumstances at grass roots. Furthermore, interrelationships between available support, discipline and acknowledged 'client rights' might affect the merits of a case for specific regulatory steps. Some restraints and persuasions are best implemented alongside positive foundations that legitimate and anchor acceptance of obligations. Various social rights have a place in such scenarios. It may help to refer here to a concept about '*entitlement to quiet enjoyment*' very briefly indicated earlier. Such a proposition (implying rules and infrastructure protecting people against invasive behaviours) might gain legitimacy if linked with an array of relatively unconditional and universalistic positive rights. These might cover access to, use of and shared control over local environments for all residents, alongside some strong security of possession and finance for every household within homes and neighbourhoods. Rights claims from different people often conflict, and there would certainly be scope for competing claims and appropriate resolution rules in such a context. Nonetheless, at the level of principle, constraints and mutual obligations might more credibly be argued for if linked to clear social, economic and environmental rights enjoyed by all. Across social policies, a sense of shared available benefits and participatory empowerment might moderate any feeling that social control was set primarily within coercive or paternalistic authority relationships, or an assault on individual dignities (for the significance of dignity and self-determination, see Grant, 2012, pp 58, 121). Additionally, making inroads on acceptable rights and resource claims in one domain in order to achieve 'behaviour change' in a different field may be morally problematic, and potentially an abuse of power. Denying someone health treatment to compel them to take up a paid job would be an instance of abuse.

A third point (connected with the second and with earlier comments) is that in some circumstances there should be reservations about relying on moral positions focused around individuals detached from real-life contexts. Formulation and evaluation of many social policy practices require systematic consideration of:

- exactly who is affected;
- how people will really react and for how long;
- how far their choices are real (with genuinely voluntary responses open to them);
- what side-effects might arise for them;
- whether there are not only expected 'third party beneficiaries' but also 'casualties' (such as children affected by policies targeted at their parents).

Fourth, moral or philosophical standpoints need conditioning by an appreciation of issues of inequality, discrimination, power and property (discussed earlier), which constitute environmental framings for options and constraints facing households. Some religious and other traditions have implied that duties should be observed especially by the wealthy in favour of people who are less so. This moral counterpart to accepting economic inequalities has fallen out of favour in UK politics (Harrison with Davis, 2001, pp 74-5), but remains salient, especially given the huge state support for better-off groups through endorsement and defence of property relations and private power.

Fifth, the present authors are concerned by the potential of regulatory mechanisms, disciplines and conditionalities to erode liberties cumulatively, and in ways that might be hard to reverse. This may threaten specific freedoms, but perhaps also diminishes possibilities of a pluralistic and integrative civic life with full opportunities for social participation across all groups. For some households, imposed restrictions may inhibit development or continuity of 'self-regulation' within day-to-day settings, of effective long-term household planning, of mutual support relationships or of interdependencies. This concern does not mean rejecting social control strategies as such, but implies great caution when they target vulnerable people and widen criminalisation (for criminalisation and the redefining of social problems as 'crime', see Wincup, 2013, including pp 13 and 17-18 on truancy and rough sleeping).

Social policy trends in changing environments

Reviews of developments in disciplinary practices and of attempts to control behaviour have been highly informative about the character and growth of interventions, and there has been valuable interpretative work (see Garland, 2001; Crawford, 2003, 2009; Dwyer, 2004; Burney, 2005; Flint, 2006c; Rodger, 2008; Nixon and Prior, 2010). Crawford (2009, p 811), for example, comments on 'hyper-active state interventionism and social engineering', noting ideas of better regulation being used to circumvent and undermine established criminal justice principles, 'notably those of due process, proportionality and special protections traditionally afforded to young people'. From a social policy perspective, the breadth and scope of reported regulatory change are striking, spanning income support, housing and homelessness, youth policies, education, 'return-to-work' strategies, managing residential neighbourhoods and more. It almost seems as if programmes of rehabilitation, discipline and retrieval had expanded out of the custodial environment – where they could not succeed against the backcloth of increased numbers, cost limits and the unremitting external conditions facing custody-leavers – and into the forum of everyday life on a wide and more regularised basis. Certainly, the 'reach' of interventions appears to have increased substantially.

Over time there has been a mix of change with continuities, but also some variation in 'subtexts' within domain discourses, even when general preoccupations move with apparent consistency. One instance concerns social segregation themes in housing. In earlier periods, social landlords might seek to educate and pressure people into better self-management in the home (a classic paternalistic illustration being available in Ward, 1974, p 12, opening quotation), with a move into social renting potentially serving to encourage 'modernised' or 'socialised' ways of being a householder. As is widely understood, respectability was favoured, there was racism and sexism, some positive collective community activities were encouraged, and rejection or banishment to a low-status estate punished lapses among those 'less deserving' or more highly deviant (for insights on grading, 'race' and respectability, see Henderson and Karn, 1987). Whereas some later rhetoric presented social mixing as a way of leavening the unacceptable habits of the poor, earlier formulae sometimes invoked strong separation. As Tucker (1966, p 50) explained, most big councils had 'apparatus to prevent what they regard as undue social mixing on their estates', and segregation here was 'a science'. As time passed, positive propositions about generating social mix became more politically acceptable. Gradually, however, negative portrayals of social housing as a whole gained ground. Key challenges supposedly now involved helping larger numbers retrieve their lifestyles from danger and part with the 'habits' of the 'failed or resistant worker', the 'self-disabling' or the incompetent parent. In this developing climate, pushing certain low-income renters away from better conditions returned to the social control agenda, operationalised through driving more people into insecure, low-status, private sector tenancies, and compelling tenants (by reducing financial support) to leave larger or higher-value properties (see Chapter Twelve for fuller explorations).

The high political profile of concerns to control behaviour was evident well before the arrival of the UK coalition government. Emphasising the need to confront anti-social behaviours was so attractive for ministers when Blair was Prime Minister that stories linked to Anti-Social Behaviour Orders (ASBOs) and other tools of control became among the most recurring images from domestic policies. Illuminating foci for reports included a woman 'given an ASBO' for singing 'glam rock' songs in her bathroom or a sex worker required not to carry condoms or enter the area where the clinic she attended was based. There appeared to be a mix of the perverse, heavily moralistic, petty and punitive with the sensible, protective or genuinely supportive. Importantly, pre-existing social and economic differentiations were often mirrored in the impact and orientations of controls (see Harrison and Sanders, 2006; Nixon and Prior, 2010). As in the preceding Conservative period, some supposedly 'less legitimate' client groups seeking support faced pressure or denial of choice. Young single parents, for instance, might be expected to 'return to' or stay in the dwellings of their own parents rather than creating independent homes with state support (note Giullari and Shaw, 2005). Meanwhile, some practices were influenced by labour market strategies, seeking to reduce benefit claimant numbers while encouraging people to move into work with incentives as well as surveillance, and a diminution of support for 'economically inactive' people (see for instance Fothergill, 2010). In effect, foundations were being strengthened in relation to both social order and benefits strategies for the coalition government to build on.

The Big Society: meanings, aspirations and limitations

As the UK coalition government came into power, much was made of the Conservatives' idea of the 'Big Society'. Responses appeared to vary from enthusiastic advocacy to 'derision, confusion and critically righteous anger', but the 'governmental impetus' behind the concept seemed likely to persist (Morgan, 2012, p 463). In Chapter Eight, Mastin highlights some political ideas evident in Big Society discourses, including decentralising state power to society and from centre to localities, alongside the intention of emphasising social responsibility rather than state control. Wallace mentions in Chapter Six the Conservative concern with rolling forward the frontiers of society, and – citing Ellison, 2011 – notes the role of the Big Society concept in providing something of a cohesive banner for a number of coalition reforms. Wallace points out links to New Labour ideas around localism and active citizenship, but also an increased emphasis on voluntarism, a more hostile perspective on state social support, and connections into the pathologising of social problems. Commentators have recognised several important components of Big Society programme aspirations, including devolution, localism, partnership working and responsibilisation, along with substantial promotion and development of voluntary and community sector organisations (cf Morgan, 2012, p 467). Yet the strongest philosophical or ideological resonances for Conservative Big Society thinking may well be with economic liberalism. For economic liberals, a Big Society may contrast with what they might conceptualise as the Big State, with its connotations about the 'squeezing out' and over-regulation of private enterprise, and diversion of national resources for collective purposes.

In specific policy contexts, of course, contradictions may arise within governmental programmes. In town and country planning, for example, the Big Society promise of passing decision-making powers to local residents has apparently been undermined by shifts of national policy favouring private developers over conservationists (for one Conservative Member of Parliament's views, see Herbert, 2013). Critics also have doubts about sustaining localism strategies, effective volunteering and support for vulnerable groups in a severely constraining austerity context, and what some see as the potential of Big Society rhetoric to provide 'a vehicle, and indeed a gloss', for introducing policies and practices based on the 'assumption that they will cost less to deliver' (Walklate, 2012, p 495). Furthermore, outcomes from marketisation and 'outsourcing' have been unsatisfactory from the perspective of some advocates of mutuals, cooperatives and the third sector generally (for insights on the involvement of the third sector, see Wincup, 2013, pp 68-70). These matters are touched on further in the next section, and briefly in the conclusion of Chapter Two. As this book's subtitle indirectly suggests, there is also a more general question to consider about the appropriateness of the term 'Big Society' itself. The concluding chapter takes that up, arguing that the 'not-so-big society' may be a more realistic descriptor of what is being engineered, when seen in terms of the social regulation of the disadvantaged.

Ongoing privatisation and revitalised enclosure processes

Although the government's central target is currently to reduce public expenditure, another key goal concerns encouraging the private sector and increasing its profitability, with privatisation an important component. Some of the forces and communities of interest that helped to sustain a 'mixed' economy and pluralistic polity in the post-war period have been in decline, and economic liberals now have freer scope in 'core' areas of education, local government and health services that once formed the bedrock of the 'old' welfare state. Numerous strategies to encourage private sector involvement have emerged, varying from complex plans affecting large policy areas to more modest innovations such as the 'social impact bond' (where tackling prioritised social problems yields financial returns linked to achieved 'results'; see Gentleman, 2012a). General arguments favouring privatisation claim that consumers are put 'in charge' through gaining the power of choice in competitive supplier environments, that bureaucratic and employee 'vested interests' lose ground and that freedoms are enhanced. The claim that freedoms are enhanced has long been important to advocates (as is clear, for example, in Marsland's [2004] *Social policy review* defence of 'Thatcherite' perspectives on welfare policy, where the word freedom is invoked twice in the subheadings themselves; 2004, pp 212, 214). Additional arguments revolved in recent decades around hopes of reducing visible public sector borrowing requirements, by transferring provider functions to non-governmental bodies that would raise on private markets part of the investment funds needed, particularly in housing.

In contrast, observers opposing privatisation have highlighted negative implications from transferring resources or their management away from collective groupings and elected representatives, and into the hands of private companies and wealthy individuals. Concerns are expressed about profit taking by businesses, their unhealthy relationships with politicians, and effects on inequalities. For some critics, a historical analogy might seem appropriate, remembering what happened to land resources in parts of Britain in the 18th and 19th centuries. It has been observed that seven million acres of land in England were enclosed under 4,200 private Acts and various general enclosure Acts, facilitating a loss of rights for smaller landholders and the poor (Shoard, 1987). Today, private 'capture' of resources and systems previously dedicated for public use and collective support is linked not with the farming of land and livestock as in earlier centuries, but with securing a return from people themselves (see for instance Morris, S., 2012), and from the services, premises or equipment previously operating in their names. Someone seeking pejorative terminology for these '*new enclosures*' might borrow from Shakespeare to argue that anyone needy, dispossessed or vulnerable now serves as a potential source of sustenance for the emerging 'caterpillars of the commonwealth' (Bolingbroke, *King Richard II*, Act 2, Scene 3), from private equity investment organisations to inadequate or exploitative contractors.

Of course, any strong judgement on privatisation may look partisan, whether favourable or unfavourable. Nonetheless, even relatively cautious interpretations are likely to raise concerns about:

- accountability and transparency;
- the effectiveness of commissioning processes, monitoring and control;
- the impact of profit motivations;
- the extent to which proposed arrangements adequately reflect complications, needs and realities of specific contexts (see for instance Vine, 2013, on legal aid; also *The Guardian*, 2 July 2013, p 4).

For present purposes, furthermore, it is important to acknowledge that social control practices are not confined to governmental institutions. The scrutiny, measurement, disciplining and exclusion of groups of people are built into many private sector activities, generating outcomes ranging from day-to-day restrictions (such as refusals to rent accommodation to tenants with children or pets), to bullying or discrimination against staff. Private control over space also excludes many poorer people from access to desirable physical environments (for 'gated communities', see Atkinson and Blandy, 2005). Despite supposed positive links between marketisation and liberties, private corporations are often 'authority systems' exercising extensive powers over employees, and in some circumstances almost systems of private government (for illustrative comment, see Gold, 2013). Certainly, it is 'normal' and 'rational' when providing private sector services and products to engage in discriminatory risk evaluation of persons or places. Furthermore, the moralising, pathologising or paternalistic outlooks found historically in some public sector support systems owed at least part of their historical foundations to private or voluntary sector practices (for Octavia Hill's approach at the end of the 19th century, see Whelan, 1998).

In any event, privatisation or outsourcing into the hands of large businesses seems unlikely to soften controls and exclusions, and may generate new orientations where penalties, selectivity, conditionality and denial are intensified to protect profit. At the same time, channels of accountability and representation for potential clients and consumers may be transformed, with fewer possibilities for effective intermediation and modification at implementation stage, and lessened hope of exerting influence through local electoral processes. For 'welfare consumers' there may be increased uncertainties in the supply process and difficulties for those seen as a risk or danger, with profit considerations playing a heightened role in relation to the measurement of, caring for and policing of the disadvantaged, 'deficient' or 'dangerous'. National debates and press comments have indicated numerous problems in privately run welfare provision, surveillance and control of people (see for instance Milne, 2012; Grayson, 2013; Sambrook, 2013; also *The Guardian*, 18 July 2012, p 9; 10 July 2013, pp 1-2, 6; and 5 August 2013, p 8), alongside the deficiencies arising in public and third sector provision from resource cuts. There may be dangers of debasement of day-to-day practices and 'cultures', following staff reductions and cost savings accompanying privatisation. There has also been pressure since 2010 to shrink public protections under the banner of reducing 'red tape', complemented by reductions in the legal aid that helped maintain some open access to the law (and sometimes permitted challenges to oppressive practices of powerful private and public sector bodies). Commitment has weakened to regulatory, monitoring, investigative and consultative arrangements previously created to moderate institutional practices in the direction of greater inclusiveness and equality of opportunity. An interesting instance in late 2012 was the Prime Minister's reference to the apparently intended removal of Equality Impact Assessment requirements developed under New Labour (Cameron, 2012b).

It might be argued, of course, that economic liberal strategies for privatisation are counterbalanced by Big Society aspirations. There is little sign, however, of any broader strengthening of voluntary sector or local community bodies' roles in controlling major services and assets, of increased capacity on their part to gain important places in the policy-making forum on behalf of the grass roots or of their representing 'difference' more successfully with government (see also conclusions in Chapter Two). There are variations between contexts, and service user participation sometimes remains an ongoing theme as under New Labour (see Chapters Eight and Twelve). For social housing, however, user participation in England still appears to be primarily a component within institutional settings established previously, including those in which third sector bodies took over public assets and sometimes enlarged these, but usually without tenants gaining real control. In general terms, new variants of 'welfare privatisation' creating systematic collective user participation in controlling services might be potentially empowering for households, especially if allied with firm community rights over inalienable assets via mechanisms such as trusts or mutuals (see Harrison, 2010). At the moment, however, privatisation models of a very different character appear dominant in the changes driven by the UK coalition government. It seems likely, furthermore, that the financial and political resources of larger businesses will 'outgun' the enthusiasm and community support of smaller third sector organisations. Perhaps hierarchies may become normalised, with subordination of less powerful bodies, and their use to 'embroider' bids, provide subcontracting and handle the riskier frontline tasks. Possible outcomes may include less effective 'quality assurance', less representation and positive advocacy on behalf of clients, and less refinement in disciplinary or therapeutic interventions. There is certainly nothing to suggest that disadvantaged people will receive fuller consideration or be subject to fewer disciplines as the outsourced or privatised components of 'welfare' grow.

The foundations for the book

Underpinning discussions leading to this collection was a shared interest in analysing the government's attempts to control, regulate or influence behaviour, and the efforts made in recent years to recast eligibilities, responsibilities and opportunities when support is provided for client groups. There was collective concern about:

- the ways in which powers associated with the state were being deployed;
- reductions in liberties previously associated with social rights and accessible common resources;
- the decline in recognition of the importance of state-organised social security and services for social cohesion, family life and empowerment.

A collaborative enterprise developed, bringing together people from a variety of specialised areas of investigation, to generate something that might 'showcase' new voices and accounts from a range of fields.[4] The focus or context for most contributors was primarily a social policy rather than criminal justice one, although these research territories overlap. Several participants saw a particularly strong case in the present period for examining or revisiting social control, given the current impact of austerity policies, changes to welfare systems and the political starting points available to the UK coalition government from New Labour's previous efforts to contain anti-social behaviours and increase workforce participation.

Authors undertook to touch on issues of social control, to explore themes relating to it or to engage with facets of the management, containment, responsibilisation or exclusion of people through contemporary social policies. It was understood that the controlling or influencing of behaviour was generally going to be relevant for chapters, but individual writings would not necessarily focus on behaviourism as such. Chapters were being finalised at a time when the main contours of social policy and 'welfare' strategies under the UK coalition government had become clear, even though details sometimes remained incomplete.

Part One of the book includes broad introductory discussions from Malcolm Harrison, Laura Hemingway and Kate Brown, on control of behaviour (and a 'new behaviourism') and on the topic of vulnerability. In Part Two, specific policy areas are discussed. Chapters deal with:

- work and welfare (Ruth Patrick);
- issues in the asylum system (Ala Sirriyeh);
- the governance of communities and urban change (Andrew Wallace);
- education for young people (Doug Martin);
- user involvement in health and social care (Gabrielle Mastin);
- 'nudge' strategies in the National Health Service (Ana Manzano);

- employment, lone parents and welfare reform (Laura Davies);
- drug policy (Mark Monaghan);
- housing (Jenny McNeill).

Part Three then presents an overview by Teela Sanders of some of the main findings from the chapters, and makes concluding observations. All contributing authors have developed their own perspectives, but there is much common ground visible when looking across the differing contexts.

Many of this book's contributors are relatively new researchers, engaged at the 'cutting edge' of investigations about contemporary social policies. Some have also been involved directly with frontline practice, working with vulnerable or disadvantaged people. Taken together, their accounts of specific trends indicate how far claims about the pervasiveness of social control and the impact of behaviourist themes hold true across domains. To engage effectively with rapidly changing environments, some chapters draw on relatively informal sources such as websites and press reports, alongside conventional scholarly writings. There is a shared conclusion that the control, influencing and managing of behaviours deserve more comprehensive and critical attention than they have so far received within overviews of social policy and welfare. Perhaps UK trends may also provide useful parallels or contrasts for analysts and policy makers elsewhere. The rise of behaviourism and the implications this has for households need to be acknowledged as crucial for present-day welfare systems and the thinking that underpins these. Readers will decide for themselves whether events and developments referred to in specific chapters are best viewed as threatening or productive. There is little doubt, however, that the trends call into question any claims that economic liberal political orientations and strategies in the UK are positively linked with achieving 'libertarian' outcomes or expectations, unless the term 'liberty' is given an extraordinarily narrow meaning. Indeed, appropriation of a libertarian mantle by some right-wing politicians and analysts appears not merely problematic but also intellectually unsustainable, given the systematic and growing imposition of surveillance, supervision and exclusion on people who are already vulnerable and dispossessed.

TWO

Social policy and the new behaviourism: towards a more excluding society

Malcolm Harrison with Laura Hemingway

Introduction

This chapter explores some general issues to complement coverage of specific policy domains later in the book. The first sections note the positioning of social control practices in welfare arrangements for disadvantaged households, mention some political underpinnings and suggest a tentative hypothesis about a 'new behaviourism' in UK social policy running from the mid-1990s through into the Cameron era. The analysis indicates that the close interweaving of support with disciplinary interventions that persisted historically in some practice areas has been reinvigorated and reinterpreted through contemporary politics, particularly for low-income and vulnerable groups. Discussion then turns to disability, where transformations in welfare arrangements illustrate the character of change, before concluding briefly with general points.[1]

Social control within welfare systems

Chapter One speculated about government's control of behaviours by suggesting that while support and 'nudges' are deployed for the better off, harsher treatments tend to be applied to the poor. This may seem strange, given the valued assistance delivered for low-income households through social policies, and the public service orientations and commitments to social justice among some professionals. Nonetheless – and despite diversity in government's targets and purposes – strategies for social control in social policy areas often do seem to have negative implications for disadvantaged groups in particular. One reason for the impact on poor and vulnerable households is the link between disciplinary tendencies on the one hand

and types of support arrangements on the other (Harrison and Sanders, 2006). Chapter One referred to the 'social division of welfare thesis', and to a characterisation of welfare systems in terms of an ensemble of mechanisms through which support and services for consumers have supplemented, substituted for or underpinned income from direct wages and private wealth (see Titmuss, 1958; Sinfield, 1978). Differing channels to welfare available for different households can markedly affect relative opportunities and access to resources, *but forms of provision also have implications for the capacity and perceived political need to discipline populations* (for the 'social division of welfare surveillance', see Henman and Marston, 2008; and for the 'social division of social control', see Chapter One, this volume). In contrast with welfare arrangements or pathways built around universalistic social rights, support focused selectively on needy clients may look more like a process of granting or giving than of responding to entitlements. Social control practices bearing down on low-income and vulnerable households in social policy contexts often seem contingent to some degree on the characterisation of welfare in this way, as a 'gift' for selected recipients rather than a right (Harrison with Davis, 2001, pp 65, 74). Appraisal and classification may be applied to clients seeking help, potentially facilitating restrictions, imposition of conditions, supervision or refusal of support. There is a substantial difference between such situations and those where strategies to influence behaviours aim at broad populations possessing rights to use a service (as when policies 'nudge' health service users to act responsibly).

Later chapters refer to themes deployed to justify or frame policies, so discussion now on political foundations can be brief. Social constructions of appropriate lifestyles and behaviours are important for social policy thinking, with increasing 'normalisation' of positive approval for economically successful and financially independent people. Although being dependent on others is experienced by everyone at particular times, the label of dependency when applied to poor or vulnerable people often signifies either something inherently unacceptable or a personal misfortune deserving charitable responses. Themes on human agency promulgated by economic liberals (and finding support among powerful business and political interests) include the idea of the 'culpable human agent', sometimes supposedly relatively unbounded by structural constraints, who needs 'activating' or 'responsibilising'. This contrasts with analytical approaches that portray the exercising of agency as 'overlaid onto structural inequality' and refer to understanding 'agency within structure' (Orton, 2009, pp 487, 496).

At the same time, economic liberal perspectives on agency itself seem partial, giving little attention to moral commitments, perceived rationalities, interdependencies and constructive roles (including informal support-giving) that arise locally among disadvantaged groups (for insights, see Fletcher, 2008; Dunn, 2010). People at the lower end of the income slope may be characterised by market institutions and contemporary governments primarily in terms of the relative risks such households and individuals represent, their central importance being their value (or lack of it) to employers, and their greatest threat the levels of 'vulnerability' or challenge they are perceived to manifest. As Chapter One indicated, governments sometimes reinforce rather than inhibit negative perceptions about lower-income households portrayed as 'different' or less deserving, and there may be convergence here with parts of the popular press (for analysis of misrepresentations, see Turn2us, 2012).

The new behaviourism under New Labour and the coalition government

In approaching behaviourism, this chapter touches on two linked territories. First, there are behaviourist aspects of social policies, where politicians and professionals explicitly seek to modify or control behaviours among individuals and households (or cite anticipated behaviour changes to justify preferred strategies). Methods used to encourage compliance sometimes include imposing penalties on people whose behaviour does not change appropriately. Second, behaviourist preoccupations may affect policy or practice environments more generally (and parallel economic liberal thinking), as key participants emphasise individual or group behaviours when considering socioeconomic circumstances, trends or events. The present analysis does not isolate or comprehensively inspect those policies overtly pursuing behaviour change, but notes behaviourist components while exploring a larger landscape. The discussion considers shifts in social regulation within which the control of behaviour has had increasing prominence, and argues that recent periods have been distinctive. No claim is made for innovation by the present authors when asserting the significance of changes in social control as such, or in the politics of behaviour (or of the 'governance of conduct'), since many writings comment on these (see for instance Burney, 2005; Flint, 2006a, pp 174-6). Rather, a limited hypothesis is proposed about a particular combination of trends.

As differing policy strands and emphases occur simultaneously, divisions over time are rarely neat, while practices in England are not necessarily duplicated elsewhere in Britain (Scottish divergence on homelessness being an important example). There has also been long continuity of interest within social policy contexts in controlling disorders, social pathologies and behaviours (see for instance Gallagher, 1982; Clarke, 1983), and scholars have provided some highly informative historical accounts of developments (see for example Welshman, 2013). In classic work at the end of the 1950s, Wootton noted the recurring theme of a choice between environmental and individualistic approaches to social problems, and the preference 'to analyse the infected individual rather than to eliminate the infection from the environment' (Wootton with Seal and Chambers, 1959, p 329). Governmental documents from post-war years certainly reveal an interest in therapeutic and rehabilitative concerns, alongside conceptual overtones from preoccupations such as the assumed transmission of problems across generations, or the managing of 'unsatisfactory' families or tenants (see for instance Housing Management Sub-Committee of the Central Housing Advisory Committee, 1955, reprinted 1968). As far as methods are concerned, specific high-profile 'modern' strategies may to some degree mirror past techniques. Even the 'intensive family support projects' or 'family intervention projects' publicised in the New Labour years (and in effect being built upon under the current government) may somewhat echo earlier approaches such as those noted by Tucker (1966, pp 100-12; for current practices, see Flint, 2012; also Wincup, 2013, pp 113-30).

Despite continuities, however, there are interconnected features particular to the recent and present period, pre-dating New Labour but becoming more pervasive in welfare systems after 1997, and in some ways intensifying under the coalition. First, there have been increased tendencies to attempt persuasion, reclamation or redirection of very large numbers of people through domains of social policy. Whereas it was understood in the 1950s and 1960s that numbers targeted were relatively small, scrutiny today is more widespread. Sometimes intervention has involved powerful supervisory, surveillance or therapeutic emphases where behaviour and lifestyles are at issue, not focused on causation in any broader sense but on persons and households. This has not been confined to those whose actions have been judged to pose substantial threats to the safety of friends, family and neighbours, or have attracted attention from mental health practitioners. Government's gaze extends well beyond the 'dangerously ill' or the individual 'problem families' referred to by Tucker (1966, pp 93-131). Neither has the reach of this new behaviourism been limited to 'classic extreme estates normally associated with inner-city crime and breakdown' (Power and Tunstall, 1997, p 5), although there are spatial connotations. In some ways, debates on housing from the 1990s onwards exemplified a broader attack, as social housing as a whole began more often to be socially constructed not only as being for the vulnerable and failed, but as itself promoting dependency and worklessness (for expert commentaries, see Murie, 2012a; Robinson, 2012). Meanwhile, social engineering has been envisaged for groups or quite large geographical areas under various banners, including community cohesion. Serious urban disturbances during the coalition period further stimulated debates about failing neighbourhoods and people (although events did not call forth substantial new resources to improve socioeconomic conditions).

A wider casting of nets to cover perceived threats or risks (and not just actions) connected under New Labour with criminalisation of more behaviours, and some erosion of distinctions between criminal justice work and social development or support (note Rodger, 2008, on the blurring of professional boundaries and paradigms, and subordination of social policy objectives). Specific categories of people were frequently a focus, including misbehaving and 'alienated youth'. Children became and remained more exposed to punishments akin to those previously reserved for adults, with England and Wales seeing an average of six arrests per day of primary school-aged children in 2011, although there was a fall from the 2008 rate (news release, Howard League for Penal Reform, 3 December 2012). Ideas about penalising parents for young people's difficult behaviours also received ongoing support, sometimes implying imprisonment or loss of a tenancy (see also Chapter Seven). For disabled people, local strategies to tackle anti-social behaviours could have some negative consequences as well as potentially positive ones (Harrison and Sanders, 2006, pp 160-1).

Perhaps partly because disciplinary practices received so much attention from New Labour (and were not necessarily connected with punishment for direct criminal acts but with goals such as increasing 'respect'), a myriad of interventionist ideas snowballed, sometimes generating bizarre press headlines.

A particularly striking one in 2007 read, 'Unborn babies targeted in crackdown on criminality', responding to the then Prime Minister's launching of policy to intervene during pregnancy and head off later anti-social behaviour (*The Guardian*, 16 May 2007). This was not as novel as it looked, however, given established wishes to intervene actively during pregnancy and early years, alongside identifying households posing threats to social order. The coalition's emphasis on 'troubled families' treads adjacent ground (see for instance DCLG, 2012a), although there is currently little to match New Labour's constructive initiatives for poorer households and children. In any event, it is unsurprising to find a headline similar to the 2007 one – 'Intervene before birth in problem families' – on a press report about coalition ministers responding to riots and gangs (*The Guardian*, 21 October 2011). Indeed, there seems some broad continuity from New Labour on tackling anti-social behaviour and households that pose challenges, despite ideas for streamlining and changed tools (see Chakrabarti, 2012).[2]

Across social policies overall there has been an accumulating repertoire of concepts and aims, along with measurement, targeting, surveillance, therapies and imposed 'reciprocal' obligations. Perhaps an ongoing reworking of interconnections between dependency, vulnerability and the threats groups or individuals pose helped to distinguish policy and practice environments in the New Labour period from previous ones. Nonetheless, because interrelations between support and discipline have been amenable to varying local, institutional and domain effects, opportunities have existed within or around specific enterprises for some expression of alternative discourses or narratives by project workers or by the targets of policy. Sometimes, scope might have remained for resistance or subversion (note especially chapters in Barnes and Prior, 2009a), while the visibility of the control or 'risk-containment' elements within an intervention package could help to legitimate funding for the more supportive engagements simultaneously included (see also discussion in Chapter Three).

Terminologies linked to specified behaviours and associated goals have ranged from 'responsibilisation' to improved 'wellbeing', and from better parenting to incentivisation and 'work capability'. 'Contractual governance' and conditionality have become more widespread (Dwyer, 2004), and rights more often subject to denial or devaluation (for control opportunities linked to rights delivery, see Chapter Five). Some critics suggest that welfare contractualism is 'conducive to a moralistic, populist and censorious political discourse' (Freedland and King, 2003, p 471), an unsurprising conclusion since contracts often cannot involve equality of parties or consent in any reasonable sense, while discretionary power, surveillance and coercion may be present. In discussing New Labour's 'New Deal' and 'workfare', Freedland and King (2003, p 475) noted the 'illiberal effects' and the tendency of the 'workfare regime to function as a quasi-criminal one'. The priority increasingly given to propelling people into paid work has helped to emphasise the direct responsibilities of 'inadequate' individuals and has been accompanied by a widening of focus to increased populations (see Chapter Four).

Perhaps both the prominence given to the supposedly recalcitrant unemployed and the rise of behaviourist perspectives in other policy areas have heightened awareness of deviance, dysfunction and social divisions, while undermining solidaristic concerns for basic standards of living and equalities. A key factor is the near-consensus frequently visible across the main UK political party leaderships, and perhaps this too represents something distinctive to recent times (relevant commentaries include Cochrane, 1998, pp 321-5; Bochel and Defty, 2007; Millie, 2010, p 9; Patrick, 2012; for recent illustrations, see *The Guardian*, 27 September 2011, 18 December 2012, 4 January 2013, but also 8 January 2013). Leaving aside possible exceptions around support systems for people in older age, there seem few influential voices currently from the main UK political parties arguing for any strengthening of universalistic social rights systems, although that does not necessarily imply unqualified advocacy or implementation of economic liberal prescriptions in particular contexts (see Murie, 2012a, pp 1041-6). In UK politics, the observing, incentivising, restricting and conditioning of behaviour have moved closer to centre stage (Osborne and Thaler, 2010), while a variety of bodies have been enlisted as participating agents in implementing controls across numerous policy domains. Growing recognition has been given to behaviourist themes and recipes, including so-called 'choice architecture' and nudge strategies (see Manzano, this volume), and a Cabinet Office Behavioural Insights Team has been established, building on earlier New Labour arrangements (Wells, 2010). Rather than exploring and responding to complex needs and circumstances experienced at grass roots, some ministers now reportedly prioritise a 'social return' on governmental investment, to be achieved through 'life change' (see a feature on Iain Duncan Smith, *The Guardian*, 27 May 2010, p 20). Organisations implementing policies may be incentivised to secure particular measured outcomes from clients, who are themselves rewarded or penalised in accordance with responses they make.

Meanwhile, application of negative ideas on dependency has widened, to embrace some situations where recipients of support were previously perceived as relatively 'deserving' and 'respectable'. Examining discourses on home improvement grants in recent times or on in-work benefits today might uncover examples, although dependency labels have not been applied for discounts on right-to-buy social housing purchases or help given to businesses. In any event, behaviourist ideas can legitimate negative approaches to selected lower-income 'strivers' alongside 'shirkers'. Box 2.1 summarises key indicators related to the hypothesis suggested in this part of the chapter.

Box 2.1: Indicators of a *'new behaviourism'* affecting social policies

- Increased and widened attempts to incentivise, reclaim, redirect, discipline or exclude people, often underpinned by strong preoccupations with failures or problems at individual, family and neighbourhood levels.
- Broadened applicability of negative ideas of dependency.
- A strengthened emphasis on influencing behaviours through imposed duties, responsibilities, conditionality and contracts, rather than on enhancing social rights.
- A growing repertoire of concepts and intervention ideas, with ongoing reworking of interconnections between dependency, vulnerability, risk and threat across diverse policy domains, and an impact on practice cultures.
- Overt political leadership consensus, especially in England, with downgrading of 'structural factors' in favour of a focus on individual 'agency' and social pathologies.

Disability and social control; a troubled history and difficult present

Recent approaches to disability provide strong examples of themes and trends discussed previously in this chapter. There have been increased governmental preoccupations with behaviours among disadvantaged disabled people, accumulating strategies to challenge their 'welfare dependencies', and considerable political consensus from New Labour onwards. Before summarising recent developments, however, this section refers to the past, since control and discipline have long histories within public policies for disabled people. During the Victorian period, many with impairments or labelled as 'deviants' were incarcerated in asylums, workhouses or prisons (see Lund, 1996; Allen, 1999). As Drake (1999, pp 47-8) points out, until the end of the 1880s laws concerning disabled people 'did little other than provide regulations for their incarceration'. Asylums might aim to provide 'therapeutic environments' for inhabitants (Picking, 2000), but this was balanced against practices of concealment and the managing of potential risks posed to society; implying exclusion of people with some conditions from wider populations. Although much has changed since the Victorian era, ideas about separating disabled people off from non-disabled people sometimes persist, while struggles continue around conditions, rights, autonomy and support. As regards 'treatment', it has been argued that strategies for long periods remained focused on either altering people's physiology, 'through aids, adaptations or surgical interventions', or 'putting in place specialised welfare services whose goal it was to adapt disabled individuals to the non-disabled world' (Drake, 1999, p 54). Even under sympathetic governments, the central cause of disadvantage for many operational purposes might be taken routinely to be the impairment or condition associated with an individual, while effects of wider environments and social settings remained relatively neglected.

During the second half of the 20th century, a growing acknowledgement of principles of 'care within the community' was supported by many disabled people protesting against incarceration via institutional living (Dartington et al, 1981; Hunt, 1981; Finkelstein, 1991; Morris, 1999; Barnes et al, 2002). Life inside institutions was criticised frequently (Barnes, 1990; Means, 1996; Carvel, 2007). Hunt (1981, p 38), a former resident of a residential home, described the liberties he and other residents fought for, including the freedom 'to choose our own bedtimes, drink alcohol if we chose, freedom for the sexes to relate without interference' and 'freedom to leave the building without having to notify the authorities'. Even today, institutional living can impose humiliating restrictions, limit people's potential (Beresford, 2011; JRF, 2011, p 2) or involve alarming abuses (although for some people the accommodation and services remain useful). On a more general front, local authorities have catered for housing needs of many people registered as disabled (Imrie, 2003; Milner, 2005), while services offered as alternatives to residential care came to include support and assistance with arranging adaptations in people's own dwellings. 'General' and 'special' needs in housing could be somewhat separated conceptually (Milner and Madigan, 2004), with the latter potentially implying specially designed properties but some risk of isolation. This differed from increased availability of accessible, flexible and affordable properties within general housing stocks, an alternative in line with more universalistic concepts about meeting housing needs rather than focusing primarily on the assessment of impairment-related limitations.

In the 1970s, views of disability centred around medical and individualising perspectives were challenged, with activists arguing that it was in fact society that was creating disability (UPIAS, 1976). Advocates of a social model or socially grounded understanding of disability drew attention to socioeconomic factors and processes that helped to account for persistent patterns of disadvantage (Oliver, 1983, 1990). Disabled people's choices seemed bounded not only by wider environments and economic situations, but sometimes also by the very practices ostensibly designed to give support. Eventually there was some shift in policy debates, away from top-down service-led approaches to more needs-led ones, with needs ideally defined by disabled people themselves (Priestley, 1999). Changes made to financial support via the Independent Living Fund and Disability Living Allowance (a benefit available for people with mobility and care needs) meant monies for managing needs being paid directly to disabled people, even if subject to demanding eligibility criteria and medical assessments (for a broad history, see Hemingway, 2011). Under New Labour there were moves towards highlighting choice, equality, independence and greater consultation, although Brown (this volume) indicates that understandings of vulnerability became more salient in the governance of welfare (see Chapter Three). Meanwhile, the feasibility of improving environments through universalistic measures affecting all service users was demonstrated when building regulations were amended as a step towards making dwellings more accessible for disabled people (Hemingway, 2011, pp 33-4, 72-3, 132). Government also supported equalities of opportunity and inclusiveness through developments in regulation and monitoring (although official commitment here lessened after the General Election of 2010).

As Chapter Four indicates, New Labour made efforts to assist those in work through the minimum wage, tax credits and help towards childcare. Yet the government also restructured the treatment of disabled people in receipt of benefits, as part of a broader welfare transformation, and this domain provides strong evidence supporting the hypothesis on 'new behaviourism' offered earlier. Certainly, policies here showed little recognition of the agenda that disabled people's histories and struggles had confirmed as central (prioritising social and economic rights, tackling broad environments and facilitating autonomous pathways). With disproportionately lower incomes overall than across the non-disabled population, disabled people frequently relied on support, and the selectivist or 'special needs' bases for much of this offered New Labour ministers opportunities for tightening arrangements on testing and exclusion. Ideas about welfare dependency, fraudulent benefit claims, combating 'worklessness' and moving people from 'welfare to work' – in part reflecting previous Conservative themes (see Clarke, 1983; Cochrane, 1998) – were foundations for considering abolition or narrowing of access to some benefits, and anti-fraud initiatives that supposedly might distinguish 'real' from 'spurious' disabled claimants (Drake, 2000; Roulstone, 2000, p 434). As Riddell et al (2010, p 53) indicated, objectives affecting disabled people included not only social inclusion but also a 'welfare to work agenda, geared towards reducing levels of expenditure on benefits' (see also Drake, 2000; Grover and Piggott, 2005, pp 706-7).

The therapeutic and behaviourist leanings in practices envisaged for disabled or ill claimants attracted criticism (see Ravetz, 2008), while performance of programmes was questioned (Riddell et al, 2010), and relying on personal or employment advisors could imply changing individuals rather than improving labour markets. The government reviewed Incapacity Benefit (IB), introducing the All Work Test, later renamed the Personal Capability Assessment, to determine eligibility. Employment and Support Allowance (ESA) was to supersede IB and Income Support as the main form of income replacement benefit. One intention was to 'encourage' disabled people into employment, building on the idea that these benefit claimants did not want to work (although evidence supporting this was poor). Following a Work Capability Assessment (WCA), claimants would be categorised into those immediately 'fit for work' (seen as able to start work immediately), those destined for work-related activity (who could apparently start work with further support) or those not expected to look for work because of the 'severity of their impairment' (note Piggott and Grover, 2009). Access to support would be strongly affected by a person's categorisation. The strengthening of scrutiny and discipline caused concern among disabled people's organisations, especially given the disabling barriers in labour markets (including employer attitudes, inflexible hours, discrimination and inaccessible workplaces) and what some felt was a history of misrepresentation over the supposed 'problem' of disabled people's unemployment (Roulstone, 2000, p 429). Doubts and criticisms continued into the coalition period, including worries about the WCA and the disastrous personal circumstances precipitated by some negative decisions (Disability Alliance, 2010a; note also Work and Pensions Committee, 2011).

Under the UK coalition government; harder times for disabled people

The implications of developments under the coalition government are touched on in later chapters, and have been widely discussed (Disability Alliance, 2010b; Essex Coalition of Disabled People, 2010; Grant and Wood, 2011; Marsh, 2011; Sumpter, 2011; Wood and Grant, 2011). Present coverage therefore mainly synthesises and summarises. Points to acknowledge at the outset are that retrenchment in 'welfare' spending is ongoing and cumulative, with deteriorating conditions and reduced support for disadvantaged households. There are also intentions announced at the time of writing to limit future increases that would update benefit levels, although with some exemptions for disabled people (for some distributional analysis related to initial plans for cuts, see Horton and Reed, 2010; for later material, see Hill, 2012; NEF, 2012). Tax and benefit changes have appeared regressive overall, while some spending areas weighted towards poorer households have been targeted for substantial reductions (for housing, see Phelps, 2010; Murie, 2012a). Disabled people on low incomes with care and support needs are strongly affected by declining public and voluntary sector services, as well as by measures such as Value Added Tax (VAT) changes (Disability Alliance, 2010b), and many live in urban local authority areas facing especially large spending cuts. In late 2012, findings highlighted numerous problems for disabled people, including worsening health, stress and people left without adequate support (The Hardest Hit, 2012). There have been concerns too about a possible reversal of the trend for growing numbers of people being able to live independently (Essex Coalition of Disabled People, 2010).

Within the legislative programme, the Welfare Reform Act 2012 was central for disadvantaged groups. Policies included introducing the Personal Independence Payment (PIP) for disabled people, changing Housing Benefit and ESA, and moving to 'Universal Credit'. There would be a strengthened approach to fraud and error, and a new (quasi-contractual) 'claimant commitment' showing what would be expected of claimants (DWP, 2012a). In Chapter Four, Patrick discusses policy issues, including:

- the planned welfare 'benefits cap';
- sanctions on people failing to participate in particular 'back-to-work activities';
- financial pressures on single parents and claimants working part time.

Capping benefits meant limiting total benefit receipt for individual households, potentially affecting larger families negatively (but with exemptions in relation to disabled people) and undermining principles linking a family's entitlement with its scale of needs. Under the government's Work Programme, contracted organisations would be incentivised to assist people back to work, utilising methods including mentoring and work experience (see Patrick, 2012, for links to New Labour thinking). Some small-scale specialist personalised assistance was also to be targeted on people with severe impairments. Mandatory Work Programme requirements for claimants might be interpreted as useful back-to-work experience, or alternatively look reminiscent of 'community payback' punishments for convicted criminals. Toynbee (2012) notes the 'extraordinary power' to make some disabled people take unpaid work indefinitely (note also *The Guardian*, 1 December 2012, pp 22-3).

On the housing front, benefit restrictions seemed likely to compel some households in high-rent accommodation to relocate to cheaper places (with potentially damaging disruption of local connections), while reduced support for working-age tenants supposedly 'under-occupying' dwellings (the so-called 'spare bedroom tax') seemed likely to affect large numbers of disabled people in accommodation suited to their needs (Hodge, 2011; Wood and Grant, 2011, p 28; Harris, 2013a). Both these policies implied behaviour change in terms of households reducing their housing expectations, but might generate significant debt and homelessness. The prospect of fixed tenancy terms for social renting also implied a downgrading of rights to a stable, satisfactory and secure home environment, and perhaps some disabled people losing appropriate homes and going into inaccessible private rented accommodation because of income assessments (Muscular Dystrophy Campaign, 2010; for vulnerable groups and housing, see also Chapter Three). Specific policies appeared to pose difficulties for disabled people with carers and for some single people such as mental health service users (especially if forced into occupying only a room in accommodation shared with strangers). The government also planned reduced spending on supporting poorer households in relation to paying Council Tax. The idea of low-income people paying local taxes has had behaviourist resonances in the past, given its supposed potential to 'responsibilise' voters into opposing local government spending.

Plans linked directly to disability included transferring people from IB to ESA, and reducing numbers in receipt of ESA, with moves onto lower Jobseeker's Allowance incomes (Patrick, 2012). Categorisation remained a key methodology, with the WCA determining fitness to work, and existing IB claimants being reassessed. There has been a high rate of successful appeals against WCA decisions (Grant and Wood, 2011), and critical debate about assessment (note Work and Pensions Committee, 2011), but sanctions have been applied extensively to claimants judged to have some limited capability for work (Gentleman, 2012b; Malik, 2012a, 2012b; Patrick, this volume). Policy to apply time limits and means-testing for 'contributory' ESA (the form of ESA based on National Insurance contributions) seemed to undermine the principle that those contributing over their working lives should expect protection when experiencing illness or other difficulties (Marsh, 2011;

Wood and Grant, 2011, p 64; Patrick, 2012, pp 314-15). In addition, Disability Living Allowance (DLA) was to be replaced with PIP. The government directly sought to reduce spending, with assessment (and regular re-testing) determining who 'really needs' this benefit. Coalition strategy here illustrates the widening application of concepts of unacceptable dependencies (note also *The Guardian*, 14 March 2013, p 32 on the Independent Living Fund). DLA has recognised extra costs associated with daily living for disabled people, and many recipients are in employment (Disability Alliance, 2010b; Essex Coalition of Disabled People, 2010). However, assessment for PIP may not bring resources adequate to meet the 'additional disability costs' that clients incur (Wood and Grant, 2011, p 28), while restrictive criteria may affect people with physical mobility support needs. Reduced help for mobility implies disabled people becoming more dependent on others (such as care staff), and difficulties for them in 'getting out and about' (Carter and Peck, 2011; DBC, 2011, p 2; Wood and Grant, 2011, p 25). A government minister has reportedly indicated that out of an initial 560,000 people being reassessed by October 2015, 330,000 are expected to lose their benefit or have it reduced (Cassidy, 2012).

Also likely to affect many disabled people's lives is Universal Credit, intended to replace the range of received benefits with a single payment (although not incorporating some locally managed finance). It was claimed that this would:

- 'reintroduce the culture of work in households where it may have been absent for generations';
- provide a basic allowance with additional elements for children, disability, housing and caring;
- support people both in and out of work (DWP, 2010a, p 3).

Whether bringing benefits together would in itself reduce or extend stigma was uncertain, but clearly there would be strong conditionality for unemployed people, who would be expected to try to move into jobs (DWP, 2010a, p 4). The proposals generated numerous critical responses or cautions, including concerns about the impact on vulnerable or disabled people (see Wood and Grant, 2011; Tarr and Finn, 2012; Work and Pensions Committee, 2012). Critics worried that controversial testing would remain the gateway to disability components of Universal Credit, and that claimants would be subject to revised sanctions (including compulsions under a new mandatory work activity scheme). It could be argued, furthermore, that rolling benefits up together aids retrenchment and exclusion, by making more distant any alternative ideas about distinct rights, such as those to a secure, stable and adequate home, or to independent living in terms of accessible and appropriate services and linkages. If people's claims eventually can be reduced to time-limited and changing scores on a continuum of measurable relative 'deservingness', then social rights might be collapsed into an opportunity to be appraised periodically for a temporary income supplement at a level the government decides to permit, and subject to whatever behaviourist prescriptions are imposed.

Conclusions

This chapter has suggested that trends from the mid-1990s through into the present decade look distinctive enough to justify thinking in terms of a 'new behaviourism' affecting social policies. Despite continuities from earlier periods, there have been significant shifts. Markers include:

- New Labour's anti-social behaviour strategies;
- the widening scope of conditionality and contractarianism;
- politicians' embrace of behaviourist themes.

Disabled people have been much affected by the recent intensification of controls and exclusions, and the growing governmental preference for incentivising or enforcing behaviour change rather than tackling barriers and economic disadvantage. The capacity to increase surveillance and restriction rests in part on resourcing traditions linked to top-down selectivist methods constructed around individualised concepts of disablement rather than universalistic rights. It might be argued, furthermore, that with social security and support for disabled people repositioned within an increasingly negative political terminology of 'welfare', 'national burden' images of disability and chronic ill-health have gained wider currency. In this climate, even essential aids to independent living may be linked with ideas about unacceptable dependencies.

An important remaining question concerns how far the government's disciplinary orientations are offset by 'Big Society' goals, localism or factors such as the growth in the number of cooperatives (Co-operatives UK, 2012). A developed answer lies beyond the present chapter's scope, but overall indications seem negative (for issues, see Ellison, 2011; *PPPOnline*, 2011; Blond, 2012; Butler, 2012; NEF, 2012; Twivy, 2012). For disabled people, cuts have affected valuable supportive and advisory bodies, while the future of many user-led organisations and Centres for Independent Living may have become more uncertain (Roulstone,

2011). Suggestions that third sector organisations would benefit greatly as the government's programmes developed – being enlisted to provide specialist support or drawn in as partners on behalf of disabled people – may have proved over-optimistic, given the contracts awarded to private firms (Kerr, 2011). Certainly, there seem few signs of systematic empowerment via collective service user ownership of resources or new participatory rights in England, although much of social housing remains potentially distinctive on participation even if less so on user ownership (see Chapter Twelve for a fuller commentary). More generally, as the management of needy, vulnerable or 'difficult' people becomes increasingly subject to profit-maximisation, fragmentation of functions or outsourcing, there may be an impact on the quality of social interventions, and on advocacy for clients. At the same time, as Patrick (2012, p 309) puts it, the coalition government appears 'committed to a programme of welfare residualisation', differentiating it from New Labour despite similar behaviourist leanings. Outcomes within specific policy contexts must be matters for ongoing empirical enquiry, but perhaps in general terms the present coalition period of social policy will be summarised retrospectively as a time of increased social control, widespread exclusions and severe hardships.

THREE

Beyond protection: 'the vulnerable' in the age of austerity

Kate Brown

Introduction

The concept of 'vulnerability' has come to play an important role in shaping policies and interventions targeted at intervening in the lives of certain social groups. In times of economic austerity, ideas about vulnerability and the prioritisation of 'the vulnerable' have particular significance in the allocation of welfare resources in the UK. As one example, pledges to afford special protections to 'the vulnerable' appeared 13 times as the coalition government announced its first major public spending cuts in the 2010 Comprehensive Spending Review (HM Treasury, 2010b). Despite increased tendencies to organise welfare, resources and policies on the basis of vulnerability, this strategy rarely seems to come under scrutiny. This chapter examines the implications of a focus on 'the vulnerable' in UK social policy, situating vulnerability discourses within a context of behavioural regulation, social control and decreasing welfare resources. It is argued that although ideas about vulnerability seem to resonate strongly with the pursuit of social justice and the protection of those who need it most, notions of 'the vulnerable' move beyond protection, operating in a much more complex way; especially in relation to supportive and controlling interventions, inclusion and exclusion, and in 'qualifications' for welfare.

There are many different respects in which a person or group can be identified as vulnerable, with manifold implications. Although most often not clearly defined (Chambers, 1989; Mulcahy, 2004; Daniel, 2010), vulnerability tends to function in official arenas as a summarising concept that alerts us to the need and moral obligation to take action (Goodin, 1985). It can be used in ways that imply that it is innate or natural (as in the case of babies or pregnant women, for example) or it can be configured in terms of being situational and tied to certain predicaments or transgressions such as homelessness, domestic violence or involvement in sex work. Where it appears in its situational sense, the notion often refers to people who might be facing negative circumstances, with the implication that situations or events are not the fault of the particular person experiencing them. 'Vulnerability' is therefore a concept that is closely connected to judgements about human agency and 'deservingness', raising questions about how far the concept might be significant within selectively focused welfare systems.

The chapter now goes on to consider how vulnerability has been used in social policy since 1997, focusing on selected policy domains where it has been particularly significant. Developments under the coalition government are explored in relation to each policy domain. Three significant themes are then examined in turn:

- social control, vulnerability and the professional management of risk;
- paternalism, neoliberalism and vulnerability;
- the prioritisation of 'the vulnerable' in times of shrinking welfare resources.[1]

The analysis highlights that although there are certain benefits that individuals or groups may enjoy as a result of being classified as vulnerable, such benefits may come at a price. Viewed in a wider context of increasing behaviourism and social control through social policies, focusing attention on 'the vulnerable' can act as a conceptual mechanism that reinforces social norms and emphasises personal accountability for the difficulties experienced by individuals. How far this approach might be at odds with rights-based standpoints on welfare and citizenship is a key concern.

New Labour, the coalition government and the rise of the 'vulnerability rationale'

'Vulnerability' as a concept has appeared in UK social policy for several decades now, particularly in nursing (Appleton, 1999), in housing (discussed later) and in conceptualising responses to natural hazards or disasters (Watts and Bohle, 1993; Bankoff et al, 2004; see Schiller et al, 2001, p 5 for a useful summary). It has also evidently been drawn upon in official responses to certain social problems for some time. For example, the Wolfenden Report on 'prostitution and homosexual offences' published in 1957 made reference to the need to provide safeguards for those who were 'specially vulnerable because they are young, weak in body or mind, inexperienced, or in a state of special physical, official or economic dependence' (Wolfenden, 1957, pp 9-10).

Under New Labour, vulnerability came to play a fundamental role in the governance of welfare for adults who were seen to lack the capacity to protect themselves (Beckett, 2006; Dunn et al, 2008; Hollomotz, 2011; McLaughlin, 2012). The seminal *No secrets* guidance (DH, 2000)[2] enshrined vulnerability as one of the key criteria in the assessment and 'processing' of disabled adults (Dunn et al, 2008; Fawcett, 2009; Hollomotz, 2011). Although *Safeguarding adults* (ADSS, 2005) revised the language used in policy making, the legacy of the idea of vulnerability has endured in legislation (see Hollomotz, 2009, 2011; McLaughlin, 2012). As noted in Chapter Two, various other initiatives were developed under New Labour that addressed the presumed vulnerabilities of disabled people. Disabled people had won the right to receive 'direct payments' in 1996, with a view to this group arranging some of their own services and purchasing help they wanted. However, Hasler (2004) highlights that New Labour then altered initial plans for the direct payments scheme, with vulnerable disabled people excluded from the right to make such choices on the basis that they were deemed incapable of making appropriate judgements.

The vulnerability status of certain citizens was brought closer to the centre of New Labour policy in social care with the passing of the Safeguarding Vulnerable Groups Act 2006 (see McLaughlin, 2012). This legislated for a Vetting and Barring Scheme (VBS), which would involve extra checks for people who work or volunteer with children and vulnerable adults, as well as a national database of the details of these workers/volunteers.[3] McLaughlin (2012) uses the VBS to argue that ideas about vulnerability have spread from a grounding in disability and mental health provision, moving to the forefront of individuals' relationships with government. For some commentators, 'vulnerable identities' have come to characterise contemporary social policy and society (Furedi 2007, 2008; Waiton, 2008; McLaughlin, 2012). The utilisation of 'vulnerability' in the pursuit of policies that seek to control the potential threat that some people pose to others links the concept to a more general management of risk, a relationship explored further later in the chapter.

The coalition government made significant changes to the plans for the VBS after it came to power. The Protection of Freedoms Act 2012 has now been passed, which outlines a scaled-back employment vetting scheme for those working with vulnerable groups. The justification for this move was a need to 'redress the balance' of risk to be less in favour of protecting vulnerable people, and more in favour of avoiding the constraints and implications of this for the rest of society (DfE et al, 2011, p 3). This represents a more cautious approach perhaps, but a discourse of vulnerability nonetheless remains institutionalised within this particular policy domain. In the wake of the Savile sexual abuse scandal, debates about the best ways to protect vulnerable people appear to have resurfaced, with questions raised again about how far vetting schemes should seek to address individual vulnerability at the expense of individual freedoms.

Special protections have been extended to children for some time, often based on assumptions about their innate vulnerability (James and Prout, 1997). However, under New Labour, vulnerability took root in more formal policy and processing mechanisms for those under the age of 18 (Daniel, 2010). *Every child matters* (DfES, 2003, p 15) drew on theoretical notions of all children as positioned along a spectrum of vulnerability, as did the Common Assessment Framework designed to standardise the assessment of children's 'additional needs'. Various other New Labour initiatives targeted resources at specific groups of children perceived as particularly vulnerable because of their adverse circumstances. Introduced in 2003, the Vulnerable Children Grant was initiated with the intention of improving access to education for vulnerable children and encouraging local authorities to develop their strategic approach to dealing with this group (Kendall et al, 2004). Targeted Youth Support was also introduced, a multi-agency working initiative aimed at earlier intervention in the lives of vulnerable young people (DfES, 2007).

Classifications of children and young people's vulnerability also appeared within the processing and management of young people involved in crime. Within youth justice policy and practice, the assessment of vulnerability came to play a role in determining interventions for young offenders. Youth justice interventions were initially designed on the basis of addressing the risk that young people posed of reoffending, but vulnerability (defined as the risk of young people being harmed) then became a key focus for Youth Offending Service assessments. The vulnerability status of a young person came to be deemed highly relevant when determining a suitable response to young people's actions (Youth Justice Board, 2006, appendix 12, p 7). How such developments might play out in the lives of young people who offend is an issue given further consideration later in the chapter.

The influence of a vulnerability rationale in the provision of children's services is still evident under the coalition government, with the Education Minister, Michael Gove, centring his defence of the coalition's education bursary scheme for 16- to 19-year-olds on the premise that New Labour's Educational Maintenance Allowance has been replaced by a fund that 'targets' the 'most vulnerable' in full-time education (Gove, 2011b). However, the Education Minister quite tightly defined his 'most vulnerable' children as those in care, care leavers and those on income support,[4] perhaps a narrower view of vulnerability than that informing New Labour's initiatives. The Department for Education has also announced streamlined funding for children and families in the new Early Intervention Grant, funding that can be used for targeted support for vulnerable young people, with local authorities having greater flexibility to allocate this resource (DfE, 2012a). With some critics arguing that this grant represents a cut of around 11% (Puffett, 2010), it seems possible that we may be witnessing a narrowing of entitlement in relation to children's vulnerability under the coalition.

Moving on to consider policies that tackle crime and deviance, responses to incidents of 'hate crimes' have been increasingly regarded by police as requiring a different approach in cases where victims were deemed vulnerable (Roulstone et al, 2011). Following the inquest into the death of Fiona Pilkington and her daughter Francecca Hardwick in Leicestershire,[5] the protection of vulnerable adults seems increasingly to be used as one of the justifications for the continuation of strong control mechanisms to deal with those seen as perpetrating anti-social behaviour. Under the coalition government, the idea of criminal proceedings being informed by a victim's or perpetrator's vulnerability continues to thrive. Obligations to 'vulnerable victims' (as opposed to victims generally) and those 'least able to protect themselves' seem to be taking on even further significance (see Home Office, 2011, p 1). Exceptions are also made in the criminal justice system in the case of vulnerable witnesses, who are those under the age of 17, or people deemed to have mental health problems or 'physical disabilities' (Hoyle and Zedner, 2007).

There is evidence of an implied relationship between notions of vulnerability and transgressive or criminal behaviours (see Harrison and Sanders, 2006). For example, despite responses to the sale of sex becoming increasingly punitive, referring to women who worked in prostitution as vulnerable (rather than criminal) became increasingly popular during the New Labour period (Phoenix and Oerton, 2005; Carline, 2011; Phoenix, 2012). Richards (2011) notes that even potential terrorists are 'vulnerable', according to government policy and rhetoric. The anti-social behaviour agenda has often been couched in terms of 'tackling troubled families' (DCLG, 2011a) or 'problematic populations' (see Flint, 2006a), but a cluster of other terms is also used to describe populations and behaviours that are governed by this agenda, among which the phrase 'vulnerable families' often features (cf Centre for Social Justice, 2010; Flint et al, 2011; Morris, K. 2012). As Flint (2006a) has argued, these discourses highlight the problematic behaviour of particular individuals or households and distinguish the actions of these populations from the behaviour of 'ordinary' people.

Finally, vulnerability is also one of the three defined predicaments that triggered priority need under the Housing (Homeless Persons) Act 1977, making 'the vulnerable' among those classified as needing special fast-tracking through the social housing application process. The Act was given renewed support and updated during the New Labour era, most recently in 2002, and developments in this period continued to refine what did and did not count as vulnerability into one of the key dividing lines in the provision of social housing resources. Decisions about vulnerability status were to some extent guided by precedents in case law,[1] yet – although they offered some parameters for decision making – legal precedents left ample scope for housing practitioners' discretion in judgements about whether a housing applicant was vulnerable or not (see Niner, 1989, p 96; Lidstone, 1994). Vulnerability is therefore particularly important in terms of the more informal ways in which people are managed within the housing system (Cramer, 2005). Under the coalition government there have been radical changes to housing services and allocations of social housing. In terms of the ideas related to vulnerability under the Localism Act 2011 authorities will continue to be obliged to ensure that social homes go to 'the most vulnerable in society' (DCLG, 2011b, p 15), but how those who qualify for priority based on vulnerability will be affected by matters such as overall allocations of fixed-term tenancies is as yet unclear. At the time of writing further potential changes were also on the agenda.

Vulnerability and the management of risk: subtle social control

An overview of policies related to vulnerability raises questions about how far an emphasis on protection might shade into more subtle mechanisms of social control. Often, policies that extend special exceptions or exemptions to people on the basis of perceived vulnerability would seem to enhance the power of welfare professionals to make decisions on behalf of those they support. The 'power of welfare professionals' here refers to the operation of welfare practitioners within particular policy environments, rather than the actions of individuals independent of each other or of certain contexts. A more critical reading of government attention to vulnerability might consider this in the context of a trend towards behaviourism or the growing repertoire of therapeutic concepts and interventions by which people are monitored and reviewed as well as supported and assisted (Harrison, 2010). Given that ideas about vulnerability are most often applied by those in more powerful positions to define those in less powerful ones (Chambers, 1989; Parley, 2011), it might also be the case that elements of stigma or labelling may be involved in demarcations of who is vulnerable.

There are indications that notions of vulnerability sometimes operate to strip further power from populations who are already marginalised. Daniel (2010) has argued that the construction of children as vulnerable imagines them as passive recipients of our concerns, resulting in practitioners within the child protection system frequently overriding the wishes of children. Hasler (2004) and Hollomotz (2009, 2011) argue that the conceptualising of disabled people as vulnerable has acted to reinforce the power of disability professionals at the expense of disabled people. In her empirical work with adults with learning difficulties, Hollomotz (2011) found that vulnerability classifications actually serve to augment risk, stifling the development of networks and relationships that might offer disabled people protection from abuse. Dunn et al (2008) point to creeping social control via recent extensions of the High Court's power to intervene in the lives of vulnerable people instead of simply 'mentally incapacitated' adults. One of the most concerning things about this enhancement of official power based on the vulnerability of certain individuals or groups is that it would appear to have taken place somewhat by stealth and 'in the name of protection' (see Phoenix, 2002). Although pursued in line with ideas about social justice, making exceptions on the basis of vulnerability would also appear to shield official bodies from risk to some extent.

By classifying individuals as vulnerable, it would seem that there is also the potential implication that they need to be controlled. Taking account of research in social care settings, emphasising situational vulnerability would appear to be a way of indicating the risk posed *by* individuals as well as *to* them (Moon, 2000; Warner, 2008). Some of the terrorism literature illuminates links between vulnerability and threat particularly clearly. In his analysis of government policy on terrorism, Richards (2011) argues that government has tended to position those who cause a threat to the safety and security of the UK via terrorist activities as vulnerable people. Indeed, Richards (2011, p 150) notes that in the updated version of the government's strategy document on terrorism (*Contest 2*, or 'Pursue, Prevent, Protect, Prepare'; HM Government, 2009), the words 'vulnerable' and 'vulnerability' were used a total of 32 times. The use of 'vulnerability' in this terrorism policy functions to imply 'diminished capacity for rational behaviour'

(Richards, 2011, p 51). To put it another way, vulnerability discourses here would seem to serve to underline that people who disagree with mainstream ideas cannot be of sound mind.

In the context of a social policy agenda that has become increasingly preoccupied with conduct (Burney, 2005; Flint, 2006b; Squires, 2008), vulnerability classifications can be seen as linked with the pursuit and maintenance of social order and the encouragement of particular behaviours. Prostitution policy is an interesting example. Some liberal feminist writers have indicated that in this arena there has been an 'unethical mobilization of the vulnerability' of women who work in the sex industry (Carline, 2011, p 331). Carline (2009, p 53) argues that vulnerability has been used 'perniciously' to construct women who sell sex as victims, justifying the adoption of a 'moralistic agenda' and the criminalisation of women who work in prostitution (p 38). Scoular and O' Neill (2007) similarly maintain that the construction of sex workers as always and inevitably vulnerable is a governance technique that has reproduced binary and idealised notions of citizens, justifying stronger controls where women transgress accepted behavioural norms. Phoenix (2012) applies these ideas to policies that target young people involved in 'sexual exploitation', arguing that policy in this area has been increasingly based on the policing of working-class young women's sexual transgressions. Again, vulnerability is closely connected to increased governance of the behaviours of groups who do not fit in with mainstream ideas about conduct.

Based on the work of Giddens (1990), Beck (1992) and Bauman (2000), a growing body of empirical work has developed about the role of risk in social policy and welfare (Alaszewski et al, 1998; Culpitt, 1999; Kemshall, 2002; Parton, 2007). This may be usefully drawn on in relation to preoccupations with vulnerability. Something of a consensus has emerged about the pervasiveness of the concept of 'risk' and its link to institutional power. The proliferation of information that promotes risk-avoiding behaviour by citizens[7] could be seen as a moral enterprise occurring within a context of the increasing responsibilisation of individuals (Culpitt, 1999; Lupton, 1999). Kemshall (2002) asserts that the concept of 'vulnerability' functions in a similar way. In her work examining risk, she argues that as services became increasingly preoccupied with the auditing and assessment of individuals and with bureaucratic systems of risk management, so the concept of 'vulnerability' was taken on by local authorities to further enable the implementation of top-down priorities and selective systems (p 78).

Despite similarities, there are a number of ways in which attention to vulnerable groups might be considered to be conceptually distinct or different from the pursuit of risk management. As highlighted in the ethics and human rights literature, the concept of 'vulnerability' has perhaps even greater moral weight attached to it than notions of risk (cf Goodin, 1985; Turner, 2006; Mackenzie, 2009). If the coalition government pursues moral regulation with even greater tenacity than New Labour (see Blond, 2011; Brown and Patrick, 2012), it could be that the concept of 'vulnerability' flourishes further under the present government. Furthermore, given that vulnerability might be associated more with *potential* for negative outcomes rather than *likelihood* (Sarewitz et al, 2003), vulnerability may be more contingent than risk as it may be hard to anticipate or even hidden. This raises questions about the potentially far-reaching ramifications of social policy based on addressing vulnerability. Where interventions are calculated on the basis of vulnerability, it could be argued that this may lead to more pervasive state intervention than in instances where responsibilities are generated by responding to risk. This echoes Dunn et al's (2008, p 241) concerns that where an individual is not deemed sufficiently capable of making decisions, court-sanctioned 'substitute decision-making' on the basis of an individual's situational vulnerability could lead to state actions that are 'potentially infinite in scope and application'.

Vulnerability, neoliberalism and paternalism

Due to its connotations of weakness, vulnerability would often appear to be tied to paternalism. Policies that are associated with the protection of 'the vulnerable' have received special criticism from those committed to the social model of disability (Barnes and Mercer, 1996). Wishart (2003, p 20) argues that the use of the concept creates images of people with learning difficulties as limited, deficient and having a 'tragic quality'. In his view, the label 'vulnerability' paints those with learning difficulties as inevitably at risk of sexual abuse because of their impairment, which he indicates amounts to 'victim blaming' (p 20). Roulstone et al (2011) argue that where disabled identities are constructed as vulnerable in policies related to hate crimes, disabled people are denied the right to be taken seriously in the criminal justice system and their entitlement to legal protections is diminished. The suggestion advanced by Roulstone et al (2011) seems to be that where the criminal justice system is preoccupied with a focus on supporting and protecting the vulnerable victim, this negatively affects the apprehension and prosecution of perpetrators. If accurately interpreted, such developments have implications beyond disability, as the policing of hate crimes is employed to deal with a range of other social problems such as 'racial' tensions, homophobia, religious intolerance (see McGhee, 2005) and now also prostitution in some cases (see Boff, 2012).

Viewed within the policy context of advanced liberal democracies such as the UK, the increased use of the idea of vulnerability can be seen as part of the trend towards the characterisation of welfare as a gift rather than a right. Notions of vulnerable groups serve to underline the particular construction of individuals that is central to economic liberal models of citizenship; the citizen as capable adult, unbound by structural constraints, who needs activating or responsibilising (see Chapter Two; also Rose, 1999; Clarke, 2005; Flint, 2006b). In this sense, calling groups 'vulnerable' focuses attention on the individual *and detracts attention from the structural forces* that disadvantage people (see Wishart, 2003; Hollomotz, 2011). Campbell (1991) suggests that attitudes to vulnerable people are coloured by the demands of contemporary economic liberalism, shaped by popular desires to be rational, free, independent beings, and by a dislike of dependency. Despite gesturing towards notions of mutuality, the idea of the 'Big Society' would seem premised on these notions of the otherness of 'the vulnerable'. As is the case with philanthropic approaches, the rationale here seems to be that those capable and least vulnerable should help those who are 'less able'. Additionally this agenda involves reductions in the responsibilities of the state to accommodate 'the vulnerable', with this obligation moved from a public duty to the sphere of individual responsibility.

This is not to say that 'vulnerability' as a concept is always tied to paternalism. How the rise of a vulnerability rationale connects with and maps onto notions of citizenship is particularly contested and complex. As summarised elsewhere (Brown, 2011), some writers from across ethics, philosophy, legal studies and social policy have argued that vulnerability is a potentially transformative notion, able to function as a theoretical basis for achieving equality, autonomy and freedom in society (Goodin, 1985; Beckett, 2006; Turner, 2006; Fineman, 2008). Emphasising human interdependence, such 'vulnerability thesis' writers contend that when vulnerability is seen as part of the personal, economic, social and cultural circumstances within which *all individuals* find themselves at different points in their lives, it is able to offer a powerful model for relations between citizen and state (Goodin, 1985; Kittay, 1999b; Turner, 2006; Fineman, 2008). Applied universally, the concept of 'vulnerability' is seen as able to emphasise structural causes of people's varying degrees of fragility and need, as it helps enable a society-wide and blame-avoiding rationing of resources.

Butler (2004, p 31) also draws on the idea of a 'common human vulnerability' in her work responding to the September 11 terrorism attacks on the United States. For Butler (2004, p 44), human vulnerability is inescapable and innate, but constituted politically and according to 'norms of recognition' (see also Butler, 2009). As in the works of the vulnerability thesis writers, Butler uses the concept of vulnerability in a universal sense in order to advance the development of theoretical ideas that might be deployed in the pursuit of a fairer and more just society, emphasising the interconnectedness of human existence. This vulnerability-orientated ontology has been used as a basis for placing importance on the role of caring for dependants within society (Kittay, 1999b; Dodds, 2007), and has been put forward as a uniting citizenship model that would benefit disabled people (Beckett, 2006).

Vulnerability, then, is not intrinsically and inevitably linked to paternalism and 'gift-based' approaches to welfare (note Chapter Two for welfare characterised as a gift rather than a right). If deployed universally and viewed as constituted politically, the concept of 'vulnerability' can be used to focus on social inequality and 'livable lives' (Butler, 2004, 2009). However, this universal idea of vulnerability is rarely drawn upon officially in advanced liberal democracies such as the UK. Due to the dominance of neoliberal citizenship models based on the ideals of active and capable citizens, 'vulnerability' tends to be conceptualised as 'other' and as 'deficit-orientated'. Thus, the attention to 'the vulnerable' in contemporary social policy tends to be aligned with selectivism.

Prioritising 'the vulnerable' in the age of austerity

Labelling people as vulnerable can circumvent them being to blame for their problems, or act as an appeal against the impulse to condemn them for their actions or lifestyles, thereby legitimating claims on resources. Undoubtedly, for some individuals or groups, vulnerability classifications can function as a lever to vital and much-needed assistance and support. Yet where vulnerability is not constituted universally, but as something that differentiates people based on differences or deficiencies, it is a concept that is more aligned with the rise of specific interest groups and selectively focused welfare systems (McLaughlin, 2012). This has important implications for the distribution of resources in an age of financial austerity. In her work on housing, Levy-Vroelent (2010) argues that the expansion of the 'designation of vulnerable groups' in European housing policy places an emphasis on targeting particular groups, with the treatment of these becoming increasingly specialised.

The implication of targeting resources at particularly vulnerable categories, she argues, is that individuals and groups are placed into competition for rare state resources, diverting attention from overall reductions in welfare (Levy-Vroelent, 2010). This may go some way to explaining the popularity of the concept of 'vulnerability' in times of welfare austerity.

Offering a convincing account of the connection between vulnerable groups and particularism, McLaughlin (2012) argues that social activism in contemporary society is now based on 'vulnerable identities', and that this trend runs contrary to collective approaches and wider social movements such as unionisation. Associating vulnerable identities with the individualisation of social problems, McLaughlin argues that configuring particular groups as vulnerable means that the wider social, cultural and economic factors that shape experiences are left un-interrogated. Such an analysis might lead to a reconsideration of instances where vulnerability is mobilised in research or highlighted in campaigning work with the intention of highlighting that a particular group is deserving of more support or resources. In some senses, vulnerability classifications might be seen as a rebranding of the old paradigm of the deserving and undeserving poor. Without attention to wider distribution of resources, as support is awarded on the basis of vulnerability this would appear most likely to be at the expense of other groups who are seen as comparatively less needy.

Given the subjectivity involved in decision making about who is vulnerable, 'vulnerability' may be especially significant in the distribution of resources at points in welfare and disciplinary systems where professionals exercise judgement. In increasingly selective welfare systems, service users who conform to commonly held notions of how vulnerable people should behave may find their entitlement to be more secure. As one example, researchers have noted a gendered approach to classifications of vulnerability in housing allocations, with women located more firmly within vulnerability classifications due to their being more inclined to behave with deference and accept dependence (Cramer, 2005; and Passaro, 1996, reporting from New York). We might question whether the vulnerability assessments undertaken in the youth justice system operate with similar unintentional effects. Exploratory empirical research has highlighted that young people who 'perform' their vulnerability more adeptly might be those who enjoy more sympathy in sentencing, or less punitive sanctions (Brown, 2013). How such classifications might shape interventions differently for young men and young women might also be an area worthy of further investigation. Value judgements are at work behind decisions about who is vulnerable, and such judgements may become increasingly influential as the coalition government pursues its localism agenda (see Brown, 2012).

Concluding comments: beyond protection

At first glance, a focus on 'the vulnerable' at policy level would seem to resonate with principles of social justice and would appear to protect disadvantaged groups. However, on closer inspection, the implications of drawing on notions of vulnerability move beyond protection, shading into more regulatory practices. Due to links with 'deservingness', discourses of vulnerability subtly but pervasively serve wider policy mechanisms that establish what is appropriate and correct behaviour, and that subject people to sanctions should they fail to conform. Although they help some individuals to avoid blame for their difficulties, vulnerability discourses emphasise personal reasons for difficulties experienced by individuals, diverting attention from structural issues. Within the context of neoliberal social policy, targeting resources at 'the vulnerable' unintentionally helps to justify overall reductions in entitlements to welfare and is part of the tapestry of increasingly selective welfare systems, which undermine universal citizenship rights. For a summary overview, see Box 3.1.

Box 3.1: 'Vulnerability' as a conceptual tool in social policy

- 'Vulnerability' is a concept closely connected to judgements about human agency and 'deservingness', making it important within selectivist welfare systems.
- Where people are deemed vulnerable, this may also imply that their behaviour is problematic in some way.
- Due to the dominance of neoliberal ideas about active and capable citizens, vulnerability tends to be conceptualised as 'other' and as 'deficit-orientated', undermining universal citizenship models.
- Where resources are awarded on the basis of vulnerability, this can detract attention from the wider distribution of resources across society, and thus has the effect of placing different vulnerable groups into competition with one another.
- Under the coalition government, we appear to be seeing something of a narrowing of vulnerability classifications, with these being more tightly defined in some cases.

Deciding who is vulnerable is not easy, and where the behaviours of vulnerable people are also problematic or transgressive in some way, such judgements would appear to be further complicated. This was brought sharply into focus in the case of the sexually exploited young women in Rochdale, which received widespread media attention in September 2012. Social workers judged that the young women (some of whom were considered to be highly problematic to agencies) had been 'making their own choices' and 'engaging in consensual sexual activity' with older men, yet the local safeguarding board returned a verdict that perpetrators of abuse had exploited 'vulnerable victims' (Rochdale Borough Safeguarding Children Board, 2012, p 9). Which people are deemed eligible for services and resources on the basis of vulnerability is closely tied to the views of governmental and local professionals from across the public, private and voluntary sectors. How these actors interpret demand for resources and express claims about legitimacy and vulnerability may become even more significant in a time of limited welfare resources. In the age of austerity, it could also be the case that those vulnerable people whose behaviours are seen as more problematic might well be those who are less well served as provision is narrowed. In line with the contours of the rest of welfare provision in the UK, even vulnerability seems set to become increasingly conditional.

In the current context, the 'vulnerability rationale' seems to serve on the whole to 'otherise' rather than to include. However, this is not to deny that vulnerability discourses also work to the benefit of certain selected groups or individuals. 'Vulnerability' is not a concept that is intrinsically paternalistic and tied to selectivism, but given the hegemonic ideal of the capable agent in Western economic liberal democracies, 'the vulnerable' seem set to be singled out, judged and 'gifted' resources for some time to come. Were vulnerability notions to be conceptualised within policy in a more universal way, this could highlight politically constituted lived experiences of precariousness (Butler, 2004, 2009) and could lead to the reorganisation of state resources in a more just way. Perhaps one starting point might be that impact of the vulnerability rationale should be given further consideration by those who make use of it. Most concerning about the advancement of discourses of vulnerability is that their implications are largely taken for granted. In UK social policy, the concept of 'vulnerability' has a seemingly benign and therapeutic emphasis, behind which lie more controlling forces that should not be ignored.

Part Two
Policies, practices and implications in specific domains

Welfare reform and the valorisation of work: is work really the best form of welfare?

Ruth Patrick

Introduction

With clear links to this collection's exploration of the possible emergence of a 'new behaviourism', this chapter considers the coalition government's welfare-to-work strategy and explores the valorisation of work in which much of the policy agenda and related discourse are rooted. Welfare-to-work measures encompass a wide range of policies intended to encourage, enable and even compel benefit claimants to seek paid employment. In most recent years, welfare-to-work policies have centred on efforts to ensure that claimants are taking all reasonable steps to return to work, with a notable increase in the use of both incentives and sanctions to promote working behaviour. Indeed, activation measures that utilise welfare conditionality (attaching behavioural conditions to benefit receipt) have been employed with increasing vigour in the UK since Margaret Thatcher's social security reforms in the mid-1980s, and are today in evidence across the Organisation for Economic Co-operation and Development region (Gilbert and Besharov, 2011). Within Britain, a new welfare settlement operates across the political spectrum, which sees all three main parties in broad agreement about the 'problem' of 'welfare dependency', the policy prescription (benefit conditions and tough sanctions for non-compliance) as well as the hoped-for outcome: higher rates of employment (Deacon and Patrick, 2011).

Given its reliance on attaching behavioural conditions to benefit receipt, the UK welfare-to-work policy project is inevitably focused on seeking to engineer behavioural change. Indeed, 'welfare-to-work policies ... [bring] issues of motivation, choice and behavioural change to the forefront of policy design and public debate' (Wright, 2012, p 310). Underlying policy pronouncements are clear – and often explicit

– moral judgements about which behaviours should be encouraged and promoted (paid work) and which should be discouraged and changed (claiming out-of-work benefits). While politicians often treat this moralising as non-contentious, it is important to critically engage with the arguments underlying welfare-to-work policy and rhetoric. Therefore, this chapter provides a critical analysis of the coalition government's welfare-to-work policies, outlining relevant policy developments before highlighting shortcomings with the approach taken. It is argued that a policy agenda rooted in simplistic and stigmatising binary distinctions between those exhibiting the behaviour the government wishes to promote (workers), and those who apparently still need reforming ('welfare dependants'), is unlikely to succeed.

Theoretical frames – social citizenship

It is helpful to ground an exploration of the government's welfare-to-work agenda in theories of social citizenship. Citizenship can be understood for present purposes to denote membership of a community (Marshall, 1949), and for this chapter we are most interested in membership of the nation state, and the social rights and responsibilities attached to that membership. Critically, social citizenship is of value precisely because of its bounded nature: membership of the citizenry grants an individual certain rights and privileges that are not awarded to those judged to be outside of the citizenship community (Lister, 2003). Policies and rhetoric that differentiate and demarcate subgroups within any population will inevitably have consequences for such groups' inclusion (or exclusion) as citizens.

Citizenship theorising can be divided into two broad traditions: liberal and civic republican. The former construes citizenship as a status, with emphasis placed on both the rights and responsibilities of citizens (Dwyer, 2010). Contractualist thinking often suffuses liberal ideas of citizenship with rights and responsibilities bound together and made mutually dependent. This can be seen in welfare conditionality where the 'right' to social welfare becomes contingent on an individual fulfilling certain 'responsibilities', for example seeking and being available to work. Civic republican citizenship theories – which have their roots in Ancient Greece and the expectation that individuals would be actively involved in running the Polis – conceptualise citizenship as a practice, and thus focus more attention on the duties and obligations of citizenship (Dwyer, 2010).

Commentators on the New Labour regime consistently observed the single-minded focus on paid work as the primary social obligation that citizens should be expected to fulfil (see Dean, 1999; Lister, 2001; Prideaux, 2005; Dwyer and Ellison, 2009), an observation that validly can be extended to the coalition government. Today, we find evidence of both liberal and civic republican arguments operationalised in defending an emphasis on the duty to work. Given Blair, Brown and now Cameron's determination to end the 'something for nothing' culture by creating a 'new contract for welfare' (DSS, 1998; Conservative Party, 2010a), we have become familiar with promises to make the 'right' to social welfare conditional on individuals fulfilling their side of the bargain. Although deploying welfare conditionality and contractual rhetoric suggests recourse to liberal citizenship theorising, there often seems to be an undercurrent of more civic republican ideas where the duty to work arises regardless of government intervention. While work has long been held as a central citizenship obligation (see Marshall, 1949), what is marked about the contemporary era is the frequency with which this responsibility to work is drawn upon in government discourse and policy justification. Observers have also seen the duty to work mainstreamed as it has gradually been extended to encompass ever more of the adult population. As well as targeting the traditional groups of jobseekers, work-related welfare conditionality now affects many single parents, partners of unemployed people, and disabled people judged to have some capability to work (Wright, 2009).

Understanding work

With work hailed as the hallmark of the responsible citizen, recent governments have focused welfare reform efforts on seeking to create a nation of dutiful workers. The importance reserved for paid work is conceptualised as largely non-problematic, given politicians' representation of work as *the* activity most central to life and wellbeing (Newman, 2011). Indeed, government speeches and policy documents repeatedly proclaim the transformative potential of paid employment in the formal labour market as extending beyond pecuniary remuneration to improved physical and mental health, rising self-esteem and wellbeing, better family life and greater opportunities for children (DWP, 2008a, 2010b). Work is presented as the ultimate policy panacea – a silver bullet – that can not only end 'welfare dependency' but also deliver people from substance addiction and help Britain's most troubled families back on their feet (HM Government, 2012).

In understanding the prominence given to paid employment by all mainstream political parties, it is critical to recognise that employment often does seem to improve individual outcomes, as well as reducing government expenditure by boosting taxation revenues and decreasing spending on out-of-work benefits (Brown and Patrick, 2012). Unemployed households are at a greater risk of poverty and are more likely to experience ill-health, while communities where unemployment is high are also disproportionately affected by crime, family breakdown and anti-social behaviour, although the patterns of causality remain unclear. Furthermore, opinion polls consistently record a significant hardening of attitudes to benefit claimants, with less public support for generous welfare provisions (Harkness et al, 2012; National Centre for Social Research, 2012). It is perhaps not surprising, therefore, that welfare-to-work programmes have been so central to the welfare reforms of both New Labour and now the coalition government.

More conditions: the coalition government's welfare-to-work offer

Before problematising the coalition government's approach, it is important to outline its welfare-to-work strategy in its first two years in office (see Box 4.1). Although the coalition promises a 'new' approach to welfare reform, there is in fact marked continuity with that of its New Labour predecessor (Lister and Bennett, 2010), most notably in welfare-to-work where a reliance on welfare conditionality and benefit sanctions continues along a reform trajectory well trodden by Blair and Brown (Deacon and Patrick, 2011).

Box 4.1: The coalition government's welfare-to-work offer

More 'support'
- The Work Programme – a single programme of back-to-work support.
- The Youth Contract – a package of measures aimed at reducing the level of youth unemployment.
- Efforts to 'make work pay', particularly via benefit simplification and Universal Credit.
- Programmes of work placement and work experience. Given the mandatory nature of these, they could also be understood as part of the package of 'conditions'.

More 'conditions'
- The introduction of a 'claimant commitment' to embed the idea of a welfare contract between benefit claimant and the state.

- A ratcheting up of possible sanctions for non-compliance with the conditionality regime, including an ultimate sanction of three years without benefits for those who three times fail to comply with certain job search requirements.
- Mainstreaming conditionality within the benefits system, by increasing the number and type of benefit claimants subject to work-related conditionality via disability benefit reform and lowering of the age of the youngest child at which single parents are transferred from Income Support to Jobseeker's Allowance (JSA).
- Plans to introduce in-work conditionality to promote full-time employment.

Delivery mechanisms
- A reliance on the private and third sectors for programme delivery, most notably in the Work Programme.
- Emphasis on payment by results, on the basis of successful outcomes in moving people from welfare into work.

Employing contractualist rhetoric, the coalition promises that with more expectations will come more support, seeking to position its government as the one to finally deliver on ending supposedly entrenched welfare 'dependency'. Certainly, the coalition has ratcheted up possible sanctions for non-engagement with the welfare-to-work regime, with the Welfare Reform Act 2012 legislating for the ultimate sanction of three years without benefits for those who three times fail to participate in particular back-to-work activities such as applying for jobs or engaging in Mandatory Work Activity (DWP, 2012a). Furthermore, the coalition plans to introduce a 'claimant commitment', which will require all benefit claimants to promise to fulfil work-related conditions if they are to continue to receive social welfare (DWP, 2012b). Building upon the Jobseeker's Agreement first introduced by John Major's government in 1994, the claimant commitment will further entrench conditionality within the benefits regime, and is also a notable mainstreaming of the expectation that all claimants who receive out-of-work benefits (as well as many receiving in-work support) must enter into a written contractual agreement with the government.

Despite high-profile challenges from critics, the coalition also remains committed to a variety of programmes of work experience designed to assist people to get into the 'habit' of work. Sanctions are threatened for non-engagement in many of the schemes, meaning that the possibility of a referral on to a mandatory work placement can operate as a tacit threat to encourage individuals to terminate their benefit claim(s). Media coverage of the schemes has unveiled examples of benefit claimants working without remuneration as security stewards at the Diamond Jubilee celebrations, while there have also been cases of work experience participants being used as unpaid cleaners in homes, offices and council premises (Harris, 2012; Malik et al, 2012). Although the government recently reduced the compulsion within its scheme for young people, the Mandatory Work Activity Programme – which involves claimants doing work for the benefit of their community such as cleaning up rubbish or wiping off graffiti, 35 hours a week, for four weeks – is being extended so it can handle an estimated 70,000 referrals per annum (Malik and Ball, 2012). The government has also announced that disabled people judged to have some limited capability for work can be expected to participate in unpaid work experience or risk benefit sanctions (Malik, 2012a).

The coalition is also legislating to introduce in-work conditionality, where those receiving in-work benefits, but judged not to be reaching a minimum earnings threshold (equivalent to working full time at the minimum wage unless a claimant has caring commitments), are given work-related conditions to increase their levels of employment (DWP, 2012b). At the same time, the coalition has extended the level of conditionality faced by single parents and disabled people by continuing reforms introduced by New Labour. From 2012, single parents will be moved onto JSA when their youngest child is five, at which point they have to engage with back-to-work measures or risk benefit sanctions. When Prime Minister Tony Blair entered Downing Street in 1997, a single parent qualified for Income Support – which includes only limited work-related conditions – until their youngest child was 16. This has been reduced in a series of stages and, in a recent speech on welfare reform, Cameron (2012a) suggested that there is also scope to go further; by looking at what additional welfare-to-work conditions can be applied to single parents when their children start to receive free childcare at the age of three (see also Davies, this volume).

Particularly controversial are the reforms targeted at disabled people, which involve the migration of some 1.5 million Incapacity Benefit (IB) claimants onto Employment and Support Allowance (ESA) (Disability Alliance, 2011). Introduced by New Labour in 2008 for all new benefit claimants, ESA requires individuals to undergo a Work Capability Assessment (WCA) to determine fitness for work. On the basis of the test, performed by the private contractor ATOS Healthcare, claimants are placed in one of three groups (DWP, 2012c):

- Those who are found fit for work are refused ESA and instead advised to apply for JSA, providing they are eligible.

- Those judged to have some limited capability for work are placed in the work-related activity group (WRAG), where they are expected to participate in welfare-to-work measures or risk benefit sanctions.
- Those with the most severe impairments are placed in the support group, where they receive a higher level of benefit with no conditions attached to its receipt.

Under the IB to ESA migration, all existing IB claimants are being reassessed to see if they are entitled to ESA. The most recent government statistics show that 36% of those reassessed between December 2011 and February 2012 were found fit for work (DWP, 2012d).

The WCA has been dogged with complaints, and there is a high rate of successful appeals against WCA decisions, leading many to worry that people are incorrectly being found fit for work and then pushed into a welfare-to-work regime with which they are simply not well enough to comply. Despite ongoing controversy, the government is committed to continuing the IB to ESA migration, and has legislated to increase the possible sanctions faced by ESA WRAG claimants. Previously only threatened with reductions in the level of their ESA, claimants now face the withdrawal of 70% of their benefit for fixed periods of seven, 14 and 28 days in addition to the time it takes for them to re-engage with the work-related requirements made of them (DWP, 2012a). Statistics demonstrate that sanctions against disabled people are increasingly being employed, with 8,440 sanctions applied to claimants in the ESA WRAG between October 2010 and August 2011 (Malik, 2012a).

Supporting claimants to enter paid work

The coalition argues that as well as increasing the conditions attached to benefit receipt, it has increased available support in tandem. Government ministers point to 'radical' plans to simplify the benefit system and the introduction of the 'biggest back to work programme this country has ever seen': the Work Programme (DWP, 2012e). With regard to the former, the government is introducing a new benefit – Universal Credit – which is designed to simplify the benefit system while also sharpening work incentives by making sure that work always pays (Bennett, 2012). Universal Credit, intended to be introduced in a phased process from 2013 to 2017, will replace a number of benefits (including ESA, Income Support, JSA and Housing Benefit) and integrate out-of-work and in-work support by also incorporating tax credits. In an effort to deal with the problem that arises when individuals who leave benefits for work receive only a very small increase in their income, Universal Credit will be withdrawn at a single taper rate of 65%, meaning that individuals will keep 35 pence of every additional pound earned (Bennett, 2012). The government promises that Universal Credit will reduce poverty and increase the numbers in employment, as people are better incentivised to enter work. While a critical analysis of Universal Credit is beyond the remit of this chapter, it is worth noting that commentators have questioned whether the reforms will actually increase incentives, reduce poverty or deliver the 'holy grail' of benefit simplification (Toynbee, 2010; Simmons, 2011).

Marketed as a new departure, the Work Programme in fact shows substantial similarities with New Labour's Flexible New Deal, which was about to be rolled out just as New Labour's period in government came to an end (Deacon and Patrick, 2011). The programme is delivered by third and private sector agencies that are paid by results and encouraged to take a 'black box' approach in assisting those referred onto the programme back to work (DWP, 2011a). What this means in practice is that agencies can utilise whatever mixture of assisted job search, mentoring, work experience and training they think is most likely to be effective in getting participants into sustainable employment. Significant payments are available for positive outcomes, with a maximum fee of £14,000 for helping someone previously on IB into work that they sustain for two years (Wintour, 2011). While it is as yet too early into the programme's life to evaluate its effectiveness, a government-commissioned report by the National Audit Office (2012) described its targets as 'overly-optimistic'. Furthermore, recent figures have shown that in the 14 months to July 2012, only 3.5% of Work Programme participants were found a job that lasted six months or more (Ramesh, 2012a). Given ongoing fears regarding particularly high levels of youth unemployment and the proportion of young people not in education, employment or training (NEET), the government has also launched a Youth Contract. This is a package of measures to try to reduce youth unemployment, which encompasses employer subsidies for firms that take on young people as employees and apprentices, fast-tracked help from the Work Programme and guarantees of work experience placements for 18- to 24-year-olds (HM Government, 2012).

In its efforts to reinvigorate the welfare contract, the government – like its New Labour predecessors – has continually promised that its administration will be the one that will make work pay. Put simply, there are two ways to make work pay: policy makers can either increase the rewards attached to work or reduce those attached to benefit receipt (Lawton, 2010). In office, New Labour put marked emphasis on the former and in doing so developed some of the most progressive and socially just policies of its administration, including the National Minimum Wage, tax credits and financial assistance with the costs of childcare (Lister, 2001). While the coalition has preserved the 'making work pay' rhetoric, early signals suggest that it is rather more wedded to policy measures that cut the levels of benefits, with the coalition's austerity measures including an £18 billion reduction in the benefits bill by 2014–15. Most recently, the Chancellor George Osborne's 2012 Autumn Statement included plans to freeze benefit increases below inflation at 1%, a measure that will ensure that benefits fall relative to wages, which Osborne explicitly justified on the grounds of being 'fair' to working people (Osborne, 2012a). Furthermore, the controversial benefits cap can be understood as one mechanism for making work pay (Puttick, 2012). Introduced in April 2013, the cap imposes a limit on total household benefit receipt at the level of median household income for working households (after tax), with exemptions available for households with an adult or child in receipt of Disability Living Allowance. Capping the total household income available to those reliant on out-of-work benefits is one – admittedly rather crude – way of trying to ensure that work always pays more than welfare.

Recognising the importance of demand-side barriers to work?

The government's reliance on welfare conditionality suggests that the supposed problem of 'welfare dependency' can most effectively be tackled by changing the attitudes, incentives and ultimately behaviour of those reliant on out-of-work benefits. Such a discourse endures despite an economic climate of recession and high rates of unemployment. The corrective lens is firmly focused on the supply side of the labour market, with a concurrent neglect of enduring demand-side issues that can make the transition from benefits to work problematic (Standing, 2011a). Policy energies are committed to supply-side strategies such as increasing individuals' employability, work-readiness and motivation to find a job, while demand-side issues, such as the availability of work and suitable child care, and employers' behaviours, are consistently neglected. This neglect of structural barriers to work individualises the problem of unemployment – 'individualizing the social' (Ferge, 1997) – and operates to tacitly blame unemployed and economically inactive people for their 'welfare dependency' (Crisp et al, 2009; Newman, 2011). The supposedly impaired agency of out-of-work benefit claimants is the focus, while the ways in which agency is constrained and shaped by structural barriers are given insufficient policy attention. Such an approach can seem politically tactical in a period of welfare retrenchment, but becomes ever harder to justify against a backdrop of high rates of both unemployment and underemployment.

Under the coalition, we can see particular parallels between its poverty strategy and its agenda on welfare-to-work, with both seeming to individualise the 'problem', and foreground paid work as the seemingly transformative solution. Influenced by the Centre for Social Justice, which he founded while in opposition, Secretary of State for Work and Pensions, Iain Duncan Smith (2012), has developed a discourse on poverty that outlines five central pathways to poverty:

- worklessness;
- welfare dependency;
- drug and alcohol addiction;
- educational failure;
- family breakdown.

Dismissing the idea that solving poverty requires income redistribution, Duncan Smith argues instead for sustained interventions to address these five pathways. The pathways are easily individualised, and conceptualised as 'problems' of 'the poor', with posited policy solutions tied to an understanding that 'life change is the key to moving people out of poverty' (Duncan Smith, 2012). Importantly, worklessness is positioned as the central pathway to poverty, with work repeatedly described as the most effective route out of poverty and into independence and self-sufficiency. Aside from the issue that a one-sided analysis of the welfare-to-work problem is unlikely to prove effective, there are also consequences in terms of the negative impacts of a discourse that so squarely locates the 'problem' of unemployment as a 'problem' of individuals' behaviour and motivations. A supply-side emphasis can operate to exclude benefit claimants from the citizenry, at least until they take remedial action to show 'responsibility' and find paid work.

Problematising the 'work is the best form of welfare' mantra

Perhaps unsurprisingly, government discourses are largely silent on the ongoing problem of in-work poverty, which serves as a pertinent challenge to the 'work is the best form of welfare' soundbite (Newman, 2011). Sixty per cent of children in poverty and around half of working-age adults in poverty live in households where someone works (Harkness et al, 2012; Ramesh, 2012b). Given these figures, employment is better conceptualised as the surest route – but not a guaranteed one – out of poverty (Crisp et al, 2009). Frequently contained within the ranks of the working poor are the 1.3 million 'frustrated part-timers' (Aldridge et al, 2011; Oxfam, 2012) – those who would like to work full time but are only able to secure part-time employment. Underemployed part-time workers do not fit easily into the government's policy analysis, given that their existence suggests that the labour market 'problem' will not be solved by welfare conditionality and sanctions alone; instead implying a role for demand-side interventions around job creation and economic stimuli (Aldridge et al, 2011).

In repeatedly proclaiming the transformative potential of paid work, the government also seemingly ignores its own research that shows that the *type* of work in which individuals are engaged is important in determining whether the much-quoted positive outcomes around improved health, wellbeing and family life are actually realised (Wadell and Burton, 2006; Overell, 2011). While government rhetoric deploys a flat and simplistic conceptualisation of work as innately good and rewarding, the reality is that the nature of work can determine whether it delivers rewards beyond pecuniary remuneration. Research shows that those in insecure and menial jobs can actually find their health and wellbeing adversely affected by the work they are doing (Wadell and Burton, 2006), with parents also finding that family life can suffer when employment is uncertain and unstable (Ridge and Millar, 2011).

These findings are particularly relevant given that the current economic climate has seen a considerable growth in the number of 'vulnerable' workers in Britain, with the Trades Union Congress (2008) estimating that there are now two million individuals engaged in insecure and short-term work (cited in Crisp et al, 2009). Britain now has the highest number of 'zero hours' contract jobs in Europe (Oxfam, 2012) – innately unstable roles where employment contracts do not specify any number of hours that the employee is required to work, instead stating that the employee must be ready to work whenever asked. A growing proportion of the economically active population also experience a cycle of low pay/no pay, a cycle that can persist across the working life (Shildrick, 2012). Such is the instability of the economic and employment context for such part-time, contingent workers that Standing (2011b) has described a 'class in the making' – the 'precariat' – which includes those in insecure jobs whose lives are characterised by fragility and uncertainty.

Arguably, the reality of working life for many Britons suggests that more needs to be done to address issues of 'poor work' (Crisp et al, 2009; Shildrick, 2012), while the promise that 'work is the best route out of poverty' remains rather hollow for those who continue to experience poverty alongside paid employment. These issues are underexplored in both government policy and rhetoric, which rely on simplistic narratives that imply that work always delivers transformative outcomes by enabling people to both leave 'welfare dependency' and escape poverty. These shortcomings are only magnified as we turn to explore the divisions and dichotomous distinctions utilised by the government to segment the population along a work/non-work axis.

'Strivers and shirkers' – drawing divisions between the 'deserving' and 'undeserving'

Making distinctions between the 'deserving' and the 'undeserving' has a long history (Warren, 2005), with means-tested, selective benefit provision inevitably leading to governments engaging in a continued revisioning of who should be deemed 'deserving' of state support. Importantly, however, the contemporary climate has seen an increase in both the frequency and intensity with which such demarcations are made and utilised. The government creates and reinforces distinctions between those behaving as it would like by working, and others who 'need' the threat of sanctions, and the push of conditions, if they are to leave their much-stigmatised 'welfare dependency' behind. Work is associated with responsibility and independency, while non-work is implicitly equated with irresponsibility and dependency. Admittedly, the government repeatedly promises to protect the 'most vulnerable', those who cannot work, but this category appears to become ever more residualised as increasing numbers of those on out-of-work benefits are moved into the welfare conditionality regime.

At the same time, all three main political parties compete to offer the greatest praise to the 'hard-working majority' who are depicted as valiantly battling to survive in 'credit-crunch Britain'. Indeed, the past two years have seen the emergence of new discursive categories such as Ed Miliband's 'squeezed middle' and Nick Clegg's 'alarm clock Britain', intended to celebrate and elevate the actions of workers who are unproblematically assumed to be fulfilling their duties as 'good' citizens. Most recently, the government has been promising to support the nation's 'strivers', implicitly contrasting their hard-working behaviour with that of the 'shirkers' whom Osborne (2012b) describes as passively 'sleeping off a life on benefits'. Arguably, the government is deliberately creating and sustaining these binary divisions in order to justify and defend a policy approach that is squarely focused on residualising welfare and increasing the level of welfare conditionality faced by the large majority of those on out-of-work benefits.

The government's uni-dimensional approach too often seems to suggest fixed groupings of hard workers and passive benefit claimants, ignoring that these groups are in fact fluid, with frequent movements between work and benefits unfortunately the norm for those stuck in the low pay/no pay cycle (Shildrick, 2012). As soon as analysis looks beyond rhetoric to lived reality, it is found that the simplistic binary dualisms collapse and are replaced instead with a picture that is far more nuanced and complex. Indeed, the present writer's ongoing qualitative research into the lived experiences of welfare reform is finding that working-age benefit claimants frequently draw on strong work ethics, have experience(s) of paid work and are often actively engaged in efforts to move off benefits, where this is a realistic aspiration. Presented with the government's discourses around benefits as a 'lifestyle choice', research participants reflect on the challenges and hardship associated with reliance on benefits as well as the very real 'work' that getting by on benefits demands.

Conceptualising those on out-of-work benefits as 'dependent', and contrasting this with the supposed 'independence' of those in paid employment, may be politically convenient, but it is based on a simplistic and arguably unsustainable understanding of dependency. As Titmuss (1958) argued, we are all welfare dependants if welfare is conceptualised as encompassing not just the most visible forms of social welfare but also occupational and fiscal welfare (which include benefits linked to employment and tax relief). While government analysis suggests (see Cameron, 2012a; Duncan Smith, 2011, 2012) that those in work are independent and self-sufficient, the reality is that many millions receive forms of social welfare via the tax credits regime and financial assistance with the costs of childcare. It can also be argued that there is real scope in undertaking a fundamental re-evaluation of the meanings of both autonomy and independence, in order effectively to challenge the idea that human dependency is necessarily and always a negative characteristic. Much can be learnt from ethic of care theorists (Mink, 1998; Kittay, 1999a; Williams, 2012a), who argue for a celebration of human interdependence and an associated reconsideration of the place of both work and 'care' in people's lives.

Given the regularity with which workers are praised, and non-workers stigmatised and undermined, it seems likely that this will have impacts both for how welfare claimants are seen and for how they see themselves. With regard to the former possibility, a government rhetoric that is comfortable employing stigmatising and derogatory language to describe those reliant on out-of-work benefits seems to give licence for a tabloid media that is even more forthright in its censure and critique of those people who are out of work. Furthermore, it seems inevitable that the instrumental moralising in which the coalition is engaged will have some impact on public attitudes and opinions. As individuals and society are increasingly conditioned to see unemployment as being the fault of the individual, the 'economically inactive' may well face increased public condemnation and discrimination from prospective employers (Newman, 2011). Additionally, there is an under-researched question regarding the impact of the 'welfare dependency' discourse on those on out-of-work benefits, who may find their own identity challenged by the media and government onslaught. The government's stigmatising has a moralising character, which may ironically serve to *de*moralise those reliant on benefits, who could internalise and respond to the negative depiction of benefit claimants in ways that further exclude them and make their return into formal employment less likely (Brown and Patrick, 2012). Indeed, it seems possible that welfare claimants will become conditioned to see their own behaviour and supposed 'dependency' as flawed and symptomatic of deeper personal failings. This could lead to a shift from welfare conditionality to self-conditioning, where claimants amend their own behaviour in ways that the government would like, not in response to incentives and sanctions, but as a result of a pervasive rhetoric that suggests the necessity of work and the importance of making the welfare-to-work transition (Dwyer and Ellison, 2009). This area is undoubtedly a fruitful one for further research, and this author's own research into welfare claimants' experiences of welfare reform has found individuals internalising the idea of the 'welfare scrounger', as well as becoming increasingly desperate to move off benefits, perhaps suggestive of welfare 'conditioning'.

Citizenship and work – an exclusionary approach

Government efforts in the welfare-to-work arena are often justified as measures to help those reliant on out-of-work benefits become socially included as citizens, seeming to neglect the ways in which a citizenship discourse that gives such primacy to paid work may operate to exclude many from the national citizenship community. Situating paid work as the central citizenship obligation of the good citizen has inevitable exclusionary consequences for all those not currently working (Lister,

2003). All those subject to work-related conditionality are also subject to the suggestion that they are failing to fulfil their citizenship duties, with meeting welfare conditions characterised as not only helping such individuals escape benefit 'dependency' but also enabling them to secure a more certain citizenship status. Citizenship thus becomes a disciplinary tool to promote behavioural change and regulate individual behaviour, with social citizenship becoming 'increasingly conditional, exclusive and selective in recent years' (Lister, 2011, p 78). Although the government promises to protect those who 'really' cannot work, those receiving less conditional social welfare will nonetheless also experience a more precarious citizenship status given that they are not performing the prescribed role of the dutiful worker-citizen. Meanwhile, those best buffered from the obligation to work are rich non-workers, who seem to be given a tacit get-out clause by their supposed 'independence' from social welfare. It is possible that rich non-workers are included in the broader civic republican emphasis on the duty to work, but they certainly do not face the interventionist and sometimes punitive approach that is the lot of those reliant on out-of-work benefits.

By prioritising paid work, the government's citizenship approach also serves to neglect other forms of socially valuable contribution in which many non-workers are so often engaged, such as volunteering, 'care' work and the activities of parenting. While paid work is consistently valorised, 'care' work is devalued and all too often rendered invisible, with the suggestion that single parents must be subject to welfare-to-work carrying with it the implicit message that parenting does not constitute work (see also Davies, this volume; Fraser and Gordon, 1994). The economic imperative of welfare-to-work seems to crowd out the ethic of care (Williams, 2012b), with paid work given prominence over other forms of contribution that individuals may themselves want to prioritise. Ironically, Cameron's much-maligned and misunderstood 'Big Society' vision is of a society where individuals are more active in their local communities, with volunteering praised and widely encouraged (Ellison, 2011). Arguably, there is a lack of fit between this deepening and widening of personal responsibility and the government's continued emphasis on paid work, which downplays and undermines the very forms of contribution on which any Big Society would depend.

Conclusion

The government's valorisation of paid work has the potential to exclude those not in paid work but reliant on out-of-work benefits, who effectively become second-class citizens. Based on simplistic and unsustainable divisions between the deserving workforce and undeserving 'welfare dependants', this approach stigmatises and 'others' a significant proportion of the British working-age population. Further, a flat conceptualisation of paid work as 'the best form of welfare' neglects the endurance of in-work poverty and the questionable rewards of temporary, insecure and menial employment – 'poor work' (Shildrick, 2012). Work, and its undoubted importance and value in individuals' lives, needs to sit alongside (and not above) the importance of the right to both receive and give 'care', which should be incorporated as central elements of both citizenship and social justice (see Kittay, 1999a; Williams, 2012a). Celebrating and even valorising 'care' as a collective social good in which we are all engaged at some point in our lives (whether as recipients or givers of 'care') should also help to move us away from flawed conceptualisations of self-sufficiency and independence, instead embracing the fundamental reality of human interdependence (Williams, 2012a).

The coalition's welfare reform approach, with its tying of paid work to citizenship status, suggests that the only way to enable the social inclusion of out-of-work benefit claimants is by assisting them to make the transition into paid work. While this may well be the right direction of travel for many, there is also real scope for reappraising and reconsidering just what should be the duties of a good citizen. A conceptualisation of social citizenship that moves away from a uni-dimensional focus on paid work, and is perhaps more fluid and embracing of other forms of contribution such as volunteering, parenting and caring, has the potential to deliver a more inclusive form of citizenship. Given the coalition's avowed commitment to its welfare reform project, such a shift in citizenship theorising – by government at least – does not currently appear a likely prospect.

FIVE

Sanctuary or sanctions: children, social worth and social control in the UK asylum process

Ala Sirriyeh

Introduction

This chapter examines how discourses on asylum and childhood intersect in policy and practice in the UK asylum process, and explores the role of judgements on 'social worth' (Morris, L., 2012a) and mechanisms of social control. In May 2010 the Conservative/Liberal Democrat coalition government declared that it would end the detention of children for immigration purposes. This followed campaigns that had highlighted the psychological and physical health impacts on children being held in immigration detention (Campbell et al, 2009; Burnett et al, 2010). This initial coalition declaration was later modified by Immigration Minister Damien Green, who said that the intention was now to 'minimise' child detention (McVeigh and Taylor, 2010). Deputy Prime Minister Nick Clegg (2010) had described concerns for the welfare of children as the 'starting point' of the coalition's approach to this issue. However, with a commitment to maintaining the restrictive asylum system that currently operates in the UK, the end point of government policies appears more complex.

Debates on child welfare and on the reception of asylum seekers share some parallels, as each centres on concepts of 'vulnerability', the 'ethical responsibilities of society' and 'rights to recognition'. However, asylum-seeking children are subject to inherently conflicting policy and practices on child welfare and asylum. While child welfare discourses are increasingly inclusive (Giner, 2007), asylum seekers have been marginalised and excluded over the last two decades. Asylum-seeking children occupy a contradictory status between these two policy agendas.

This chapter explores how claims for recognition in the asylum process are formed around notions of 'social worth' (Morris, L., 2012a) and vulnerability, and examines how these are identified, ordered and regulated through the asylum process. It is argued that claims for recognition are acknowledged according to a judgement of social worth based on an accepted 'performance' of passive vulnerability and absence of perceived threat. People are positioned as vulnerable and in need of protection, or framed as deviant and in need of exclusion or expulsion. The chapter explores how mechanisms of social control operate using surveillance, conditionality and sanctions to mark out those to be included or excluded. Through a focus on the experiences of asylum- seeking children there is an analysis of how understandings of the social worth of children are engaged in these processes in ways that reinforce or challenge restrictive asylum policy and practice. It is argued that while more inclusive child welfare approaches have been incorporated within aspects of the asylum system or have enabled modifications to some of the most exclusionary aspects of asylum policy, more radical transformations are constrained when the broader restrictive asylum framework remains firmly in place.

Background to asylum policy

The *United Nations Convention and Protocol Relating to the Status of Refugees 1951* (hereafter the UN Refugee Convention) states that in order to claim refugee status, people must prove that they have 'a well-founded fear of being persecuted for reasons of race, religion, nationality, membership of a particular social group or political opinion'. The term 'refugee' refers to a person who has been granted asylum on the basis of these claims, while 'asylum seeker' refers to a person who has applied for asylum and is waiting to hear the outcome of their claim.

During the 1990s the numbers of people claiming asylum in Europe rose, reaching a peak in the UK in 2002 when 84,000 people claimed asylum there (Sirriyeh, 2013a). The numbers have since been in decline, although 2011 saw a rise of 11% (19,804) compared with 2010 (17,916) (Home Office, 2012a). The UK government has responded by introducing increasingly restrictive immigration controls and reception conditions. There was no specific asylum legislation until the Asylum and Immigration Appeals Act 1993, although this built on earlier rounds of restrictive immigration policy. Since 1993 there have been a further eight Acts on immigration and asylum, each imposing more restrictions and conditionalities to direct the behaviour of asylum seekers.

Asylum-seeking children may be dependants on their parents' asylum claim or may be claiming asylum in their own right if they are in the UK alone. Unaccompanied asylum-seeking children are under the age of 18, claiming asylum in their own right and with no adult relative or guardian in the UK to provide care. In 2011, 6% (1,277) of asylum applicants were unaccompanied minors (Home Office, 2012a). Of these applicants, 30% were males from Afghanistan and overall 82% of unaccompanied minors were male. Local authority children's services departments hold responsibility for the welfare and resettlement of unaccompanied minors under the Children Act 1989. Where an unaccompanied minor is assessed as being 'in need', they are entitled to the same level and range of services as 'citizen' children (Wade et al, 2012). They are supported in a range of placements, including shared housing, foster care and children's homes. Those under the age of 16 are most commonly placed in foster care, while those aged 16 and above are usually placed in shared housing with floating support (Wade et al, 2012).

Claiming rights: social worth

Children and asylum seekers both feature prominently as key populations within contemporary debates on rights, recognition and citizenship. Both are viewed as incomplete citizens, often deemed in need of 'citizenship education' (Cockburn, 1998; Sirriyeh, 2010). They are either to be moulded into model citizens through protection and guidance or, in the case of refused asylum seekers, judged as lacking citizenship potential and rejected through abandonment, confinement or expulsion. Children in general are regarded as an investment in the future of the nation (Hendrick, 2003) while asylum seekers and other unwanted migrants are often framed as jeopardising that future.

Although they have been the subject of divergent discourses and policy frameworks with distinct historical genealogies, both populations have been framed in terms of their ethical demands on the nation and have been signified as 'moral touchstones'. Nick Clegg (2010) declared that the 'test of civilised society' is in 'how it treats its young children', while the UK's welcome and offer of sanctuary to people fleeing persecution is held as a marker of its status as a good 'host' (Sirriyeh, 2013b). The welfare conditions of asylum seekers and children are used to interrogate the ethical status of the nation and test and secure its boundaries. However, the moral status, social worth and borders of the categories 'asylum seeker' and 'child' have also been contested and redrawn over time. This has influenced the basis on which these populations can gain recognition.

Drawing on the writings of Honneth (1995) and Lockwood (1996), Lydia Morris (2012a) has recently explored the 'moral grammar' of claiming and recognising rights in the case of asylum claimants and the withdrawal of welfare. She (Morris, L., 2012a, p 42) discusses Honneth's proposition that 'full membership within a rights-granting community' signifies recognition of 'social worth', which is defined as making a positive contribution to the society and, therefore, depends on what is acknowledged as socially useful. Definitions of social worth are open to reordering when exclusion leads to morally motivated struggles against it and an assertion of claims for recognition. However, Lydia Morris (2012a) observes that in considering the dynamics of these potential struggles, it is important to understand who is able to claim and be recognised as having social worth. Referring to the work of Lockwood (1996), she suggests that this is dependent on the level of access people have to moral or material resources that enable claims-making. Some groups are disadvantaged because they have an unequal access to these resources.

In welfare systems, social worth is commonly acknowledged on the basis of (a) recognition of social contribution or (b) being 'vulnerable' and therefore someone whom society has an ethical obligation to protect. Brown (2012, p 42) suggests that in social welfare practice 'the vulnerable' are often constructed 'as those who are less accountable for their circumstances or actions, and as those who have less "agency" in the development of perceived difficulties in their lives'. Migrants, including asylum seekers and refugees, are frequently viewed in terms of their contributions or vulnerabilities, which determine whether they are seen as 'deserving' or 'undeserving'. Policies on asylum originated in a rights-based approach enshrined in the UN Refugee Convention. However, in recent decades there has been a narrowing and qualification of this discourse, with a reassessment of the social worth of people seeking asylum and the ethical responsibilities of 'host' societies. This has been marked by exclusions from full membership of these societies and the curtailment of rights and welfare support. The former 'morally untouchable' category of 'deserving political refugee' (Cohen, 1994, p 82) has been redrawn, fragmented into the subcategories of 'genuine refugees' who are those deemed to have legitimate claims of fleeing persecution, and 'bogus asylum seekers' who are threats to the nation's security and socioeconomic wellbeing. This undermines asylum seekers' social worth as human beings who are subjects of ethical responsibility and moral obligation.

As a consequence of migration, people who live in a country and are subject to its laws may not be full citizen members (Benhabib, 2004). While those with full membership status benefit from the social and economic rights aligned to national citizenships, these markers of citizenship simultaneously establish boundaries for exclusion. Just as citizens have been categorised as 'deserving' or 'non-deserving', this moralising approach has also been applied to migrants (including asylum seekers) in the allocation of resources, but more fundamentally over access to citizenship and the 'rights to have rights' (Arendt, 1958). Soysal (1994) states that the growth of international institutional arrangements established to guarantee and protect rights at a supranational level in the 20th century led to an expansion in the recognition of rights claimed through universal personhood. However, while these developments had an impact, the significance of national citizenship as a marker of rights has not diminished. Lydia Morris (2012a) contends that claims for recognition go beyond a dualism of citizenship rights and rights of universal personhood. She suggests instead that there 'has been the elaboration of a hierarchical system of legal statuses with different rights attached' (p 41). The nation-state border is drawn through a hierarchy of entitlements to social, political and economic rights. In an era of globalisation and increased international migration, the borders of rights and entitlement have become increasingly significant in establishing and marking out membership of communities and the boundaries of belonging. In this hierarchy, asylum seekers have assumed 'an almost para-digmatic status as the outsider par excellence' (Darling, 2009, p 649).

Any acknowledgement of the social worth of asylum seekers is commonly made on the basis of being a vulnerable subject rather than being socially active. In order to be vulnerable, people must appear to be passive and non-instrumental. Attempts to exert agency and to be a decision maker are often discouraged. 'Refugees' are no longer imagined as the brave political émigrés of the Cold War era and instead are transformed into the social category of dependent asylum seeker. As a consequence, campaigns seeking to redress exclusions and reassert asylum seekers' social worth have often used discourses of vulnerability in response. One way in which some asylum seekers can be included within 'the vulnerable' is through their status as children, and asylum-seeking children have been the focus of several high-profile campaigns.

In the 19th and 20th centuries, the protection of children became a major public policy aim in the UK, with the expectation that it was the responsibility of adults and the state to protect children (Cockburn, 1998; Giner, 2007). In this process, different understandings of the nature of childhood developed, which had implications for the kinds of models of social control that emerged. Jenks (2005) identified two broad understandings of the characteristics of 'the child': the wild and sinful 'Dionysian child' who requires strict discipline from adults, and the innocent and intrinsically good 'Appollonian' child who is 'naturally perfect but needs to be safeguarded from the corrupting influences of the adult world' (Smith, 2012, p 34). Recent legislation and supranational conventions focused on the welfare of children have been based largely on the latter. The *UN Convention on the Rights of the Child* (hereafter CRC) 1989 enshrined the universal rights of the child (Article 2) and state duties to protect children (Article 4). Article 3 of the CRC declares that the 'best interests' of children must be the primary concern in making decisions that affect them. The UK ratified the CRC in 1991 but held a reservation on Article 22, which requires states to ensure that refugee and asylum-seeking children receive appropriate protection and humanitarian assistance. The UK finally withdrew this reservation to CRC in 2008 following criticism that it was not compatible with the object and purpose of the convention. In UK legislation, the Children Act 1989 established a duty for local authorities to safeguard children's welfare, especially children 'in need', which includes unaccompanied minors. Child welfare also featured as a central policy agenda for New Labour. The Children Act 2004 drew on notions of children as inherently vulnerable. It established a duty on state agencies to safeguard and promote the welfare of children. This exempted immigration removal centres, although *Every Child Matters* guidance in 2009 stated that 'every child matters even if they are someone subject to immigration control' (Dorling and Hurrell, 2012, p 5). The precarious status of asylum-seeking children in these policies and legislation has been a key area of contention, while the growth of a children's rights discourse has simultaneously enabled campaigns to centre on the welfare of children in asylum policy. Asylum-seeking children enter into a relationship with the state on the basis of their identity as asylum seekers, but also as 'children'.

Social control in the asylum process

Mechanisms of social control are used to create and maintain forms of order based on the notions of social worth referred to earlier. Innes (2003, p 3) defines social control as 'the purposive mechanisms used to regulate the conduct of people who are seen as deviant, criminal, worrying or troublesome in some way by others'. This section outlines some key examples of the mechanisms of social control used to categorise asylum seekers and asylum-seeking *children* into deviant risks or innocent vulnerable beings requiring different forms of social regulation. Three broad approaches to control discussed are surveillance, the imposition of conditionalities and, tied to this, the imposition and enforcement of sanctions.

Surveillance

There has been a proliferation of work on the experience of surveillance in recent years within debates on securitisation. However, not everyone is monitored to the same extent. Bigo (2008) highlights this through his concept of the 'ban-opticon dispositif', combining Foucault's analysis of Bentham's 'panopticon' (the all-seeing mechanism of surveillance) with Jean Luc Nancy's and Agamben's theories on the 'sovereign ban'. The subject of the 'sovereign ban' is denied the rights of the political citizen, 'held within the purview of the law's censure but excluded from its protection' (Farrier, 2011, p 12), abandoned yet still held by the law. Bigo (2008, p 32) suggests that the concept of the 'ban-opticon dispositif' 'allows us to understand that the surveillance of everyone is not on the current agenda but that the surveillance of a small number of people, who are trapped into the imperative of mobility while the majority is normalised, is definitely the tendency of the policing of the global age'. Asylum seekers are a key group within this monitored population. At a time when governments are plagued with perpetual anxiety that they have lost control of immigration, various tactics of surveillance are deployed to ensure that the solidity of their borders is maintained. These tactics have been utilised within the asylum system to make sure that certain people are visible and marked as out of place, and to prevent them passing through undetected and merging into the wider population. Through the 'upstreaming' of migration policies these processes begin even before people arrive in the UK through the use of extra-territorial border controls. Reynolds and Muggeridge (2008, p 4) point out that 'since there is no legal way to travel to the UK for the specific purpose of claiming asylum, asylum seekers ... are forced to travel irregularly in "mixed flows", and hence encounter the same border controls as other irregular migrants'. The very act of travelling independently outside of official refugee resettlement programmes becomes defined as suspect. Surveillance continues at the UK border and is then built into the asylum support system.

As representatives of members of the Schengen Group, European Union (EU) government ministers develop joint policies on border control. In 2003 they introduced the Dublin Regulation (known as Dublin II), which prohibits asylum seekers from making an application in more than one EU state. This is an attempt to prevent 'asylum shopping' whereby applicants are said to select more favourable destinations in terms of welfare provision or asylum claim success rates (Hynes and Sales, 2010). In order to enforce this policy, people aged 14 and above applying for asylum in an EU country are fingerprinted and the prints are entered onto the EURODAC database. This means if they subsequently claim asylum in another EU state they can be detected through the database and removed back to the 'safe third country' (the first country in which they claimed asylum) (Schuster, 2011). The concept of 'asylum shopping' implies that a level of strategic planning is undertaken by asylum seekers and connects to concerns that asylum seekers are 'pulled' to particular destinations because of the draw of welfare and economic benefits, whereas 'genuine' refugees are content to remain in the first 'safe country' they reach. Researchers have countered arguments on the pull of the welfare system in Britain through study findings which indicate that asylum seekers know little about their destination or the UK welfare system (Gilbert and Koser, 2006; Crawley, 2010). They conclude that most asylum seekers do not come to the UK with the specific aim of benefiting from the welfare state. While this may be the case, governments' attention to 'asylum shopping' and official responses made in counter-arguments can risk reinforcing the discourse that those who assert their agency and actively 'strategise' exist in polar opposition to 'vulnerable' and 'genuine' applicants who are characterised instead by their passivity.

A series of legal cases has been brought against the UK Border Agency's (UKBA) Third Country Removal Unit around its attempts to remove asylum seekers from the UK to 'safe third countries', notably Greece and Italy (*The Guardian*, 7 October 2011). Among these there have been several cases involving unaccompanied minors. In addition to the assertion that the conditions under which some removals took place were unlawful, the legal team acting in a series of cases involving the removal of unaccompanied minors to Italy have further argued against removal using a discourse of childhood vulnerability, for the need for stability rather than mobility, and for appropriate supervisory care and protection (*MA and Ors, R v SSHD* [2011] EWCA Civ 1446). They have asserted that the 'best interests' of the child need to be considered and that the UK should ensure that reception conditions adequately meet the needs of unaccompanied children. This followed criticisms that in Italy unaccompanied minors had not been adequately cared for and had been left to fend for themselves.

Once it is decided that the asylum claim will be processed in the UK, surveillance continues during the asylum interview where applicants are questioned about the grounds of their asylum claim. A young woman in a research study conducted by the present author was asked 192 questions in her asylum interview in an attempt to determine who she was and whether her claim was genuine (Sirriyeh, 2013a). While assumptions about the vulnerability of childhood can act as moral leverage at various points in the asylum process, it has often been argued that in the asylum claim itself, such discourses on childhood actually impede the chances of children being granted refugee status. In 2011 only 20% of child applicants were granted refugee status while 62% received Discretionary Leave to Remain, which usually allows them to remain in the UK until they are 18 years old. For the latter, when their protected status of child comes to an end it has proved difficult to receive a decision to remain in the UK, and for decisions on the asylum claims of former unaccompanied children who have reached the age of 18 there was an 83% refusal rate in 2011 (Refugee Council, 2011). Bhabha (2004) argues that the UN Refugee Convention has an implicit assumption that adults, and not children, are political activists and does not recognise child-specific forms of persecution. She notes that in the convention, children and young people are only mentioned in relation to their welfare as part of the family and in reference to the need for the protection of unaccompanied minors.

As asylum seekers enter and live in the UK in communities alongside citizens, internal borders are reasserted through a continuation of surveillance, conditionality and the regulation of entitlements. The Nationality, Immigration and Asylum Act 2002 introduced the need for regular reporting for all asylum seekers at immigration offices and the 'application registration card' (ARC), which contains the biometric data of the asylum applicant. The Immigration and Asylum Act 1999 introduced a dispersal process whereby destitute asylum seekers waiting for their claims to be determined are supported under section 95 in accommodation in regions outside of London and the South East (Hynes and Sales, 2010). In order to receive support with accommodation in this system, asylum seekers must agree to be housed on a *no choice* basis, which makes their location easy to track. In March 2012, the UKBA awarded security firm G4S Care and Justice Services the new regional contract in Yorkshire and the North East for the provision of initial and dispersed housing and transport for asylum seekers in the region, marking a new level of surveillance. This has been critiqued by some practitioners and campaigners who argue that G4S has a poor track record of running immigration detention centres and providing transport services linked to detention and deportations (including allegations of abuse and violence). They also note the firm's lack of a track record in the provision of social housing and the inappropriateness of a security firm delivering this service (Grayson,

2012a). Where challenges to G4S or their subcontractors have been made, these have predominantly been on the basis of the protection of children's rights and safeguarding issues, as will be discussed below.

In the process of determination of access to welfare support, many young people face an additional layer of surveillance if the UKBA suspects that they are older (or occasionally younger) than the age they claim. Minors are cared for through children's services in the local authorities in which they present rather than through the adult dispersal system. It is suspected that some young people claim to be a child because of perceived advantages in levels of support provided to children and opportunities for remaining in the UK. Authorities guard the borders of childhood, demonstrating they are protecting vulnerable children while filtering out instrumental asylum seekers. Young people who are age-disputed undergo an age assessment to determine their 'true' age. Age is assessed by social workers based on the young person's appearance, behaviour and interaction with the social worker, documentation, social history, health, level of independence and developmental considerations. An 'unchildlike' child who challenges these socially constructed conceptions of childhood can face difficulties (Crawley, 2011).

Conditionality

As asylum seekers wait for their claims to be decided, control is also exercised through the use of conditionalities and sanctions that are attached to rights and provision of services. Lydia Morris (2012a, p 48, 2012b) has discussed how rights may be used as a tool of governance, observing that 'both conditional conferral and deterrent denial of rights' are linked to social control and judgements of social worth. The delivery of a right creates opportunities for surveillance and control while the *mode* of delivery of a right (such as the use of the dispersal system or provision of vouchers rather than cash payments) can act as a deterrent. Rights can be impaired by a deficit in their delivery, such as the devaluing of a right through stigma (as with the 'bogus' asylum seeker). The retraction of a right, such as removing financial support, can be used to enforce particular behaviour (see also Chapter Two).

In *Fairer, faster and firmer* (HM Government, 1998) – the White Paper that preceded the Immigration and Asylum Act 1999 – the government argued that welfare benefits acted as incentives for economic migrants to enter the UK via the asylum system (Sales, 2002). The reforms introduced in the Act created the new social category of 'asylum seeker', separated in policy from recognised refugees. The Act introduced the dispersal system, which established a separate system of housing support for asylum seekers. As mentioned earlier, in order to receive support, asylum seekers have to accept accommodation on a no choice basis, usually in socioeconomically deprived areas where there is available property. Asylum seekers also face a host of restrictions on their ability to actively engage in their communities in the UK, including limitations on access to education and no rights to work (except for some who have waited 12 months or more for an initial decision on their claim). Although allowed to volunteer, asylum seekers risk the withdrawal of financial support if they are discovered in paid employment (Sirriyeh, 2013a). Engagement in employment and education are key measures of integration; yet while people with refugee status are actively encouraged to become involved in these activities, the integration of asylum seekers is discouraged and segregates this group of people from the wider population. Conversely, these restrictions on the ability to work further embed challenges to claims of social worth.

'Genuine refugees' are expected to be willing to put up with hardship in the asylum process (Hynes and Sales, 2010), establishing a test of moral status, while adverse conditionalities serve as deterrents to those 'less worthy' who might consider claiming the right to apply for asylum in the UK or staying beyond their 'welcome'. In this context, only basic essentials are provided and these begrudgingly as a controlled service rather than through an offer of hospitality (Darling, 2009). With the new round of asylum housing contracts awarded in 2012, asylum seekers living in accommodation in dispersal areas are being moved to housing provided by the newly subcontracted housing companies, with some people being relocated to different cities. Challenges to moves and poor housing conditions have taken place on the basis of safeguarding issues focused on the vulnerability of children. For example, when a three-month-old baby was moved with her mother from Bradford to substandard accommodation in Doncaster, interventions from campaigners and the lodging of an application to Doncaster Children's Safeguarding Board about the health and welfare of the baby led to them being returned to Bradford and placed in improved accommodation (Grayson, 2012b).

Sanctions

Sanctions are used in combination with conditionalities in the asylum system. Three of the most documented forms of sanctions are destitution, detention and deportation. Destitution functions as abandonment through the withdrawal of financial support and accommodation.

Asylum seekers may also be confined through detention at any point during the asylum process and, finally, may be expelled from the UK through deportation. Refused asylum seekers have 21 days to leave their accommodation and no entitlement to any financial support (Lewis, 2007). Therefore they are at high risk of destitution, although some people who have reasons that temporarily prevent them from leaving may be eligible for financial support through section 4 of the Immigration and Asylum Act 1999. This support is provided on the condition that the person who is refused asylum agrees to return to their country of origin if a route becomes available. The introduction of section 9 of the Asylum and Immigration (Treatment of Claimants etc) Act 2004 gave the Home Office powers to withdraw all welfare support to refused asylum-seeking families (who had previously been exempt) who were deemed to be in a position to leave the UK. This threatened children with destitution or removal from their families into care if their families were unable to support them. Cunningham and Tomlinson (2005) described it as 'a blunt instrument of coercion, designed to coerce families into leaving the country by plunging them into destitution'. The government co-opted safeguarding and 'best interests' arguments to refocus on parents, rather than the government, as instigators of potential risks to their children should they opt to remain in the UK in these circumstances rather than return to their countries of origin. Meanwhile, the government claimed that its policy of withdrawal of financial support was compatible with Article 3.1 of the CRC because it was not in a child's best interests to continue to be supported in a country they had no future in. Section 9 was piloted in 2004 in three cities, but was not rolled out, although it has not been repealed.

The Asylum and Immigration Appeals Act 1993 allows for the detention of asylum seekers while they wait for claims to be resolved. People can be detained at any point in the asylum process. Following the expansion in numbers in detention under New Labour, the UK 'detention estate' became one of the largest in Europe with 2,000 to 3,000 migrants held at any given time between 2009 and 2011, including children (Silverman and Hajela, 2012). Since November 2009, a duty has been placed on the UKBA under section 55 of the Borders, Citizenship and Immigration Act 2009, to safeguard and promote the welfare of children. In May 2010 the new coalition government announced plans to end child detention. On the basis of evidence that detention was damaging to children's psychological and physical wellbeing, the coalition's policy was presented as the protection of children's wellbeing in a civilised society. However, in contrast, the human rights of adults appear to carry less moral weight. Despite research evidence and campaigns highlighting the negative impacts of detention on the health and wellbeing of adults, the flouting of guidance that no victims of torture should be detained and the fact that asylum seekers are held in detention without having committed a crime, there has been no end to the detention of adults (Tsangarides, 2012).

The numbers of children in detention have decreased considerably since the introduction of the coalition government's new policy and alternatives to detention (UKBA, 2010). In 2009, over 1,000 children were detained for the purpose of immigration control (Silverman and Hajela, 2012). In 2011 this declined to 99 (64 of whom were asylum seekers) (Refugee Council, 2011). However, child detention has not been eradicated. Although children are not held in 'detention centres', from May to August 2011 697 children were held at Greater London and South East airports. Almost one third were unaccompanied minors (Children's Society, 2011). Children are also detained in the newly opened Cedars House, designated as a 'pre-departure accommodation centre'. Cedars opened in August 2011 and co-opted the children's charity Barnardo's to deliver a service at the centre to ensure the wellbeing of children held there (Gentleman, 2011). Cedars can hold families for up to 72 hours and up to a week in 'exceptional cases' (Silverman and Hajela, 2012). As with previous government declarations on the best interests of asylum-seeking children, while the phrase 'best interests' is embedded within policy language the meaning it acquires is flexible, and the concept has been moulded to fit with and support government immigration objectives. This is illustrated in the following statement within the UKBA's review on ending detention:

> Any new system has to ensure that families with no right to be in the UK continue to leave. Failure to deliver this would damage not only the credibility of the immigration and asylum system but also create real risks for children: if migrants believe that families with children will not be removed from the UK, the risk of children being trafficked or otherwise exploited for immigration purposes is heightened. (UKBA, 2010, p 7)

The next section makes brief concluding comments for this chapter, but before that Box 5.1 provides a summary note of key mechanisms and practices that have been discussed.

Box 5.1: Mechanisms of social control in the UK asylum process

Surveillance
- Exporting border controls
- Dublin Regulation and EURODAC
- Asylum interview questioning
- Age assessments
- Housing.

Conditionalities
- Limits on entitlements to work
- No choice in housing for asylum seekers
- Financial hardship.

Sanctions
- Withdrawal of financial support and destitution
- Detention
- Deportation.

Conclusion

The formerly morally untouchable social category of 'refugee' has in recent years been divided into 'genuine refugee' and 'bogus asylum seeker'. In order to gain social recognition as genuine refugees, asylum seekers are increasingly required to perform as passive, dependent and vulnerable, while at the same time critiqued for their dependency. Marked as an undeserving and undesirable group, they are excluded through a host of mechanisms of social control. In contrast, a discourse of childhood based on 'vulnerability' and 'best interests' has extended the rights claims of children, which have been characterised by expansiveness and the language of universalism. Child asylum seekers are positioned across both these discourses, policies and practices, holding an ambiguous status.

In the recent case, *ZH (Tanzania) v Secretary of State for the Home Department* in the Supreme Court, Lord Kerr stated that the best interests of children who are affected by immigration decisions is a factor 'that must rank higher than any other' and not be 'merely one consideration that weighs in the balance alongside other competing factors' (Dorling and Hurrell, 2012, p 5). Arguments based on child welfare and the 'best interests' of the child have been used to push for and achieve some greater protection and access to rights for asylum-seeking children in the UK. However, the statements by New Labour on the withdrawal of financial support to families under section 9 of the Asylum and Immigration (Treatment of Claimants, etc) Act 2004, and the evidence above on the continuation of detention by another name under the coalition government show the level of resistance to changes that potentially undermine exclusionary asylum policy. The recent histories also indicate the ways in which the language of 'best interests' has been co-opted by New Labour and now the coalition government to continue to push forward their asylum policy agendas while appearing to foreground a concern for child welfare.

SIX

New Labour, the coalition government and disciplined communities

Andrew Wallace

Introduction

The role of geographical area or place has long been central to some social policy strategies, initiatives and tensions. When considering governmental interventions, there are perhaps three main approaches to note:

- targeted reforms and investments in schools, health services and transport facilities serving a local geographical area;
- empowerment strategies to build the moral and social capacity of individuals residing in a local community;
- social order policies to enforce security and control 'problem' behaviour within residential communities.

Under the New Labour governments (1997–2010), a combination of all three of these approaches was evident in a range of urban welfare programmes (see Imrie and Raco, 2003, for an overview). However, in step with a wider critique, which argued that New Labour pursued conditional and punitive welfare (see for instance Levitas, 1998), place-based policies were often analysed as disciplinary mechanisms implemented to build 'responsible' and 'orderly' communities (see for example Atkinson and Helms, 2007). This perspective, which fits with the broad premise of this chapter, is underpinned by two key strands of thought. First, there has been a critical social policy tradition (Mann, 1998) that has tended to conceive of policy interventions in the lives of the poorest people in society as relying on behaviourist explanations of poverty, and which therefore consider controls, incentives and frameworks for behaviour change ethically and politically problematic. Second, there are also aspects of a critical urban studies literature arguing that the political economy of urban space involves the rolling out (Peck and Tickell, 2002) of disciplinary and punitive state strategies within poor residential communities. From such a standpoint, policy interventions – underpinned by an anti-welfare ideology (MacLeod and Johnstone, 2012) – seek to police, exclude and displace troublesome populations in order to enable profit-seeking projects of urban renaissance (Ward, 2003; Wacquant, 2008).

This chapter examines the enduring behaviourism that underpins much recent welfare and communities policy. It begins by briefly situating governmental discipline of individuals and communities within a broader agenda of neoliberal regulation, before proceeding to analyse the approaches of New Labour and the coalition government, and identifying the fresh agendas through which behaviour-shaping has been authorised and textured. Drawing on some primary research conducted within a recently 'empowered' residential community, the chapter offers critical perspectives on these agendas and their weakness both as wider projects of societal discipline and as theories and practices of civic governance.

Neoliberalism and governing through community

The state, no matter who is in power politically, plays a central role in the articulation of behaviour management strategies and the naming of geographies through which these processes occur. As Peck (2001, p 449) has noted: 'Policy responses are ... inevitably tweaked and struggled over, at the level of the national state.... In contrast to the script of state powerlessness, governmental intervention ... may actually be stepping up in some areas ... just as it is reduced or reorganised in others.'

In order to unpack the continuities and tensions in the New Labour/ coalition social policy programme, it is perhaps useful to identify and situate an increasing policy concern to scrutinise and govern citizen conduct within a literature that has addressed the neoliberalising of urban management at the level of state policy. It is fair to say that the governing of responsible citizen conduct *through* community has not gone unnoticed by sociologists and urban researchers (see for instance Rose, 2000; Flint, 2003; Ward, 2003). These perspectives have tended to suggest that neoliberal free market ideology has colonised social spheres and been deployed to assemble ordered communities comprised of responsible citizens to act as partners in social regulation and capital accumulation (Larner and Craig, 2005). In such accounts there is a shift away from readings of welfare state roll-back (associated with the classic neoliberal New Right) towards the surreptitious rolling out of the state in ways that seek to civilise society and police troublesome citizens (Ward, 2003). Once these powerful cleansing projects have been implemented, then disciplined, remade communities (Wallace, 2010a) become important spatial fixes for urban restructuring and the creation of more orderly and profitable social terrain. If this reading of neoliberal roll-out is acceptable, successive governments have been engaged in the (re)formation of responsible communities in particular disciplinary directions through the implementation of a range of formal and informal incentives, sanctions and 'nudges'.

It is also possible to situate, within this reading of neoliberal regulation, how the 'authorisation' of welfare (Skeggs, 2005, p 977) has been reframed by UK social policies under both coalition and New Labour governments in a generally more prescriptive, more invasive direction. Shades of this shift could be seen in New Labour's community engineering projects such as Neighbourhood Renewal and the Sustainable Communities programme, just as resonances can be found in the coalition's appeal for a 'Big Society' of voluntarist, orderly citizens. While the backdrop of neoliberalised social policy is pervasive, it is also important to draw out the differing readings, filterings and approaches to disciplined community building apparent under these two political regimes, thereby identifying, following Raco (2005, p 326), a hybridity of approaches, rather than essentialising different governing projects within straightforward accounts of neoliberal regulation. To this end, the chapter now examines the specific ways in which social citizenship in the UK has been entangled not only in the regulation of space and capital accumulation, but also by attempts to generate responsible communities. By adopting this focus the chapter hopes to move beyond merely depicting, to critiquing *how* communities and social relations are imagined by these neoliberal state programmes, and to contrast them with some grassroots realities.

New Labour's behaviourism

New Labour formalised and intensified behaviourist strategies as part of its welfare reform agenda. The Blair and then Brown governments tried to reconstruct welfare citizenship along more morally inflected lines enacted through a range of interventions designed to activate, regenerate and responsibilise behaviour. These interventions tended to be focused on the poorest people and towards the extension of disciplinary approaches within the lives and communities of the poor. An array of area-based initiatives was introduced, measured and evaluated, which sought to revitalise inner and outer city districts, deploying an amalgam of physical, political, social, cultural and moral regenerations. With its 'bewildering myriad' of policies targeted at urban populations (Imrie and Raco, 2003, p 4), New Labour constructed communities as spaces of civic opportunity but sutured with codes and parameters of 'appropriate' individual conduct and civility.

Communitarianism is a political philosophy broadly emphasising the fundamental embeddedness of individuals within communal relations, and New Labour, in its efforts to articulate a punitive discourse, drew on a North American functionalist strand popularised by thinkers such as Etzioni and Putnam to stress the importance of instilling civic respect and tackling anti-social behaviour in order to build strong local networks and relationships (Wallace, 2010a).

The panoply of behavioural interventions that framed New Labour's agendas of activation and social inclusion went beyond the traditional arenas of individual responsibilisation such as labour market participation and social welfare conditionality. There were also programmes designed to inculcate responsible citizenship by strengthening communities' roles in decision making, resource allocation and behaviour control (Rose, 2000). These were ambiguous agendas that offered citizens opportunities to participate in circuits of local governance, but which also coupled community living (for some) with a number of conditions and expectations. Therefore, under New Labour, where individuals lived and how they inhabited their communities went some way to determining people's capacities as responsible, governable subjects (Wallace, 2010a).

A New Deal: a case study of New Labour's behaviourist agenda

Under New Labour, the strengthening of the moral and social fibre of communities was implemented through policy initiatives such as Neighbourhood Renewal and the New Deal for Communities (NDC). These sought to summon 'liveable' neighbourhoods populated by engaged and responsible citizens (see Imrie and Raco, 2003; Wallace, 2010a). This agenda placed growing pressures on communities to promote cohesive identities and police themselves to ensure their continued viability and profitability (Ward, 2003; McCulloch, 2004). Between 2001 and 2010, New Labour implemented the NDC programme in 39 disadvantaged neighbourhoods across England. This was an initiative designed to build networks of public, private and third sector agencies to tackle some of the structural disadvantages that had befallen areas of post-industrial England. In keeping with the rolling out of community reform identified above, however, the NDC also sought to enact the moral and cultural renaissance of groups and populations who lived in these areas of assumed welfare dependency and breakdown (Wallace, 2007, 2010b). To this end, the NDC programme was part of the engineering of sustainable, liveable places and encompassed a range of social and behavioural interventions related to community engagement, management and security (see DCLG, 2007, for NDC national evaluation data pertaining to these goals).

The present author undertook field research in an NDC neighbourhood in England, which included exploring how the regeneration of behaviour through community initiatives played out in practice. This research was designed to investigate aspects of the lives of residents living in a neighbourhood defined as 'socially excluded', and involved interviewing a sample of residents to examine experiences of living in this particular 'community' and engaging with the NDC process. A key finding of the research was that, far from being a robust basis for behavioural reconstruction, community as understood through the NDC programme was an unstable site of social, cultural, economic and political exchange consisting of 'multiple publics' (Amin, 2002, p 972) and a range of disunities. The instability and complexity of the local community threw into question the entire project of strengthening the character, moral vitality and order of local people and place.

Nonetheless, NDC practitioners and New Labour policy makers appeared to conceive of a behaviour change agenda based on the 'warm associations' (Herbert, 2005, p 851) of community, a theme that has continued to resonate through much policy thinking (Day, 2006). As many authors have noted, the key problem with such accounts and conceptions of community is that they are deterministic and depoliticised in their understanding of how social relations develop and (dys)function (see for example Brent, 1997; Fremeaux, 2005). Indeed, there is a tendency for some policy makers and contributors to popular debate to reify the neighbourhoods and estates of people living in poverty as a priori communities by virtue of their structural conditions, and to assume that a particular brand of vibrant social relations and proletarian bonhomie is generated by limited geographical mobility and a sharing of poverty and struggle. In theory, this should precipitate consensus and processes of community strengthening. However, there are scholars who have rightly challenged the failure to acknowledge that localities are not 'fixed communities', but actually sites of 'processes [and] fragile and temporary settlements' (Amin, 2005). Similarly, others have identified the ways in which local spaces can be significant sites of contestation, division and social closure (see for example Elias and

Scotson, 1994 [1965]; Hoggett, 1997; Watt, 2006; Wallace, 2007). The tensions generated by constructing arbitrary boundaries of community as a means of turning humanised places into governable spaces has been highlighted by some writers (see Raco and Flint, 2001). Indeed, the expectation that multiple and often oppositional groups will identify with the same spatial identity and unite in the cause of local transformation might help to generate new (and make real hitherto latent) divisions, as groups feel the pressure to belong, not to mention tensions over funding and planning decisions (see for instance Lawless, 2004; Dinham, 2005; Wallace, 2007). Such divisions are particularly salient in the context of inadequate services and opportunities, and where some groups experience a lack of cultural autonomy in the first instance (Watt and Wallace, forthcoming).

Another key finding of this research resonated with other work, which has found that meaningful local action is often constrained by government-determined policy outcomes (Furbey, 1999; Taylor, 2003; Diamond, 2004; DCLG, 2007), and unrealistic official expectations for individuals as active citizens who can drive a 10-year regeneration partnership (Lawless, 2007). Programmes like the NDC often failed to facilitate 'journeys of empowerment' for citizens (Warren-Adamson, cited in Dinham, 2005, p 303), the ostensible goal of community regeneration, and to overcome the 'persistence of oligarchy' at the local level (Somerville, 2005). In 2005, the National Evaluation of the NDC programme asserted that 'probably no Area Based Initiative has ever achieved as much engagement' (NRU, 2005, p 281), but it is unclear how and what type of engagement was measured, and difficult to assess whether that engagement was meaningful for the lives of the majority of residents (see for example Dinham, 2005), particularly in terms of what Brenner and Theodore (2002, p 342) call an ability to select and pursue 'developmental pathways'. In the NDC neighbourhood researched by the present author, a possible mismatch between policies and the grassroots was illustrated by:

- the limited engagement of local residents in official NDC business;
- the setting up of alternative community-run events to undermine those organised by the NDC;
- tensions between the community-led ethos of the NDC and the broader strategic goals of central and local government.

More generally, efforts to develop responsible communities in which residents have a stake in the management and future of their neighbourhoods might be undermined by broader policy considerations, circumscribing the voices of local citizens. In the NDC neighbourhood referred to in this chapter, an example of this emerged with the issue of housing redevelopment, which led to a series of conflicts with residents, many of whom did not share the local authority's or NDC's long-term vision (involving redevelopment, loss of social housing and the building of a mixed-tenure neighbourhood). One of the important issues a tension of this kind raises is not only how far citizen empowerment can be genuinely realised when it is bounded and undermined in this kind of way, but also how a background of exclusion and neglect may structure micro-conflicts between residents.

According to Davies (2005), a weakness of the NDC programme lay in the presumption of consensus within poor communities by policy makers. Indeed, the engineering of imagined local consensus was bound up in the competitive funding process that awarded NDC status to 'appropriate' forms of community (Wallace, 2010a). In fact, as Craig (2007, p 354) notes, regeneration and its goals of sustainability and capacity building are potentially always an arena for political contestation, not just passive, grateful obedience. However, New Labour's community model allowed little scope for forms of social action that bred resistance to or disruption of government projects and planning priorities (see also Mooney and Fyfe, 2006).

Illustrations of contestation could include residents resisting and objecting to official structures of regeneration and partnership; that is, refusing to submit to the normative image of the dutiful participatory citizen, or contesting the meanings and priorities of regeneration projects as well as meanings of empowerment and representation (McCulloch, 2004; Hanley, 2007; MacLeavy, 2009). There is evidence from the NDC programme that under New Labour there remained a failure to acknowledge that there was a structural and experiential backdrop shaping how citizens conceived, managed or resisted the enforced social/physical transformation of their localities (an official approach that implied some inherent condemnation of what had gone before and an explicit belief in the need for the forces of newness to be brought to bear on the area). Such failures of recognition could undermine the broader goals of engineering stronger communities and reshaping citizen behaviour.

A further aspect of New Labour's rationale of community discipline and responsibility was the construction of safer neighbourhoods. An important element of this agenda was to operationalise a perceived behavioural fault line extant in poor areas between the decent, responsible majority and a deviant, anti-social minority (see Wallace, 2010a, 2010b). Mobilising around this line was seen as necessary, following communitarian logic, to support the agency of responsible residents in policing 'anti-social people' who cause low-level nuisance. Through anti-social behaviour telephone hotlines and other innovations, citizens were responsibilised to report anti-social behaviour, while a wider agenda of community safety was implemented in order to enhance the liveability of poor spaces (seen as a key feature of the strengthened, ordered neighbourhood). However, there were problems with this approach attributable to both the localised and the depoliticised nature of governing behaviour through community. Primarily, the presumption that there is a clear division of values and norms of conduct within a community that can be mobilised to tackle low-level disorder downplays the extent to which poor neighbourhoods consist of aforementioned social divisions, relations of power and dynamics of difference (Millie, 2007). There is a danger that some groups will be consistently labelled as troublesome, and the scrutiny of behaviour will be absorbed into the repertoire of those who exert 'social closure' against others, leading to the exacerbation of existing divisions (Watt, 2006; Johnstone and MacLeod, 2007).

Such approaches may also generate or worsen a climate of mistrust and suspicion within communities, as groups and individuals continually scrutinise the behaviour of those around them (Prior, 2005) and their use of public space, a resource relied on by some groups more than others (see Wallace, 2007). It is arguable that in trying to build behaviourist communities through strategies of 'naming and shaming' and community payback, and operationalising nebulous boundaries of behaviour, it becomes less likely that conflict and contestation between groups can be resolved and understanding negotiated (especially once simplistic definitions of who is not making a contribution or taking responsibility take hold). The strategies revealed New Labour's communitarianism as a rather limited framework through which to govern behaviour, failing to recognise processes of social division, defended space and marginalisation, and depoliticising 'appropriate' conduct and performance. In the frameworks adopted, socioeconomic status or political resources of a neighbour might be rendered irrelevant as what mattered was whether he or she was perceived as a 'nuisance' or a 'nightmare'.

The discussion of this case study has suggested that New Labour's focus on reshaping the behaviour of poor people through community was problematic. On its own terms of encouraging participation and empowerment it had very modest impacts. In part this was because it assumed consensus, and consistently undermined local grassroots action through local, regional or national state steering or direct interference. As regards encouraging self-policing of neighbourhoods and identifying problem behaviour, the approach could be claimed to have been more effective if consideration was given to the numbers of citizens drawn into the civic disorder system through mechanisms such as Anti-Social Behaviour Orders. However, as has been pointed out by numerous commentators, it could be argued that the bolstering of community security was based on a punitive and counterproductive approach to disorder (see for instance Squires, 2006) and should be viewed against the perpetuation of structural inequalities that New Labour largely failed to address. Interventions in the everyday lives of disadvantaged people became commonplace under New Labour, often implemented according to frameworks of community. However, it is clear that these offered, at best, very brief opportunities to participate in local programmes, and at worst risked compounding the stigma of the most marginalised, and exacerbating age-old divisions between the 'respectable' and the 'undesirable'.

The coalition government programme

The UK coalition government has offered its own approach to empowerment and control. While a slightly different filtering and orientation of communitarian-style policies has been devised, the coalition has continued with New Labour's focus on activating some citizens and controlling others through readings of community, whether in a local, residential sense or in a wider societal sense. The specific engineering of responsible communities has perhaps dropped down the policy agenda, but geographical place continues to be mobilised to identify social breakdown and to target disciplinary interventions in individual citizen behaviour.

Since the election of the coalition in May 2010, there seem to have been two dominant trends in the governance and provision of welfare in the UK that have shaped its approach. First, in the aftermath of the banking and recessionary crises that began in 2008 and in order to reduce the UK fiscal deficit, successive austerity budgets have set targets for significant reductions in government spending, including cutting a range of social welfare programmes and entitlements. Second, there has been Prime Minister David Cameron's Big Society agenda based on a vision of a more reciprocal and responsible civic culture and the recalibrating of citizen/state relations:

> For a long time the way government has worked – top-down, top-heavy, controlling – has frequently had the effect

> of sapping responsibility, local innovation and civic action....
> It has turned able, capable individuals into passive recipients
> of state help.... The rule of this government should be this:
> if it unleashes community engagement – we should do it.
> (Cameron, 2010a)

The attempt to 'roll forward the frontiers of society' (Cameron, 2009b), and develop themes of a 'post-bureaucratic' age (see Cameron, 2010a, 2010b) and a focus on 'general wellbeing' (see Stratton, 2010), has been implemented through the idea of the Big Society, which arguably has provided something of a cohesive banner for a number of coalition reforms such as neighbourhood planning, the introduction of 'free' schools and calls for greater personal and family responsibility (Ellison, 2011). While the approach of the Big Society to self-help and citizenship has deep and varying antecedents (Norman, 2010), in a modern social policy sense it follows on very clearly from familiar New Labour ideas around localism and active citizenship, and perhaps conceivably even the community development programmes of the 1970s Labour government (Power, 2012). However, despite continuities, the Big Society signifies a greater emphasis on voluntarism and a more hostile reading of the state's involvement in social support. Further, the call for civic activism has been promoted as a direct corrective for a 'dependency culture' and a 'broken society' (Cabinet Office, 2010). It is also important to note the coalition's broader emphasis on individual responsibility, and to frame the demands from the Big Society against the pathologising of social problems and a programme of cuts and enforcements driving the increasing selectivity of social rights (Lister, 2011, p 79).

Both financial retrenchment and Big Society ideas are having a significant impact on many residential neighbourhoods. First, the cuts have placed huge strains on the ability of local authorities to continue the funding of neighbourhood services and voluntary sector contracts, particularly in those areas in greatest need of support (Giles, 2010). Furthermore, there has been a withdrawal of many of New Labour's interventionist urban welfare programmes and the rationalisation of others (for instance Sure Start); although some targeted interventionism continues through initiatives such as the Troubled Families programme. The social composition of some neighbourhoods is also certain to be affected (or 'ethnically cleansed' to paraphrase London Mayor Boris Johnson) in light of caps introduced for Housing Benefit, the cutting of 'spare room subsidies' (the 'bedroom tax'), and the continuing shortage of social housing in some areas (see for example Ramesh, 2012c). In place of New Labour's targeted neighbourhood investment initiatives and policies, the coalition has instead placed emphasis on asking individuals and voluntary groups to contribute to the design of services through purchasing mechanisms such as community budgets and to the running of local authority services, as for example with community libraries (www.publiclibrariesnews.com, 2012). It can be suggested that through competing logics, individuals and communities are coming under pressure to formulate strategies of renewal and agency while at the same time being under threat of compound exclusions (including displacement) and disciplinary incursions. Both logics place responsibility on citizens to internalise, manage and enact social change, and may perhaps tie welfare citizenship and access to social rights to particular geographies of self-help and activation.

Just like New Labour, the coalition has sought actively to 'summon' identifiable, more responsible communities both through structural mechanisms such as policy frontrunners or vanguards and the use of competitive funding rounds (for instance in neighbourhood planning), as well as increasing opportunities to participate in the reproduction and performance of community. In a more coercive sense, the coalition appears to have continued New Labour's spatialised readings of dysfunction and 'moral lack' through geographies of social failure (Hancock et al, 2012), but with a concurrent decline in state-funded provision. It has deployed community as a perceived site at which cultural and behavioural deficits and declines are occurring, to define where and how society has broken down, and as a setting of concentrated worklessness, poor parenting and benefit dependency in need of sanctions and intervention (Hancock et al, 2012, p 351). As with New Labour, the coalition has had no qualms in identifying what it considers to be the failings of what are usually urban, social housing estates, and has drawn on its vision of a Big Society of responsible communities to frame those failings. David Cameron and ministers such as Iain Duncan Smith have discussed poverty and marginality in stark geographical terms, and have not been shy to constitute places such as Easterhouse in Glasgow as sites of 'broken Britain' in need of remedial action (see for instance Gray and Mooney, 2011). The riots of August 2011 helped to further cement the notion that civic dysfunction is a property of particular spaces and populations undergoing crisis, and requiring greater discipline and control. The coalition uses community, much like New Labour, not only to constitute what it considers to be broken, welfare-dependent spaces (Hancock et al, 2012), but also to convene expanded surveillance and disciplinary techniques in the pursuit of more civil, ordered space (MacLeod and Johnstone, 2012) as evidenced in the aftermath of the riots. Community has remained central therefore to the extension of not only crime control within urban settings, but also the surveillance of individual and family conduct and the tightening of the boundaries of productive citizenship.

Despite these disciplinary aspects, however, the coalition's framing of welfare citizenship is one that is also constructed as apparently rather benign, focusing as it does on volunteering, self-help and mutual aid. This reading of the Big Society is one that focuses on enhancing the contribution that individuals can make to their own communities (Power, 2012, p 7). Instances of this approach can be found in policies such as Community Organising, the National Volunteering Service and increased opportunities to participate in personal and community budgeting.

However, behind these apparently supportive agendas, it is clear that two interlinking concerns emerge. First, this voluntarism is underscored by the biggest fiscal retrenchment in recent decades. Critics might question the meaning and ethics of self-help in contexts of cuts to support services and infrastructure, and possible overestimations of how citizens and civic groups can replace or manage services previously run by government (Power, 2012). Second, like New Labour, the coalition has been clear that its social policy agenda has desired outcomes regarding the type of communities that should be 'assembled' (through for example neighbourhood planning, which assumes that local communities can articulate consensual development agendas and indeed want to 'participate' in a predetermined and often rigid planning system). In a sense, therefore, there may be a continued foreclosing of the parameters of citizenship through circumscribed terrains of social action. At the same time, the apparently 'subaltern' households are either expelled from spaces they are not deemed worthy of inhabiting, or subject to increased supervision and welfare cuts, while those considered part of the Big Society are encouraged to take on new responsibilities through delineated sociospatial units and in prescribed ways.

While involvement and empowerment of populations has been a facet of modern governance for decades, probably never before has such a weight of expectation been placed on individuals and communities, as governance partners upon whom social and moral outcomes are said to depend. The thread running through neoliberal welfare visions is that the burden of responsibility has been shifted onto individual behaviour patterns and away from sources of inequality and injustice. Seeking to condemn, manage or reconstruct particular communities is part of this shift. In contemporary political thinking, therefore, a key responsibility is for individuals to contribute to the unified agency of a community, helping towards civic and moral governance ends. Under the coalition, with its various retrenchments, roll-outs and empowerments, responsibilisation is being strengthened as individuals are simultaneously loosened and ensnared by the 'disordered' (and often under-resourced) places they happen to inhabit. However, as is known from previous community activation agendas, intervention projects tend towards depoliticised, unified models of the local, which commonly fail to provide space for fracturings of agency, non-unitarist subjectivities, and complex sociopolitical exchanges (see Wallace, 2010b; Hancock et al, 2012). This renders the Big Society project a fragile one for those caught up in its logics and interstices. To close discussion of details, Box 6.1 lists some of the most important elements in the coalition government's approaches.

Box 6.1: Summary of the coalition government's approaches to disciplined communities

Agendas and approaches
- Cuts to welfare entitlements
- Increased welfare conditionality
- Broken society: pockets of worklessness and dependency culture
- Big Society: voluntarism and self-help

Policies
- Troubled Families programme
- Neighbourhood planning
- Family intervention projects
- Community organisers
- Neighbourhood community budgets
- 'Open', cooperative public services
- Criminal Behaviour Orders

Conclusion

The invigoration of strong, active communities has recently been presented politically in the UK in benign terms, often as an opportunity for citizens to reform state welfare systems. These 'beyond the state' governance spaces (Swyngedouw, 2005) tend to be offered as opportunities for enhancing wellbeing through personal empowerment and civic participation. In recent years, a purported communicative turn in urban policy (Gunder, 2010) has stressed the need to dissolve top-down rational-bureaucratic interventions in neighbourhoods and focus on retelling the relationship between individual, neighbourhood and state along more collaborative and responsive lines. In the UK, talk of this reconfiguration of the scales and modalities of the modern state has deepened through recent political narratives stressing new localism and the Big Society (Cameron, 2010a, 2010b), as well as an array of think-tank reports emphasising the benefits of strong community networks, relationships and bonds (see for example RSA, 2010). However, there are good reasons to be wary of these new spaces of community governance, which invite greater demands on the neoliberal subject to participate in specific ways. Households' empowerment may be disrupted by pitfalls or barriers and governed by entrenched material and power inequalities. Politicians' ideas here may seek to tie individual behaviour to narrow readings of empowerment, which are often underpinned by judgements of moral lack or failure. When policies and debates construct individual subjects in this manner, the possibilities and practices of citizenship become bounded within enclosed geographies of self-improvement and moral renaissance. In many ways, despite the withdrawal of interventions such as the NDC, the song remains the same under the coalition government. There seems to be a continuing and growing expectation that citizens will play an active role in communities as co-producers of individual and collective wellbeing, but the communities that they can engage with continue to be loaded with normative assumptions that they will be cooperative, responsible and ordered. Further, low-income communities are falling prey to benefit cuts, public sector retrenchment and targeted policies of privatisation and expulsion. Overall, this leaves little opportunity for recognising the disparate practices, difficult cooperative relationships and alternative strategies for public benefit and collaborative citizenship that sit outside government-sanctioned community space, and which ultimately get written out of a predictable civic discourse favouring control, responsibility and order.

SEVEN

Young people, education, families and communities: marginalised hopes and dreams?

Doug Martin

Introduction

Education has many institutional dimensions, and diverse social control issues can arise in a variety of settings. This chapter concentrates primarily on schooling for children in England, within what has generally been thought of as the state sector, and makes reference to disadvantaged pupils in particular. The chapter begins with a brief note on the historical development and 'construction' of schooling. This is followed by discussions of approaches under New Labour and the UK coalition government. The chapter then concludes with a local example from northern England, suggesting that there might be viable alternatives to 'top-down' discipline-orientated strategies as far as disadvantaged households and localities are concerned.

The historical context before New Labour

Concern with discipline and behaviour has been important for national schooling practices across England since the 19th century. Over a long period this has been underpinned by a 'bedrock' of compulsion in terms of school attendance, although with requirements on targeted age groups open to change. Individual schools' disciplinary practices have varied over time and place, and the private sector has added to the complexities. Whatever the circumstances in a specific school, however, there have generally been some implicit contracts between parents, pupils and schools over performance, opportunities and behaviour, and usually also various formal expectations over discipline.

Historical accounts demonstrate the importance of behavioural and disciplinary codes, but it can be argued further that successive governments have used the schooling system both to legitimise differentiated educational opportunities and to aid regulation of sections of the population. In the early 19th century, Hannah More justified the establishment of Sunday Schools for children (the first substantial free schooling for the working classes) as positive in supporting reading; yet learning to write was seen as a more dangerous matter (Wrigley, 2007). The roots of today's state-funded education system can be found in the 1870s with the introduction of 'elementary education'. This schooling primarily set out to address growing concerns about the 'raggedy' working class that was being drawn towards the labour markets of expanding cities (Garratt and Forrester, 2012). Observers within the British ruling class perhaps may have shared More's concerns about workers becoming too educated, but Simon (1960) suggests that the task was in essence to assert control over a growing and seemingly uncontrollable urban population. Although there were opponents of the condemnations of the 'undeserving poor' (Frost and Stein, 1989, p 27), debate frequently drew on pejorative attitudes to disadvantaged families. Ideas encompassed some similar to those still found today about 'feckless parents' or 'feral children', and linked to the middle-class construction of 'the act of rescuing children from destitution' (Hendrick, 1994, p 70) as 'children [of these feckless parents] were thought to be unformed enough to be saveable' (Cunningham, 1995, p 135).

Compulsory free schooling for all was first introduced through the Education Act 1944, a major step in confirming universalistic rights to learn along with the principle of national direction over children's development. Nonetheless, Wrigley (2007, p 2) argues that policies remained founded on the notion that 'capitalism needs workers who are clever enough to be profitable, but not wise enough to know what is really going on'. After the Second World War, the school system continued to reflect labour market expectations and associated stratification based on social class, gender and disability, but with considerable variations of approach over time. National strategies during the 1960s and 1970s built around the idea of comprehensive schools as alternatives to a more selectivist gradation into different categories of institution. Apparently at the heart of practice were the teacher trusted to act in the best interests of all pupils (Gerwitz et al, 1995), and what was sometimes dismissively maligned as the 'bog standard local comprehensive' (Campbell, 2007). During the Conservative period in the 1980s and 1990s, economic liberal ideas gained ground, and the recasting of service users as citizen consumers affected policy thinking. Ball (1994, p 130) refers to the introduction of 'selfishness' to state-funded schooling. Parents were supposedly being empowered through choice, while schools were to demonstrate via league table positions what was available.

New Labour; mixed interventions for disadvantaged families

New Labour's mission apparently sought to make children central to service provision (DfES, 2003) to enhance their education and to improve outcomes for all young people, but particularly children from disadvantaged families. There was some continuity from the Conservatives, with continuing interest in school performance linked to educational indicators (Phillips and Harper-Jones, 2003; Cummings et al, 2011). Perhaps some older themes about accountability and responsiveness to local elected representatives and communities were giving way to more managerialist debates about how best to measure, audit and control schools through national oversight systems, the shaping of a national curriculum and the shifting of preferred teacher professionalism from that of the supportive educator to one who best served school priorities in terms of national performance measures (Power and Whitty, 1999).

In any event, while the previous Conservative administrations might have treated the family as relatively 'private', unless children appeared at serious risk of harm, thinking now shifted somewhat towards concepts of a more 'public family' for which the state had a right and duty to intervene; note for example Sure Start Local Programmes, targeted services (DfEE, 1998) and the later *Every Child Matters* policy (DfES, 2003). Some critical observers emphasised the presence of negative discourses, Scraton (1997, p vii) for example noting as New Labour took power that:

> ... a litany of deviants has been constructed providing evidence that the social and moral fabric of British society is collapsing, infected at its childhood foundations. The streets, it is argued, are inhabited by drug users, runaways, joyriders and persistent young offenders. Schools suffer the excesses of bullies, truants and disruptive pupils. Families have become dismembered, replaced by lone parents, characterised by absent fathers.

Certainly, some statements at this time might be read as justifying state intervention at the earliest stages into family life (DfEE, 1999). Perhaps government was treating schools as one important channel for intervening over a perceived 'crisis' of childhood (Wyness, 2000). As noted elsewhere in this book, New Labour re-emphasised duty and responsibility, and expanded behavioural and disciplinary frameworks and policies across several domains. A key example relevant to young people was the Crime and Disorder Act 1998, which introduced Youth Offending Teams and the Youth Justice Board (Oliver and Pitt, 2011). Rising political interest in tackling anti-social behaviour implied strategies to link schooling and youth justice arrangements, and there was growing commitment to so-called 'joined-up thinking', crossing previous administrative and practitioner boundaries (Simon and Ward, 2010). Of course, multi-agency working was meant to improve children's lives, but observers varied even when interpreting New Labour's more positively framed interventions (see for instance Giddens, 1998; Whitty, 2002). One critical line was that initiatives such as Education Action Zones (DfEE, 1997), established in response to the apparently low educational aspirations of communities, might contribute to pathologising as much as empowering communities, despite central concerns with raising educational standards (see Hughes, 1998).

Issues around anti-social behaviour and broader criminality were set in the context of young people's lives and a wider framework of behaviour (Field, 2003), in which a 'lack of respect for other people' was highlighted (Home Office, 2003, p 7). Relationships between schooling, offending and this perceived lack of respect were important to debates. Perhaps a cultural shift was hoped for, particularly in disadvantaged communities with 'poorly performing' schools, while 'good citizenship' was becoming more central (MacBeath et al, 2007), and concepts of 'good parenting' were gaining ground (Home Office, 1998). In some ways, public services organisations were being positioned more firmly to act as judges of what 'good parenting' should be. The Crime and Disorder Act 1998 gave powers to issue parents with orders making them accountable for the behaviour of their children (see sections 1 and 8). Increased intrusion into the family – and the enlisting of agencies in this – was moving towards professionalising the arena of parenting itself. For schools in disadvantaged communities, parenting expectations were increasingly becoming manifest alongside deficit models linked to the behaviour and attendance agenda (Ebersohn and Eloff, 2006; Cummings et al, 2011), while the 'net' affecting children and their communities strengthened through the exertion of increasing controls upon them (James and James, 2001).

New Labour's second term saw extension of school powers to act against young people and their families (see Anti-social Behaviour Act

2003, section 26, for example). Education authorities were increasingly charged with acting on behalf of schools. An example of methods was use of Acceptable Behaviour Contracts for parents who failed to comply with expectations in the context of children's schooling (Flint and Nixon, 2006). Momentum continued with the Education and Inspection Act 2006, which cemented links between family behaviour and schooling (see guidance DCSF, 2007). 'Responsibilisation' of parents for their children's behaviour was of growing significance. Schools gained powers to act against pupils over unacceptable behaviour and attendance by applying to magistrates in respect of Parenting Orders (DCSF, 2007). Contracts were drawn up between schools and parents at the earliest sign of unacceptable behaviour in school (see Education Parenting Contracts and Parenting Orders [England] Regulations 2007, reg 3). Local authorities could issue fixed-notice penalties against parents in response to pupil attendance and behaviour problems, while a parent or parents had to know of the whereabouts of their child while under a school-imposed five-day fixed exclusion (DCSF, 2007). The legalisation of duties bound schools to intervene directly into not just the pupil's life but also that of the family, and there was a closer drawing together of schools, police and other practitioners involved with youth offending.

New Labour did provide a base for some holistic support to young people from disadvantaged communities by bringing together schools with wider services to better support pupils succeeding in schools (Barker, 2009). At the same time, however, government was reconstructing relationships more generally between schools and disadvantaged families (Power and Whitty, 2006). Critics, including some politicians, could depict the relationship as representing New Labour's 'nanny state' (Powell, 2002; Davidson et al, 2003). Institutional practices meant school and allied services being provided subject to conditions and permissions inspired partly by a kind of 'deficit modelling' of family failings, and pointed towards reliance on behaviourist rather than economic solutions.

The coalition government, schools and disadvantaged communities

The UK coalition government's approach to schools diverged in some respects from New Labour's. Government now presented itself as reinstating 'traditional educational values' (Martin, 2012), and some observers saw policies as representing a return to education in its historically narrower senses (Fielding and Moss, 2011). The classroom and quality of teaching would be crucial, and the raising of standards very strongly about teaching itself (Gove, 2010; Wilshaw, 2012). While the approach sought to roll back New Labour's so-called 'nanny state' and some reformist themes associated with that (Facer, 2011), coalition policy nonetheless added to the political agenda of schooling as a frontline social regulation activity. Some types of avenues developed under New Labour therefore remained potentially relevant for intervening in the lives of disadvantaged families, while the construct of the 'crisis in childhood' might now complement that of the 'broken society' favoured among the Conservatives.

For schools, the coalition set in train a strengthening of powers to assert control over pupils. Families living in disadvantaged places were sometimes being portrayed as responsible for the ills of 'broken Britain' (Cameron, 2009a, 2011c). While awareness was expressed of the barriers to success that young people faced, parents were labelled for the failures of pupils to achieve academically (Gove, 2010). New Labour's Education Maintenance Allowance – which had supported disadvantaged young people remaining in education post-16 – was withdrawn. The Pupil Premium was introduced to assist households (DfE, 2012b), although initially this apparently meant only approximately £10 of service support per week for 'poorer pupils' (Martin, 2012).

One important provider of legitimation for the coalition was the five-day period of rioting in England in August 2011, which was covered widely in the press, albeit that research and reporting did not provide clear evidence actually justifying the coalition's favoured responses on schools or families (see for instance Singh, 2012). Perhaps events strengthened the leanings towards strongly disciplinary educational stances and 'traditional education'. The coalition's Education Minister, Michael Gove, had previously indicated (before the government took office) the importance of discipline and respect within the Conservatives' agenda for English schools, which was to deliver 'what every sensible parent knows is needed', proper uniform – 'with blazer and tie' – respect for authority, 'clear sanctions for troublemakers and no excuses for bad behaviour' (Gove, 2009).

In this scenario, pupils were to 'engage in traditional subjects', and when bureaucrats tried to insert 'fashionable nonsense into the curriculum' they should be told 'where to get off' (Gove, 2009). Later in this speech, Gove referred to the development of a 'Troops to Teachers' programme that apparently reflected experiences from the United States, the aim being to get ex-military personnel into schools. It has been suggested that present school policy is based on traditional education values constructed upon the 'Eton test', meaning that if a practice could be adopted by the elite private school, Eton, then it would be 'good enough for all schools' (Field, 2012). Perhaps ideas for an English Baccalaureate may have been influenced by similar perceptions of the merits of a traditionally orientated curriculum, even if at the cost of losing so-called 'GCSE equivalents', which were valued qualifications in many communities (Hodgson and Spours, 2012). New Labour's commitment to social justice (Campbell and Martin, 2011) was superseded by a rhetoric emphasising a 'broken Britain', traditional values, respect for authority and a 'blame' agenda. Some ideas voiced in the wake of the riots rather resonated with 19th-century Victorian notions of the 'undeserving poor', although updated to the 21st century. Entire disadvantaged communities were sometimes depicted negatively, as having lost their stake in society and the sense of people being able to fulfil their 'hopes and dreams' (Singh, 2012).

Meanwhile, thrusting schools into a reinvigorated market involved some apparently excellent ones being financially induced to convert to academies with more freedoms of pupil selection, potentially serving to reinforce disadvantage and existing inequalities (Machin and Vernoit, 2012). All schools were being expected to become Academies, outside the control of their local authorities. 'Free Schools' represented a further diversification and fragmentation in school quasi-markets. It appears that sponsors of free schools may have interests other than concerns about disadvantaged families. Commenting on the early rounds of free school creation, Chitty (2011) argued that they included one London school with a right-wing journalist as its chair of governors, two Jewish schools, a Hindu school and a Sikh school. He also argued that at least three of the then new free schools would have 'a predominantly Christian ethos', while one would be run 'according to the beliefs and teaching of the Maharishi Mahesh Yogi' (Chitty, 2011, p 237). Clearly, such orientations may affect the scope of choices available to families. Another key issue concerns how far the parent chooses the school or the school chooses the parent. Bearing in mind the latter possibility, and national moves towards traditional expectations (as well as governmental endorsement of religious orientations), outcomes may be very patchy as far as pupil engagement, commitment to formal education and equal opportunities are concerned.

Returning to the theme of how the coalition has been seeking to utilise schools to manage disadvantaged young people, we can note the policy on Troops to Teachers, mentioned above, and new powers for teachers (DfE, 2012e). Both have embodied claims for a shift towards 'restoring discipline in schools' (Gove, 2009). The Troops to Teachers policy is intended to bring ex-army staff into the classroom instead of existing teachers who are unable to keep order. Apparently, troops 'know how to train young men and women' (Gove, 2009). Aspects of the professionalism of the existing workforce have also been under challenge through new training arrangements, like the Teaching Schools route introduced in 2011, which provides a 'new hands-on' opportunity for potential teachers. Recruits train alongside existing teaching staff to understand classroom craft, representing a growing role for school management when compared with the historical dominance of the higher education sector in teacher training. Perhaps the aim is to enhance teacher professionalism in a recast form, with practical and disciplinarian roles prioritised rather than ones that inspire through providing insights into more broadly grounded thinking.

More generally, the coalition's approaches to pupil–teacher and home–school relationships reflect the priority premise that 'discipline has to be restored in our schools' (Gove, 2011a). Government's response in 2012 was *Ensuring good behaviour in schools*. This indicated that the government expected:

- all pupils to show respect and courtesy towards staff and towards each other;
- parents to encourage their children to show respect and support the school's authority to discipline its pupils;
- headteachers to help create a culture of respect by supporting their staff's authority to discipline pupils and ensuring that this happens consistently across the school;
- that every teacher would be good at managing and improving children's behaviour (see DfE, 2012c, p 1).

The coalition sought to secure respect through a code of discipline, while schools would be expected to provide safe learning environments. To instil respect, teachers would have rights to search pupils, restrain them, and retain them in detentions without parental consent, while obtaining a new right to anonymity if accused of misconduct such as assault (DfE, 2012c). The policy marked a shift from the child being accepted as a full member of society – having their own legitimate agency as a person alongside adult counterparts – to one of separation from society, with potential human rights ignored or downgraded (Facer, 2011). Far from schools being freed from the state and its bureaucracy (Gove, 2010), teachers and schools might be enlisted increasingly in the control of disadvantaged young people. This would be in the context of concerns about weapons, illegal drugs and articles that could be used to commit crime (DfE, 2012c), but also had potential connections with fears about wider disorders or terrorism (an issue attracting ongoing official interest under New Labour too). Headteachers have retained the right to exclude pupils, and parents retain the right to appeal in this connection to an 'independent body' instead of the local authority. However, a Conservative Party (2012) statement, *Where we stand*, indicates that appeals from pupils who request they be returned to the school they were excluded from may be prevented (see Facer, 2011, on the coalition's consideration of young people's rights).

The Department for Education's statistics reflect the influence of its policy on children and young people in relation to exclusions from schools, particularly those pupils from disadvantaged families. In 2009/10, the twilight of the New Labour reign, permanent exclusions totalled 5,740, with boys being four times more likely to be excluded when compared with girls, and those from disadvantaged families on free school meals a further four times more likely to be excluded. Fixed-term exclusions totalled 316,470 (DfE, 2012d). In 2010/11 in the first academic year of the coalition government, comparative statistics demonstrated a marginal decline in exclusions; however, boys from disadvantaged families remained four times more likely than girls to fall into this group, while pupils considered in the Special Educational Needs category rose from eight to nine times more likely to suffer exclusion (DfE, 2012d). With increased sanctions against parents of children truanting from school (at an estimated cost for sanctions of apparently over £1 billion by April 2010; Gungell, 2012), Ministry of Justice (2012) statistics indicate a growth in prosecutions of parents from under 4,000 in 2004 to over 12,000 in 2011, of which 9,000 were convicted (with some 25 given prison sentences, the longest being 90 days). Following the aforementioned riots, Gove (2011a) apparently described these measures as 'toothless' while issuing a threat to take away Child Benefit from 'recalcitrant parents' (Gungell, 2012). However, despite these approaches, truancy marginally increased again in 2010/11 from 1.0% to 1.1%, with over 4,000 children being considered 'persistently absent' (DfE, 2012d).

A fundamental question about contemporary English schooling concerns whether it is about learning as a process enabling development and personal progression, or the training of disadvantaged young people (and their families) to behave acceptably while adapting to a society where their economic prospects are limited. Analysis of coalition discourses sometimes reveals differing and perhaps opposing messages. *Positive for youth* (DfE, 2012f), for example, illustrates a more youth-centric approach, diverging somewhat from the frequently explicit messages elsewhere to restore discipline and respect. It asserts that 'government is unashamedly positive about young people' and that policy is 'centred' on them, with their needs and aspirations as starting points (DfE, 2012f, p 1). Going further, there was reference to young people's rights to have their voices heard, and apparently this might take 'centre stage', particularly for those disadvantaged or vulnerable (p 2). Some personnel within the children and young people's workforce (including staff in schools) may have been confused by mixed official messages on youth from the coalition, and this was suggested in findings from research in spring and summer of 2012 across a number of sites in the north of England (Martin, 2012). Perhaps moving schools' roles towards 'traditional educational values' and discipline was not always fitting comfortably with the commitment of some professionals to 'listening models' that hold young people as central.

Despite variation, however, it is clear that day-to-day social control of disadvantaged young people is a crucial policy component for government. Along with an explicit focus on so-called 'troubled families' (see Casey's findings in DCLG, 2012a; Casey, 2012), there has been renewed discourse around old ideas such as the supposed intergenerational transmission of disadvantage, with overtones of culpability and failure. As Casey argued in 2012, 'this requires services (including schools) who work with families to take a long term view; of what happened to the parents as children and of what happened to the children since birth' (see DCLG 2012a, p 64; and also Casey, 2012). Preoccupations of this kind may divert attention from the educational ground being lost by disadvantaged pupils in terms of opportunities, resources and support services, and possibly also through the ongoing trends towards fragmentation, traditionalism and differentiated choice within the schools system. Although it is difficult to summarise trends since the coalition took office, Box 7.1 offers a reminder of some of the key features as far as schools and social order have been concerned.

Box 7.1: Key policy orientations under the UK coalition government

- A mixture of goals, not always consistent, but with strong leanings towards 'educational traditionalism'.
- A strengthening of school/professional functions and capacities on the 'social order' front, and of some of the means for securing discipline and protecting schools and staff.
- Enlisting of schools in more general tasks of managing 'troubled families'.
- Encouraging fragmentation and competition.
- Continuity with New Labour in facilitating particularistic control of individual schools. Possible implications for disadvantaged pupils' choices and for the imposition of specific 'moral' environments within schools.

Schooling: possible options for less control and more listening

Reviewing trends in social regulation affecting pupils from disadvantaged households since the end of the 1970s, we can observe some divergent or complementary policy strands over time, but also a growing emphasis on trying to manage or contain behaviours. While conditional on academic performance, the pathways and opportunities open to pupils have often remained affected negatively by pupil behaviours as perceived by schools, and perhaps sometimes by religious affiliation or ascribed social status. On occasions there could be close alignment or overlap of support and discipline, with schools seeking both to assist students with difficulties and to maintain secure environments in which disturbance and perceived deviance were minimised or contained. Positive attempts to support disadvantaged children (by practitioners and via governmental programmes) may have sat alongside punitive and exclusive strategies.

One view of the increased emphasis on disciplinary practices seen in recent years is that there is no alternative strategy available, and that it is essential to strengthen links with the youth justice system and focus closely on individual transgressors. Before concluding, therefore, this chapter offers a challenge (albeit a modest one) to popular wisdoms about dealing with 'troubled' pupils, families and neighbourhood communities. Some schools in the state sector have explored alternatives to a narrow, school-centred and quasi-market approach. Longitudinal research conducted by the present writer from 2007 to 2012 in three schools (infant, junior and secondary) revealed how some strategies not built around disciplinary practices can work for families even in difficult contexts. The research had sought to understand why relatively 'top-down' control-orientated models in these schools appeared to have been failing, and how far innovations in an alternative direction were proving positive. The location was a disadvantaged community in a large northern English town (the area being referred to here as 'Newtown' for purposes of anonymity and the local authority as Farrington), where the schools faced closure in 2002 due to a combination of poor league table performance, negative judgements by Ofsted and falling pupil rolls. The schools came together to form a local partnership by application for Full Service Extended School Status under a pilot scheme (DfES, 2002). A post of community manager was created jointly between the schools and local authority, to explore ways of bringing together wider service provisions and to understand how links could be made with local people.

Newtown in this period was a place where young people (and their parents) apparently felt that education was "not for them", and the schools were (in some observers' views) incidental to "a life dependent on benefits". Local residents described how the schools had been "of little relevance to our community", and referred to young people not attending, and vandalising schools on a daily basis with the community passively looking on. There were claims that the community had lost hope and confidence in itself, and that local people had lost respect for teachers, who "could be regularly heard shouting at pupils in the grounds of the schools as pupils walked out". Informants indicated that the educators' perspectives on young people and their families in 2002 were based primarily on a narrow field of concerns informed by the national curriculum, standard assessment tasks (SATs) results, school league tables and Ofsted inspection reports. Despite local pupils transitioning through infants to junior and then to secondary school, the schools did not appear to communicate very systematically with each other, and frequently operated as relatively isolated, autonomous institutions, working with an eye to officially approved or quasi–market considerations of status and measurement. The community manager, local playgroup staff, local residents and voluntary sector organisations that worked on the estate where most residents lived confirmed perceptions of schools that were self-interested in a rather narrow sense. Conversations with parents illustrated how "the schools' work starts and ends at the school gates, like a bubble" and "that they [the schools] talk to us [parents] like we are children". Parents also recalled that "school only phones us when something has gone wrong [with their child]".

A key agent of subsequent change was the community manager, who referred to the "social capital" she had hoped to mobilise through her role and recognition of the value of understanding local communities. Meanwhile, the schools were using various tools approved by central and local government as parts of the armoury built up to support the officially inspired agenda based on raising standards, especially through work within the classroom (interview with community manager, 2 July 2009). A critical view was that the schools were accepting and 'internalising' the challenge of failure emerging from the preoccupations dominant within the national educational environment. The leadership adopted perspectives from the growing 'industry' of 'school improvement', which framed their professionalism, predominantly within the school, with a focus on behaviour, attendance and test scores. Young people who could not conform and perform were excluded or self-excluded.

Although based in the high school, the community manager aimed for thorough engagement with the broader local community. She described a fundamental shift in culture, which included "the schools engaging with the community and the community coming into the school". For the community manager, the professionalism of school leaders and teachers had been set within too limited a perspective, fostered through a culture of school performativity and education in its narrower sense. To combat this, she sought new alliances with the local regeneration team, faith institutions, voluntary organisations and local informal and formal education services such as the playgroup, adult education and youth service. This seems to have led to conflict with leadership figures in the schools and teachers, as it initially appeared that they could not whole-heartedly endorse the community manager spending so much time in this way in the community, when raising standards was the ultimate priority (to be achieved through better classroom practice).

Despite the divergent outlooks, however, both the community manager and school leaders had broadly similar end goals in terms of improving pupil attainment. The community manager introduced an approach to schooling that encompassed education in its broadest sense, through a combination of engagement involving both a welfare and an education agenda, and the placement of children and their families at the centre of the process. This approach generated substantial benefits. By 2008 the three schools had come together to form a 'through-school'. All three had improved significantly in their league table positions and moved from being classed as having 'serious weaknesses' to becoming seen as 'good schools'. Documentary analysis of Ofsted inspection reports across the three schools in the years 2003 to 2009 demonstrated that central to the improvements was this engagement with the community. Analysis of data provided by Farrington

Community Safety Partnership and Farrington Children's Services (the local authority-led partnerships covering Newtown community) evidenced reduced incidence of reports of behaviour issues, improved attendance, improved SATs results and steadily improving 'occupancy' coinciding with reduction of exclusions, anti-social behaviour and crime across the period. In 2009 the new Principal of the through-school noted that she "had never worked in this way with the community in my previous headships". While events in this case study history were very particular to time and place, it does suggest at least some scope for alternatives to schools working in isolation from the disadvantaged neighbourhoods they claim to benefit.

Conclusions

Schools quite reasonably expect their participants to comply with codes, such as those covering aspects of behaviour, so that environments reach an acceptable level of safety and wellbeing for all. This chapter has illustrated, however, how English schooling over recent years has become entwined in a central government agenda that is over-fixated on challenging disadvantaged families. There has been a shift from more structured and interlocking mainstream school systems to fragmentation and relative school autonomy locally (although not necessarily always in relation to central government). The shift has been paralleled and legitimated in part through ideas about activating individualised consumer choice. Given the schooling environments that have developed over recent periods, it is not clear how far commitment to a professionalism based on the individual welfare of students is holding its own. Some disadvantaged families may be losing ground if schools more frequently seek to serve particularistic interests, or respond to better-resourced or more 'respectable' families. Yet, alongside this, schools have become positioned by successive Secretaries of State for Education as components in the repertoire through which interventions might be made into the lives of disadvantaged families and their communities. New Labour's interventions aimed to influence the culture of communities through 'joined-up' working, to break young people out of supposed cycles of deprivation, and to improve outcomes. The 2011 riots provided apparent justification for the coalition government to act against disadvantaged families, but the agenda on families, 'broken Britain' and a return to 'traditional education' was already in hand (Centre for Social Justice, 2006; Cameron, 2009a; Gove, 2009). Despite the rhetoric about disorder and the degree of national political consensus over the need for disciplinary practices, it is important to remember that there are other ways forward. One potential route may be to listen to, and work more with, disadvantaged young people and their families within a wider community engagement orientation, where real attempts are made to help groups and individuals realise at least some of their hopes and dreams.

EIGHT

Choice, control and user influence in health and social care

Gabrielle Mastin

Introduction

This chapter differs somewhat in focus from others in this part of the collection. It does not directly examine disciplinary strategies or appraise incentivisation and nudge tactics (see Chapter Nine). Instead, discussion centres around the involvement and participation of service users. Encouraging people to participate and give their views is very different from disciplining them, even though it too connects with how government wants target groups to act. Indeed, systematic involvement of service users and the 'subjects' of social policy can potentially offer something positive to set against the march towards greater coercion in welfare systems, and remains potentially crucial to challenging powerful state organisations and private companies. Even in the context of participation exercises, however, there may be official expectations for preferred behaviours to assist services management, while the theme of responsibilisation sometimes runs as an undercurrent within the flow of involvement practices.

The concept of 'user involvement' has been an important area of interest for politicians and decision makers over several decades. Although the concept lacks an agreed and universal definition, the aims and values attached to the process have generally related to issues of power and control. Political discourse around the topic has drawn on a variety of powerful 'soundbites': enhancing choice, removing dependency, modernising government, renewing democracy and reinforcing the 'Big Society'. The end product of political interventions here – which have straddled some 30 years over the tenure of five Prime Ministers of both the Left and Right – has been a reinforcement of the roles of the users of public services in their relationships with the state. This has been engineered at three overlapping levels:

- *a collective level*, through the encouragement for instance of the user voice in the commissioning and provision of health and social care services using Patient Panels, pensioner forums and the like;
- *a community level*, through the community development programmes of the 1970s, the neighbourhood renewal initiatives of New Labour and more recently the coalition government's promotion of Community Challenge contained in the Localism Act 2011;
- *an individual level*, as with the regular exhortations for patient-centred care in the NHS, the development of a consumerist dialogue and the 'personalisation' agenda, and the growth of 'direct payments' and the right to choose, which became embedded in some practices of social care authorities.

Strangely, perhaps, these developments appear not to have been the products of exhaustive consultation with service users, although the direction of travel has appealed to some. The disabled people's movement, for example, and some other modern social movements, have sometimes secured opportunities for voice that the standard system of elective democracy had denied them. Yet along with personalisation there emerged new and enduring behaviourist expectations affecting users/consumers, involving:

- responsibilisation;
- taking charge of their health and wellbeing;
- self-managing of preventable disease; or
- commissioning of their own care packages.

This chapter explores the story of this transformation, and then illustrates local trends and issues from a recent case study of user involvement among older people in a northern borough in England, reviewing how user involvement had meaning in local practice.

'Participatory engagement'

The practice of involvement only relatively recently developed as an important facet across government policy, with earlier examples appearing less integrated and less comprehensively established. Past interest by governments in promoting user involvement tended to be driven by very service-specific imperatives and political expediencies. The community development projects of the Wilson government in the 1960s were faltering responses to the 'rediscovery' of poverty in the UK, and failed to last a decade. Of more lasting influence were the encouragement of participation in planning introduced in the Town and Country Planning Act 1968 and of involvement in health service activities through Community Health Councils, introduced in 1973 to counter the 'democratic deficit' in the NHS and its prevailing paternalism. Although welcome at the time, the ideas underpinning these developments did not start to be more mainstreamed and integrated into government thinking until the market reforms of the Thatcher governments. The literature on this topic has suggested a variety of drivers behind the adoption of user involvement practices in that period, which sought to remodel the responsibilities associated with citizenship, invigorate participative democracy, modernise government and respond to 'rights-based' claims to independent living and 'nothing about us without us'. Some observers have traced aspects of involvement developing from the apparent growth of 'consumerist' practices emerging from the post-war welfare state (Hodgson and Canvin, 2005), while others have identified the user movements of the 1960s and 1970s as being significant drivers (Branfield and Beresford, 2006). Examples of 'participatory engagement' included both 'officially led' practices encouraging professionals to involve users, and 'user-led' practices encouraging users to get involved on their own terms (Carter and Beresford, 2000), with some blurring of the edges between the different interests of users, the general public and professionals (Harrison, 2002).

For some decades, depictions of a ladder have been used to represent the varying degrees of influence and power that users can expect to achieve from their involvement, the assumption being that the ultimate 'goal' for successful involvement was citizen control and power (see especially Arnstein, 1969). Other views have emphasised the difference between involvement arising from service user movements (and focused on empowerment and democracy) and officially-inspired initiatives that tended to be focused on improving consumerist services (see Carter and Beresford, 2000; Beresford, 2005). A common theme in the literature is of meaningful involvement being essentially about transferring power and resources from provider to user, perhaps empowering individuals to control and manage their own lives, not least for apparently 'powerless' social groups such as older people in social care services: 'This word empowerment symbolises the delegation of authority, the assignment of responsibility and an authoritisation for elders to assume new roles – often the same roles that society has systematically denied them' (Sykes, 1995, p 49).

Along with this, a growing body of literature also recognised the complexities around 'desirable' practice and ways to achieve this.

In particular, the very notion that empowerment can flow from involvement has been challenged, with commentators questioning the ability to empower clients or service users unless they themselves want to be empowered (Oliver, 1991). Much of the literature appears to identify particular types of 'best practice', which ultimately suggest that conceding more power and control to the user is better than less, and that users are ready and willing to engage. However, as will be noted in this chapter, this rather optimistic view can be contested, with some evidence emerging that not all service users are necessarily wanting or ready to take on such power and control. The picture of involvement may be more complex than is suggested by the rhetoric of politicians. At the same time, it should also be kept in mind that the governmental agenda here can contain or reflect behaviourist assumptions or motives.

User involvement and government policy, 1979–2013

Although roots can be many and varied, a common understanding in the literature suggests that the journey of transformation towards increased involvement had particular links with the political ideology of the late 1970s that introduced radical new thinking, seeing the state as being a facilitator and arranger of 'new' health and welfare markets (through which services could be purchased from a network of pluralist providers). While there was some encouragement for collective forms of service user participation during this period, as for a while with tenant control in social housing (Bradley, 2008), this tended to sit a little uneasily alongside the preferred emphasis on individualised consumer decision making. 'The promotion of an overtly consumerist culture in public services', suggested Laing et al (2009, p 78), had generated an environment in which concepts of consumer empowerment could gain 'renewed relevance and power'.

The new tune was played to an accompaniment of new watchwords. Some referred to the introduction of market principles into the care system in the late 1980s (Ward, 2000; Hodgson and Canvin, 2005) as representing a shift from universal provision and collective decisions over welfare towards individual consumer demand and private consumption, which encouraged service users to exercise greater choice in selecting their care providers and greater independence in selecting their care packages. In addition, the changing role of the 'user' in this market was reflected in shifts in terminology used by government agencies and in wider discourses during the 1980s, as previously passive depictions of health service patients and social care recipients became displaced by advocacy about more active clients and consumers. New terms of address were developed to capture the renegotiated relationship between providers and users of care, as needs became 'commodified to some extent and converted into objects or functions to be met through the operation of the market' (Ward, 2000, p 46). At the same time, some have indicated the introduction of a 'new managerialism' (Clarke et al, 2000) into public services, which, by externalising services through quasi-markets to manage anew the remaining state functions, not only impacted on the providers of services but also changed the culture of public sector management and governance. Reflecting on the changed relationships between public and private sectors, professionals and managers, and central and local government, some have suggested that citizens and service users 'were recast as consumers, and public service organisations were recast in the image of the business world' (Newman, 2000, p 45). Such changes, however, did not always attract positive support, with Small and Rhodes (2000) for example suggesting that the Conservative government's consumerist approach remained predominantly service-centred, and arguing that the marketisation of the public sector was an insufficient basis on which to empower service users.

When New Labour came to power in 1997, its proclaimed 'Third Way' rhetoric sought 'to move beyond the old politics of organising public services in which choices were made between state control and market anarchy' (Clarke and Glendinning, 2002, p 33). The Third Way was to be about working with the new health and social care markets, but in a spirit of collaboration, partnership and joined-up government where 'purchasing' was replaced by 'commissioning', was performed in keeping with evidence-based policies (rather than the traditions of old Labour) and with the consumer/user in the centre of the frame. If the earlier Conservative governments had been about stimulating the supply side of these markets to replace the 'monolithic state', New Labour's focus appeared to be on liberating the demand side, the voices of consumers, so that they could influence quasi-market decisions. The roles of state agencies, and especially local health and social care authorities, were altered through new modernising initiatives, captured in a new mantra of 'best value' to supersede the emphasis on value for money and competitive tendering that had characterised previous regimes. It was through the 'best value' framework that local authorities were required to consult with their citizens about their policies and priorities (enshrined in the Local Government Act 1999), a requirement that was applied to health authorities in legislation passed in 2006, and which represented, suggest Daly and Davis (2002, p 99), 'a shift from politics and governance legitimised through representative democratic structures to local governance that is now increasingly seeking to be legitimised via participatory democratic techniques'. It should be added, however, that some aspects of outsourcing implied following a different track. New Labour's espousal and promotion of the Private Finance Initiative (building on earlier steps under the Conservatives) involved inviting private organisations to manage, fund or own public facilities, including medical ones. Over the 10 years from 1997, over £15 billion was invested thereby in hospital rebuilding (Hellowell and Pollock, 2009, p 14). As well as commitments to service designs, facilities and specifications being potentially 'locked in' for discrete periods under such arrangements, there were possibilities for some bypassing or reconfiguring of accountabilities and participatory opportunities.

If marketisation and consumerism had been shaping the journey for citizen and user participation, it was now being sustained by other forces too. The intention was to replace dependency with independence, to replace one-size-fits-all with individual choice, and to replace the passive service receiver with a new active citizenry. These intentions were spelled out by New Labour in 1998 in the rebranding of the Conservatives' Citizens' Charter as Service First, while the Audit Commission was to reinforce and regulate the message. The modernising of public services was to lead to a new set of expectations and new opportunities, but also responsibilities on the users of health and social care services. Service users were granted rights to be consulted about service developments, rights that might be legally enforced through the courts, and were encouraged to engage and participate. 'The aspiration for the new duty [to consult]', suggested government, 'is to embed a culture of engagement and empowerment' (DCLG, 2008, para 2.11). Government and public service agencies were required to be both energetic and innovative in their approach to user involvement, with the supposedly passive welfare recipients of the past ideally recast as active welfare consumers (Bochel and Evans, 2007). In support of this duty, self-help and self-management became themes underpinning new prevention agendas, with some social care clients encouraged to determine and manage their own care regimes through techniques of co-production, direct payments (made mandatory in 2001) and individual budgets (introduced in 2005). Pearson (2000) and others viewed direct payments as an empowering and enabling development, complementing the relative passivity of encouraging the voice of users, with the activity and control assumed to be intrinsic in transferring power to make purchasing decisions about the care services they received.

On direct payments, policy guidance (DH, 2003) highlighted the rhetoric of individual choice, flexibility and control in service provision, although as Pearson (2000) indicated, this was matched with an equal emphasis on other imperatives, including cost efficiency and service accountability. Direct payments, as an example of user involvement, can be understood as liberating the service user to purchase their own services on their own terms, while also shifting the element of accountability from the state to the user, encouraging the user to make 'active but responsible' decisions. Despite apparent support for direct payments, however, early work on older people's use of these resources suggested that they were 'unfamiliar with the idea of direct payments and, although critical of local services, were generally unenthusiastic about the prospect of individuals running their own support systems' (Barnes, 1997, p 27). Later analysis suggested that older people, despite being overwhelmingly the largest consumers of health and social care services, continued to have reservations about taking responsibility for organising and controlling their support services. In 2009/10, 9.6% of those aged 65 and over who were receiving social care services elected to do so through direct payments, compared with 22.8% of those with a 'learning disability' and 20.2% of those with 'physical disabilities' (NHS, 2010, p 12). Notwithstanding possible doubts here, however, behaviourist expectations of active consumers seemed to have become more firmly embedded, and it was expected that direct payments and personal budgets would embrace all consumers of state-funded social care by 2013 (DH, 2010a). Indeed, pilots had already been started to explore transferability to health care, under the Health Act 2009, encouraging further 'liberation' for those users who wanted to exercise this degree of control and assume this degree of responsibility.

The quasi-market was also subject to centrally defined audits, inspections and performance management approaches to complement the professional regulation of services that had been apparent before (see Barnes and Prior, 2009b). The Commission for Social Care Inspection was created in 2004, succeeded by the Care Quality Commission in 2009, with the aim of encouraging an improved service quality through regulation and inspection. Complementing these top-down initiatives were developments (including some at the local level) to create platforms for users and the public to raise their concerns about local health and social care services. Over time, these have included Community Health Councils, Patient and Public Involvement Forums and the Commission for Patient and Public Involvement in Health, each of which appeared to gain greater powers than their predecessor, including rights to 'enter and view' care premises, with the commensurate responsibility on professionals to respond. Complementary legislation included the Health and Social Care Acts 2001 and 2008, which introduced duties for organisations to make arrangements for service users to get involved in the planning of services, resulting in a proliferation of formal and less formal bodies tasked with representing the views of users.

Local Involvement Networks (LINks) were introduced in 2007 in the Local Government and Public Involvement in Health Act, tasked with promoting and supporting 'the involvement of people in the commissioning, provision and scrutiny of local care services' and 'obtaining the views of people about their needs for, and their experiences of, local care services' (section 221(2)(c)). Compared with its predecessor – Patient and Public Involvement Forums, introduced in 2006, which were focused exclusively on health-related organisations such as primary care and hospital trusts – the LINk worked to a more general health and social care brief, and was expected to have a more participatory membership, open to all local residents and organisations interested in improving local services. LINk structures – in being membership organisations open to and composed of citizens and users – vested leadership of their affairs in a smaller group of 'representatives', which could be viewed as an intermediary body, interfacing between health and social care authorities on the one hand and user–citizens on the other. These bodies were to have a short life, and have since given way to new HealthWatch organisations, introduced on 1 April 2013, having similar structures and powers but recast within a new NHS framework introduced by the coalition government in 2011. If New Labour's approach to the modernisation of public services was characterised by a refining and regulating of the role of public authorities and organisations within the new marketised, consumerist public sector economy, the coalition government elected in May 2010 was to move in a different direction, apparently towards the Big Society, not 'big government'.

The Big Society, while offering a useful rhetorical label to the political classes, perhaps represented at its simplest an alternative to the New Labour model of state-sponsored community empowerment and involvement programmes by apparently 'redistributing power from the state to society, from the centre to local communities, giving people the opportunity to take more control over their lives' (Conservative Party, 2010b). Perhaps legitimated partly by the austere financial climate, this change was to be achieved not by targeted state investment but by a renewed focus on decentralised service provision, where 'the leading force for progress is social responsibility, not state control' (Cameron, 2010b). Widely received with scepticism and uncertainty (NCIA, 2011), the Big Society initiative was interpreted by some commentators as having the primary objective of achieving 'a permanent shift to a small-state, market-centred society' (Taylor-Gooby, 2011).

The Big Society ambitions found some expression in the coalition's Localism Act 2011, and a key goal of policies was to open the public service market to community and employee interests, such as employee-controlled mutuals, as well as to private and commercial interests, with the latter generally viewed as being more likely to take advantage of the opportunities offered than the former. This same model was applied to other areas of public service reform, as with the restructuring of the NHS (under the Health and Social Care Act 2012). A key part of the Health and Social Care Act established GP-led clinical commissioning groups (CCGs) to undertake the bulk of NHS commissioning (a function that itself can be outsourced), and legislated for 'any willing provider' from the voluntary, community and private sectors to bid for contracts. Monitor, the new economic regulator of the NHS, has since been tasked with ensuring that competition in this new market is 'fair' and that it operates in the best interests of patients.

As with many of the coalition's reforms, it is too early at the time of writing to tell exactly how these new markets will operate and who or what will be the dominant players. It remains uncertain how the growing presence of private commercial companies in key areas of public service will impact on user movements and how private corporations will engage with users and citizens. Catalyst (2012), a corporate finance company, has published research suggesting that changes in healthcare policy and pressures on public finances will present major opportunities for private healthcare providers to take a stake in the new markets, estimated to be worth £20 billion. So far the healthcare market appears dominated by large contracts for which only a certain number of 'prime contractors' are able to bid. This may put under threat the roles, autonomy, authenticity, campaigning and advocacy impact of many smaller, grassroots organisations, traditionally more user friendly if not user governed (NCIA, 2011). It is equally uncertain how the user involvement and responsibilisation legacies from the New Labour governments will fare. So far as the former is concerned, the core duties on public authorities to consult with their citizens remain on the statute book, and indeed will be applied to the new CCGs in the NHS, but the duty to involve – introduced by New Labour as part of its best value guidance – has been abolished. So far as new citizens' responsibilities are concerned, the self-help and user-centred focus of public services look likely to remain, although there have been commentaries on what Beresford (2012, p 67) has called the 'apparent ending even of the Victorian poor law distinction between the "deserving" and "undeserving" poor: those historically seen as unable to work and fend for themselves – disabled and older people, and those with chronic conditions – as opposed to the feckless and idle unemployed'.

It remains to be seen whether these developments may stimulate user movements, which have flourished and been encouraged by some previous governments, to resist the cuts in services and benefits to which they are being subjected, or in effect subjugate them. The journey is not yet over. To conclude this discussion, Box 8.1 summarises some key points, before the chapter turns to case study illustrations.

Box 8.1: Participatory engagement themes, policies and changes

- Participatory engagement has a long history, with notable examples in the 1960s.
- Involvement has varying aims for government and practitioners, and across policy domains.
- Policies and practices can contain positive (empowerment) features, but also themes about persuading and activating.
- Official discourse over time shows a mix of commitments and themes. There may have been some longstanding potential for divergence between collective and individual forms of participation.
- The commercialised, market-driven perspectives of the New Right helped to drive many changes in social care provision, including development of new rights and responsibilities in community care policies, citizen charters and direct payments.
- The New Labour government focused on 'modernisation', extended regulation to enhance service quality, and offered users opportunities to influence services.
- The coalition government appears to be further encouraging the care market to deliver personalised services.
- A gradual shift may be taking shape from collective, rights-based involvement, towards individual, service-driven involvement, assuming all individuals aspire to be involved.

The 'workings' of involvement in a northern town

This section draws on insights from a case study of service user participation on the social care and health services front among older people, so as to explore what user involvement means to different actors, and how grassroots ideas compare to government expectations. The research was part of a PhD study that ran between 2008 and 2011 in a northern borough in England. Methods included individual interviews and focus groups with four kinds of respondents:

- those active and professionally engaged in user involvement practices (key informants);
- service user participants or representatives who played leading roles in the process (involvement activists);
- other users engaged as active 'older group members';
- other users engaged as 'day care service users'.

Research was conducted during the end of the New Labour period prior to the introduction of new policies under the coalition government, and aspects noted included the varying types and levels of participation associated with individual and collective forms of involvement, and the roles of 'intermediary' participants and bodies, sometimes charged with representing potentially 'hard-to-reach' communities.

Orientations towards involvement activities ranged from the 'active' to the 'passive'. This highlighted differences between how involvement was depicted by government and much of the literature – that all want to be, and therefore should be, involved – and how individuals themselves understood their roles. The local material appeared to indicate significant contrasts with government in the degrees of control, responsibility and power some individuals wanted or thought they could manage. For government, the practice of involvement is recognised as an issue associated with personal incentive and activation, and the acceptance of greater responsibility appears to be encouraged for a variety of reasons (including practical concerns with improving services). One interpretation is that there are strong 'behaviourist' assumptions and expectations here, which may not match well with local preferences or understandings of need.

The most 'active' respondents were distinctive for their intermediary and representative roles in the involvement process, often operating within 'collective' contexts such as LINks, and focused on representing the voices of other service users, some of whom were less accustomed to taking on the role of challenging the control and influence of the professional: "I look round the patient representative group, we're all older people, which we shouldn't be of course, but then 60% of hospital patients are older people, with one in four having dementia, it's a big issue" (involvement activist).

Other respondents appeared involved in more narrowly defined practices, perhaps more individually and personally rewarding to the user, such as participating in craft and leisure activities and attending interest groups. Participants in these groups appeared less interested in gaining power and control, and more in sharing ideas and social activities with similarly interested individuals: "I go dancing every week, they go dancing three times a week, we go to the theatre a lot, we do so much...." (active older group member). Those individuals who were generally not interested in getting involved appeared more accepting of their role as 'passive' service users. Whether for reasons of health, confidence or feelings of vulnerability, these people appeared to adopt a more individualist stance in terms of reasons to get involved, and generally seemed happy with being represented collectively, or by professionals and intermediaries. When asked about getting involved, these respondents gave comments and feedback that were generally satisfied, complacent or compliant:

> 'Yes, we did one [questionnaire]. It asked about meeting here every week, how good the carers are, but all the helpers are very caring. It said at the bottom "what improvements would you like?" But we couldn't think of any improvements, because it's really good as it is.' (Day care service user)

Activation to get involved was not necessarily commonly shared, but rather based on more personal judgements and attitudes reflecting different personalities and especially past experiences. The different types and levels of involvement were also acknowledged among practitioners, with consultation exercises sometimes appearing focused on broad citizen groups (such as pensioners' forums) or on discrete users of a particular service (as with service feedback forms). Differences in involvement practice reflected to some degree distinctions between user-led models whereby users themselves would decide and manage involvement on their own terms, and officially-led mechanisms whereby the subject matter of the consultation, the precise questions asked, the methods used to gather responses and the decisions made to react to them were all controlled by various professionals. The element of direction was sometimes evidenced from respondents' observations on experiences of being asked to get involved, where there was also some pragmatic awareness among clients of possible limitations to this involvement: "We had a lady come round even today – before you came – asking what we would like to do on the social side. I contribute to things like that, but we know that money is tight, so we have to think within reason" (day care service user).

Attitudes sometimes seemed to reflect an unstated realisation that it was at higher levels where decisions were being taken, and of a context in which electoral representation affecting those levels had often been absent and might be in further decline with current plans regarding privatisation. Some respondents highlighted examples of the divergence between consultation and decision making:

> 'Questionnaires asking people "Do you want to receive modernised services?" – "Yes". "Do you want [a certain hospital] to close?" – "No". They never listened to all the people who didn't want [the hospital] to close. It shows they have their own agenda despite consulting people.' (Involvement activist)

There was also the suggestion of 'therapeutic' value from practitioners' perspectives, in that engaging people, or at least offering opportunities for people to engage, might work as a tool for professionals to secure compliance generally. Although the potential divergence between involvement being a citizenship consumer right or a broader route to empowerment was not necessarily an issue of importance to my respondents, some did mention power being significant: "I wouldn't term it as being kept 'active'; it's more about keeping your grey cells alive, making you think.... Being involved does help with feelings of power" (involvement activist).

The efforts of user participants to engage in large-scale strategic debate were limited, both by the consultation processes and also by the apparently relaxed and narrowly focused perspectives of those consulted. This was particularly noticeable as an issue when talking about participation to individuals actively engaged, who sometimes assumed that all people should get involved:

> "At [our pensioner group] we have about 13 members, and of that only seven to eight come to the regular meetings. Now consider the number of older people in [this area].... At the coffee morning alone, we tend to get about 60 older people. Coffee mornings seem like the only event that they go to. At [our pensioner group] we arrange outings and meals out, but many older people just aren't interested. I like to sit next to different people, to talk to them – but they just don't appear interested in the slightest....We have

a bus pass once you get over 60, so it's not even travel that's the problem." (Involvement activist)

Those older service users most active in consultation activities, however, appeared to be well versed and experienced in community affairs, often having other leadership or involvement interests. Tending to view their role as influencing, changing and improving community services and facilities, they presented their remit as much broader than that of the majority of users or potential users, who (in the view of these activists) often did not seem to desire the additional power opportunities they might have over service providers, and instead appeared motivated more by objectives of personal betterment or companionship. Despite positive intentions, therefore, involvement mechanisms appeared to be relatively selective, and not fully incorporating or embracing for the diversity of individuals likely to benefit from the processes involved. To a large extent, consultation appeared to remain predominantly in the hands of the 'professionals', often working through intermediary bodies who, as part of their work, were required to supply evidence of the attempts they made to solicit and encourage involvement as part of the then new duty to consult. It was not so clear that the broader targeted audience had been enabled to achieve empowerment or to keep active, as strongly suggested in the political rhetoric. In effect, some key people already active in community roles and networks were being incorporated into management to some degree and expected to share responsibilities with practitioners. Positive behaviours from activists were important to legitimate and enhance decision and monitoring processes, while for service users more generally the aims were relatively modest. They could be encouraged to engage in ways that helped to fine-tune the delivery of services and to perform more personalised 'duties' of self-help and mutual collaboration. A question remains as to how significant or successful participation mechanisms will turn out to be during a period of greater austerity in public sector funding, especially given any heightened expectations among the 'baby boom' generation soon to be entering old age.

Concluding comments

As noted above, varying perspectives, positions and potential meanings have been associated with user involvement, which has been practised at both a collective level (as expressed through intermediary bodies in the case study area) and an individual level (where the perspective tends to be more personal). It could be suggested that in social care fields the practice of involvement, which perhaps began on more collective grounds via activist groups and charity associations, has become more fragmented in terms of the variety of types and forms available and encouraged. Individual involvement through direct payments and personal budgets, for example, expanded under the climate of personalisation, with individuals increasingly required to select, manage and handle the funds for their care services. At the same time, however, collective and representative roles did seem to expand under New Labour from relatively selective memberships of Community Health Councils to broader associations with LINk structures and other intermediaries, perhaps implying that involvement was both potentially more accessible to a larger range of individuals and retained an important position in British social policy.

At a time of growing austerity in public services it seems likely that fewer resources may be directed to releasing and mobilising the consumer voice than was the case earlier, especially compared with the years of the Blair government when considerable attention was paid to this in the construction of the new welfare quasi-market. Despite some initial hesitation by the coalition government, the legal duty to consult enshrined in the Local Government and Public Involvement in Health Act 2007 is likely to remain on the statute book, albeit coloured by a new commitment to localism and the Big Society, apparently enshrining greater opportunities for local communities to both take control of local services and hold to account those who provide them. This could be construed as leading to new rights and duties of citizenship, with the expectation that citizens will engage in the opportunities that will exist to participate in local consultation and involvement exercises, both individually and as members of wider collective intermediary organisations. My research suggests that if participation is to be meaningful, this will need to happen at numerous levels: at a strategic level in terms of large-scale policy developments locally (as with hospital closures, for example, or service 'redesigns'), as well as at the more personal level of individual services, where user feedback activities can be organised relatively easily and cheaply. The theme in policy discourse that responsible citizens have duties to participate seems likely to be strengthened rather than diminished by the input of the UK coalition government as far as social care and health for older people are concerned. Themes of empowerment here may well continue to be linked with obligations, whether as an individual consumer planning and choosing in marketised settings, or as a member of some local community, real or imagined. If the behaviourist leanings found in some official health and social care discourses have been pointing towards an implicit new contract with older people, then the active and reflective consumer is likely to figure increasingly prominently on an individual basis. My empirical research suggested, however, that even if there is some strengthened contract assumed between the state and its citizens, the reality for many older people (who are major consumers of health and social care services), is that the prerequisite must be a shared belief among participants that their involvement at whatever level will be personally rewarding and meaningful. Certainly, it remains unclear how far official aspirations for responsibilisation through participation can realistically be met without material or social gains that are directly perceived as such by consumers. If activating client groups through user involvement becomes primarily about saving money rather than sharing power or control over resources, then the potential for painstakingly building genuine empowerment may be lost.

NINE

Patient responsibilities, social determinants of health and nudges: the case of organ donation

Ana Manzano

Introduction

Public health history is inherently linked to the history of state power and concerned with social, economic and political relations between classes, social structures and states (Porter, 2011). Arguments for health as a social right are based partly on the causal relationships between socioeconomic inequality and differential distribution of health and disease. In the 19th century, some modern states translated health citizenship into a universal equal right for their populations to receive protection from epidemic disease. From there, states developed healthcare coverage providing some form of health benefits to their citizens, ranging from little to universal coverage. In those days, infant mortality was one strong measure that demonstrated how economic inequality caused clear health differential gradients according to class. In the 20th century, however, perhaps especially when the relationship between lung cancer and smoking was established, a shift towards lifestyle explanations began to complement or replace traditional social structural concerns in public health. The new emphasis on behavioural approaches to public health was more political than it may have looked at the time. Blaming and changing individuals contrasted with improving social circumstances, and bio-psychosocial models of health focused thinking on disease prevention through the control of individual lifestyles. As time passed, victim-blaming of already disadvantaged groups developed, rather as an adjunct of the support for healthy lifestyles in public health politics (around smoking, obesity, alcohol consumption and so on).

In the 21st century, politics and policies often seem to reflect this kind of ideological standpoint, although strategies may take multiple and sophisticated forms. In a marriage of convenience, research quite frequently focuses on demonstrating the role of individual behaviour in reducing morbidity and mortality, and many academic debates broadly centre around exploring individuals' responsibility for particular health outcomes. In the UK, the balance between the rights and responsibilities of the state and the individual has been a longstanding interest of the two main political parties (Dwyer, 2004). This chapter explores two public health programmes implemented in the UK under the 2010 coalition government, to illustrate how individualistic behavioural ideologies are embedded in them. Discussion also indicates the importance of social contexts and health service complexities when appraising policies built around 'nudge' ideas, and notes that such programmes may fail to relate effectively to health inequalities. The two programmes involve the institution of health responsibility in the NHS Constitution (DH, 2010b) and the application of specific nudges (Thaler and Sunstein, 2009). For the second, we focus on a distinctive example: organ donation. Although parts of the literature containing criticisms of behaviourist theories refer to widely known examples such as obesity, smoking and drinking alcohol, organ donation may prove an interesting illustration for present purposes, and perhaps offer less familiar insights for readers.

Health responsibilities and the NHS Constitution

In the UK, New Labour placed wellbeing at the centre of policy making, hoping for citizens to be 'happy, healthy, capable and engaged' (NEF, 2004, p 2). The pursuit of wellbeing can be linked to forms of governance that engender self-responsibility (Rose, 1999; Sointu, 2005, 2006), while the displacement of responsibility from society to the individual may shift blame. It could also be argued that the trend towards responsibilisation in health rests on a considerable degree of consensus across political interests and parties.

In 2008, the World Health Organization called on governments to lead global action on the social determinants of health with the aim of achieving health equity. A commission explored the structural factors that generate health inequalities:

> The poor health of the poor, the social gradient in health within countries, and the marked health inequities between countries are caused by the unequal distribution of power, income, goods, and services, globally and nationally, the consequent unfairness in the immediate, visible

> circumstances of people's lives – their access to health care, schools, and education, their conditions of work and leisure, their homes, communities, towns, or cities – and their chances of leading a flourishing life. This unequal distribution of health-damaging experiences is not in any sense a 'natural' phenomenon but is the result of a toxic combination of poor social policies and programmes, unfair economic arrangements, and bad politics. (CSDH, 2008, p 1)

Despite this global emphasis on the social determinants of health, current Western policies and practices seem to focus on personal responsibility for health. With population age and countries' health costs increasing substantially, rationing is the main justification for control. Physicians and politicians may try to control 'deviant' health behaviour through imposing numerous medical regulations upon everyday life. To some extent, individuals (and not societies) are sociologically redefined as bearers of the relations of health and illness (Porter, 2011). Both the state and the lucrative health promotion industries construct the healthy body into a moral crusade: societies cannot pay for health for all, and therefore health is one's own responsibility, and enhancing or protecting it is a citizen's social duty.

In the UK, the British Medical Association (BMA, 2007) advocated the need for a patient charter focusing on the individual's responsibility both in health and illness. In 2009, for the first time in NHS history, explicit individual responsibilities for patients and members of the public were introduced (DH, 2010b). The NHS Constitution for England was established by the late New Labour government. Rationing healthcare because of an individual's habits or behaviour (as with drinking and smoking) has long been an important potential theme for parts of NHS practice (Dwyer, 2004). The recognised mantra of New Labour – 'no rights without responsibilities' – was relevant to debates here. Including these ideas more formally in the healthcare arena could extend principles of conditionality within the domain of NHS rights.

In 2010, the new UK coalition government formed by the Conservatives and the Liberal Democrats supported the NHS Constitution (DH, 2012). There would be rights, pledges and responsibilities for staff, patients, the public and all providers of NHS services. Despite the legal status of patients' responsibilities being aspirational and non-binding, establishing health-related responsibilities may have the potential to undermine disadvantaged groups, while assuming that they have control over health outcomes that are, in fact, determined socially. Practices encouraging particular responses are to some extent already found in the healthcare system and public health arrangements. Pressures may take many forms, including incentives (such as NHS weight loss schemes), and disincentives like taxes, but are mainly based on 'exhorting citizens to undertake a variety of personal disciplines to manage themselves, arranging their bodies, minds and lives around the expert advice dispensed by public health bodies' (Brown and Baker, 2012, p 3). Some primary care trusts, for example, require enrolment in pre-surgery smoking cessation programmes (National Health Service Oxfordshire, 2010). Some other countries have legislated for accountability with harder approaches. Germany requires co-payments when treatment is required as a result of a criminal activity, deliberate self-harm, cosmetic surgery, tattoo or piercing (Schmidt, 2007).

Schmidt (2009) has categorised NHS patients' responsibilities into three groups:

- those generally directed towards oneself because compliance is likely to lead to personal benefit;
- obligations directed towards others ('your family') implying that actions have implications towards those people patients care for, healthcare staff and other NHS users;
- those directed towards the healthcare system as a whole because compliance will facilitate efficient operation and use of resources.

Box 9.1 shows the specific NHS expectations.

Box 9.1: Patient and public responsibilities in the NHS Constitution

- You should recognise that you can make a significant contribution to your own, and your family's, good health and wellbeing, and take some personal responsibility for it.
- You should register with a GP practice – the main point of access to NHS care.
- You should treat NHS staff and other patients with respect and recognise that causing a nuisance or disturbance on NHS premises could result in prosecution.
- You should provide accurate information about your health, condition and status.
- You should keep appointments, or cancel within reasonable time. Receiving treatment within the maximum waiting times may be compromised unless you do.

- You should follow the course of treatment that you have agreed, and talk to your clinician if you find this difficult.
- You should participate in important public health programmes such as vaccination.
- You should ensure that those closest to you are aware of your wishes about organ donation.
- You should give feedback – both positive and negative – about the treatment and care you have received, including any adverse reactions you may have had.

The second example or case explored in this chapter is linked especially to Schmidt's (2009) last category of responsibilities: those directed towards the healthcare system as a whole. This will help to illustrate how social control can take the form of individually focused policies that seek to make citizens feel ultimately responsible for social outcomes. The official expectation in the selected case is that: 'You should ensure that those closest to you are aware of your wishes about organ donation' (DH, 2010b, p 9). Organ donation is an emergent policy issue that frequently gets media attention in the UK but the issue of 'giving' is certainly not a new area for the social sciences. Titmuss (1971), in *The gift relationship: From human blood to social policy*, explored how blood donation relates to the obligations of citizenship in a modern social democracy, whether blood is a common good, and if its distribution should relate to issues of distributive justice in a welfare state. Although organ procurement organisations are dedicated to securing gratuitous donation, their institutional forms and the ways they address and mobilise potential donors are embedded in the financial constraints of the quasi-market that rules the majority of European national health services. The next section examines how the UK coalition government proposed to increase organ donation, and considers the individualistic behavioural theories deployed to approach this issue.

The coalition government and the promotion of 'nudges'

The current UK government favours 'nudge interventions' to prompt behavioural change in public health matters, an approach popularised by Thaler and Sunstein (2009). The preference is for non-regulatory interventions designed to influence behaviour by modifying the context in which people make choices (also called 'choice architecture' interventions or nudges). Nudge theory is based on a political philosophy named by Thaler and Sunstein as 'libertarian paternalism', which promotes public policies that 'push individuals toward better choices without limiting their liberty' (Hausman and Welch, 2010, p 123). This conceptual oxymoron is justified through claims that there is a middle way for the state, rather similar in fashion to justifications that were being offered as New Labour searched for a Third Way, when writings from the UK sociologist Giddens (1998) served as support.

The repetitive Third Way rhetoric of reconciliation of right-wing and left-wing politics is made explicit by the authors. Thus, 'libertarian paternalism offers a real Third Way, one that can break through some of the least tractable debates in contemporary democracies' (Thaler and Sunstein, 2009, p 253). This middle ground claim apparently has a great appeal in some modern politics and, in the United States, Thaler and Sunstein were soon employed by the Obama administration in advisory roles. In the UK, the three main parties found some common ground in behavioural theories. Wells (2010) indicates that setting up the coalition's Cabinet Office Behavioural Insights Team breathed new life into arrangements established by former Prime Minister Tony Blair (and that had focused on law and regulation under his successor Gordon Brown). The Conservative Party embraced the approach and related it to its Big Society policy idea in its General Election manifesto (Cameron, 2009b). Despite the broader evidence base for the effectiveness of 'nudges' being questioned by a House of Lords inquiry (Science and Technology Select Committee, 2011), behavioural change and behavioural economics have emerged as areas of common interest with the Liberal Democrats. The UK coalition government has endorsed the Behavioural Insights Team promoting choice architecture as a solution to common public health issues (for example obesity, alcohol consumption and smoking).

Choice architecture policies are widely contested both on theoretical grounds (Sugden, 2009) and in respect of their empirical basis. However, there is a nudge typology (Yeung, 2012, pp 130-3) that must be noted:

- *Physical architecture.* The design of the physical environment can promote particular kinds of social outcomes. For example, stripes may be painted on roads to create the illusion that a vehicle is speeding up when approaching dangerous bends.
- *Deliberation tools.* These aim to inform decision-making processes by helping the subjects of programmes to comprehend their options. They include government campaigns to provide individuals with information that will help inform their decisions, as well as mandatory disclosure laws (Ho, 2012) like mandatory calorie counts in food labelling.

- *Defaults and anchors.* These are based on individuals' tendency not to change an established behaviour unless the incentive to change is compelling. These concepts are also apparently based on a human tendency to 'anchor' on one piece of information when making decisions, and the tendency of individual decision making to be influenced by the decisions of others. In relation to the foci of the present chapter, the example most mentioned in this category is default opt-in for deceased organ donation, also referred to as 'mandated choice'. This public policy approach requires people by law to state in advance whether or not they are willing to engage in a particular action. Under organ donation mandated choice, all adults are required to decide whether they wish to donate their organs on their death (Spital, 1992).

One short chapter of Thaler and Sunstein's book explains how donor pools could be increased through 'mandated choice' interventions. As evidence, the authors refer to a mandated choice programme added to the renewal of driving licences, implemented in Illinois with apparent success (Thaler and Sunstein, 2009, pp 184-92). In line with this, 2011 saw the introduction in England of a programme of 'prompted choice' (the reader may notice how the oxymoron was softened by replacing 'mandated' with 'prompted') on the online application form for renewing and applying for driving licences. During this routine activity people are nudged into thinking about organ donation. Applicants are mandated to answer one question (with three predetermined answers) about whether they would consider joining the donor register (see Box 9.2). This question already existed in the paper application form but now online applicants have no option but to complete it before they can continue with their application.

Box 9.2: Questions about organ donation in the UK driving licence online application

Driving licence online applicants have to tick one of three options to answer a question on organ donation before they can complete their application:

- Yes, I would like to register;
- I do not wish to answer this question now; or
- I am already registered on the NHS Organ Donor Register.

Currently, many applicants for a driving licence either miss or ignore the organ donation question (prompted seemingly by the sentence included in the paper application: 'You do not need to fill in this section'). These recalcitrants are now forced to respond, prompting expectations of an instant rise in registration numbers. The largest source of people joining the UK donor register is from provisional driving licence applications (DVLA, 2006) and this younger population are thought to prefer online registration.

At the time of writing there were no published data on whether this architectural modification had led to a significant increase in the donor pool. There are questions, however, about the 'elbow power' and even the direction of the nudge described above. The possibility remains that citizens who were reluctant to answer this question in paper form may still opt for equivocation by clicking a box now labelled 'I do not want to answer this question now'. Moreover, other experiences with mandated choice suggest mixed outcomes. An early experiment in Texas was counterproductive, with 80% of individuals refusing to designate themselves as organ donors with a concomitant reduction in organ procurement (Siminoff and Mercer, 2001). The problem facing its advocates is that choice architecture is a matter of people's dispositions as well as their options. As Titmuss (1971) taught us, the 'gift relationship' can be tenuous and precarious. It is possible that altruism can be stifled if it is nudged too hard. Altruism is socially constructed, and organ donation is deeply embedded in institutional contexts. The following section illustrates the social construction of donation altruism, and addresses some of the criticisms of nudges.

Behavioural approaches to organ donation and health inequalities

Policy makers are seduced by nudges logic partly because nudge strategies appear simple ways to shape individual behaviour. At the same time, they may appear cheap or relatively readily accessible for practice purposes because they often do not require legislation. Cost-effectiveness, however, can only be appraised if we take into consideration missed opportunities (bearing in mind that short-term success may be offset by longer-term failures), and review carefully whether strategies might be missing grassroots outcomes, or have an inadequate fit with complex practice environments or varied human purposes.

In this section, we seek to interrogate the implications that health systems' complexity, inadequate understandings of social actors, and particular inequalities of outcomes might have when analysts appraise programmes built on 'nudges for organ donation'. Looking at critiques of nudges, we review three concerns using organ donation as the framework for analysis:

- complexity;
- ascribed infantilism or oversimplification of behaviour among potential target groups;
- potential limitations arising from differentiation of outcomes.

A simple solution for a complex problem

Nudge interventions do not engage deeply enough with the complexity of causality attributions in health and social systems. A quick review of the complexity surrounding 'death-to-donation-to-transplantation' processes illuminates the issues. The worldwide demand for donated organs has grown substantially, driven by the steady addition of new organs to transplantation repertoires (kidney, liver, heart, pancreas, lung, intestines, hand, face). Technical innovations generate increasing demand, but supply remains a problem resulting in substantial waiting lists. Advances in raising donation numbers have been halting, and securing more organs for transplantation presents a major challenge. This quest has met with considerable variation across countries and regions. 'League tables' of high and low performers abound in the literature, as do explanations for relative success or failure (Abadie and Gay, 2006). Spain is customarily positioned as the clear world leader in the donation league tables, with the UK and Nordic countries performing less well than expected (Council of Europe, 2012). To date, research has struggled to understand the disparities and the reasons behind them, while major policy modifications seem unable to overcome them.

Although quite unique in its procedures and practicalities, 'deceased organ donation' shares the complexities experienced in the delivery of all services in modern medicine. The ultimate outcome (transplantation) requires the coordinated effort of hundreds of players (patients, donors, recipients, families, physicians and surgical teams from assorted departments and institutions), often operating with different motivations and objectives. Understanding the requisite processes and interactions has drawn on conceptual schemas extracted from clinical, management, social science and public health theories (Steiner and Jacobs, 2008). We are confronted with a prime example of a complex adaptive system in healthcare (Plsek and Greenhalgh, 2001), operating with multiple, self-adjusting, unpredictable and interacting pathways.

The 'death-to-donation-to-transplantation' pathway is formed by many stages. Figure 9.1 simplifies them in 11 stages. Stage 4 represents the pivot of the mode: the need to establish consent for organ donation. In terms of decision making, it is the most complex component, involving a balancing act of the wishes and expectations of a variety of stakeholders. Here we note a key dynamic. Wishes to donate may have been expressed clearly by patients, but frequently this is not the case and families normally act in proxy. Families are thus confronted with the dilemma of whether to consent or to refuse donation in an enormously tragic moment. Decision making is febrile under these circumstances: type of death, age of the patient, cultural practices, parental involvement and kinship relationship of the decision maker are among the many factors conditioning the consent/refusal rate (Moraes et al, 2009).

Figure 9.1: The death-to-donation-to-transplantation process

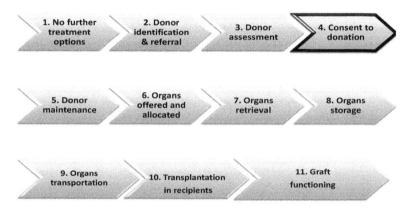

Programmes that allow individuals with strong preferences for donation to state their wishes do not guarantee that these will be fulfilled. There is a parallel and potentially greater ambiguity about the meaning of 'lack of consent'. Inaction, of course, may signal everything from intolerance to apathy to forgetfulness. It has been argued, however, that families confronting this unknown intention infer that non-registered relatives are not active supporters of donation and, accordingly, do not consent on their behalf (Bilgel, 2012). Under such an interpretation, the registers may become unintended mechanisms that act to reduce donation numbers for those (the majority of the population) who do not record their wishes formally.

Once a potential donor is identified, the individual's wishes to donate are explored. Two possible situations can occur: the person had registered as a donor, or more commonly, the person had not formally registered their wishes anywhere. Interestingly, donation wishes (implicit or explicit) have no binding impact in the process. In both situations the next of kin is asked to consent to organ donation on behalf of the individual. This conversation can end up in acceptance or refusal of organ donation. In the UK, theoretically, families have no authority to overrule the wishes of an individual to donate in the event of their death. In practice, however, clinicians, being obliged to engage in consultation with close family members, rarely ignore their objections. The British Medical Association frames this practice in their duty of care to the bereaved relatives: 'It is also questionable whether all individuals who sign up to the organ donation register would want their wishes followed if to do so would cause very significant additional distress to their families' (BMA, 2012, pp 11-12). As noted earlier, consultation with the family can be a fraught affair, its outcome dependent on many contingent factors of which a deceased person's precise donation preferences is only one.

Much of the confusion here, it seems, stems from ambiguity over what it means to 'consent' to organ donation before death. People may communicate their preferences explicitly or implicitly. 'Explicit' includes joining the official registry, carrying a donor card or using other written materials such as wills to express wishes. Explicit consent is thereby considered to signal a clear donation preference to family members who will inevitably be asked about a patient's donation wishes. However, cards and registers do not always carry legal status and their stipulations are not enforced in most countries. Physicians have also questioned whether they represent real 'medically informed consent' in the sense of the donor fully understanding the consequences of the decision. Practicalities of finding donor cards when patients are in Accident & Emergency Departments and of accessing donor registers are also at stake. Donor register consultation does not always occur (Van Leiden et al, 2010) and the effectiveness of donor databases is contingent on significant factors common to any computerised data management system. These may include:

- errors associated with pulling data together from many sources (DH, 2010c);
- software errors when the database is used as an operational tool;
- poor data quality and accuracy of information (as with out-of-date address information or incomplete donor identification details,

which can be a key factor in countries such as the UK with no identity cards).

This snapshot of deceased donation complexity demonstrates that if the nudge succeeds and the individual ticks the box accepting to be a donor, the social construction of organ donation is the complex mechanism that will facilitate or stop those wishes being fulfilled. The next section explores the reasons why the target box may not be ticked.

Simplistic views of human behaviour

Factors underpinning human behaviour are also complex, and science has struggled to identify how they interact and what can influence behaviours in specific settings (Science and Technology Select Committee, 2011). Parts of the literature discussion about libertarian paternalism refer to how choice is conceptualised and whether it is an illusion. If individuals do not consciously think through their decisions, perhaps choice may remain unexercised. Such a possibility raises questions about how far specific choice architecture strategies do build around expectations of persuading the readily compliant, and about the prospects for targeted groups raising their guard in response. Certainly, nudges gain some of their appeal by presenting individuals as actors who may be easy to manipulate or persuade by creating the right environmental factors. If the reader has booked a flight from a low-cost online air travel company, 'default intervention' may have been experienced. Default travel insurance, in-flight meals, pre-booked seats and so on nudge us into spending more money than planned. The question to ask might concern how long those nudges work for and for whom. Surely not that many people would buy travel insurance by accident on a regular basis. Most certainly, humans can be quick to learn to untick boxes and to neutralise unwanted defaults.

Nudge theories may imply that 'cognitively constrained individuals' are nudged to make 'optimal choices' (Schnellenbach, 2012, p 266). At this point, we consciously choose to ignore the issue of who (the person imposing the nudge, of course) makes the decision of what optimal choices are and for the benefit of whom. Instead, the focus is on the simplistic view of human behaviour relied on or invoked by economists, and based on experimental studies not always founded with a thorough acknowledgement of implicit assumptions or theories. Many apparently irrational decisions made by actors are only irrational at a superficial level, because individual decision-making behaviour is more sophisticated than behavioural law and economics might suggest

(Yeung, 2012). Individual motivation interacts not only with cognition but also with emotions and social norms (Amir and Lobel, 2009). We proceed now to offer a short overview of the influence of these last two concepts in relation to deceased organ donation.

The role of emotions and affective attitudes attached to organ donation are not generally approached by default architectural interventions. Family decision makers bear the emotional impact of the type of death (accidental, sudden, expected). Possible registrees deal with the so-called 'ick factor' (feeling disgust towards the idea of organ donation) and 'the jinx factor' (the superstitious belief that registration could lead to harm or death for the registrant), these being two of the most prominent instinctive reactions to registration (Morgan et al, 2008). How the ick and jinx factors are taken into account in policy designs is important.

The roles of social norms relate to some individuals being unprepared or unable to decide when prompted to make their decision. As mentioned before, regulators try to nudge people towards behaviour based on the regulators' preferences, 'correcting' misapprehensions about social norms, as when regulators seek to encourage a diet that seems to them reasonably healthy (Schnellenbach, 2012). The policy maker's strategies for deceased organ donation encounter some challenging cultural entities, including the meaning of gift-giving, brain death and non-heart-beating death, property rights, body integrity, religion and funeral practices. Certainly, removing body parts from brain-dead patients with beating hearts in the hope of prolonging the life of another human being is not a social norm or practice that can easily be imposed in multicultural societies. Linking this medical procedure to complex notions of generosity, altruism and selflessness is not a straightforward campaign. Not surprisingly, in the UK, refusal-to-donate rates among black and minority ethnic families in hospitals are high (DH, 2008).

Finally, we must not forget that nudges can reduce opportunities for people to exercise their rational decision-making capacities (Hausman and Welch, 2010). In the case of donation, to have ticked the driving licence application form box may stop individuals from discussing their donation wishes with their families. In summary, interventions directed at increasing organ donation registrations are preliminaries that impinge on our model only at stage 4 in Figure 9.1 and as a side channel entering the flow at the moment of 'consultation with register'.

Potential complications arising from inequalities and differentiation

Critiques point out that nudges give no attention to issues of inequality, welfare and redistribution (Prabhakar, 2010; Wells, 2010). The state nudges individuals, implying that the responsibility for decisions and the consequences of those decisions lie with them and not with the state. The state, therefore, might be seen in some ways as withdrawing from responsibility in addressing any adverse consequences. One risk is that by overlooking the health organisation macro-structures, while focusing on nudging individuals, policy neglects population-level interventions (Marteau et al, 2011). We need to consider what these macro-structures look like for organ donation.

As explained previously, different cultural attitudes and organisational structures for organ donation and transplantation are at play. In the UK, organ allocation systems are sustained by a national registry for organ matching and selection criteria (concerning who gets onto the transplant list). Allocation policies (regarding who is prioritised to receive organs) are decided according to geographical and clinical principles. Distribution policies follow diverse demand management models (based on need and/or outcome), which are supposed to ensure equity of access, justice and fairness (Neuberger, 2012). However, black and minority ethnic groups are at greater risk of developing organ failure and they also experience differential access to transplantation lists and organs (Randhawa, 2011). Some structural factors that offer insights beyond the lower organ donation rates from black and minority ethnic groups follow. These factors highlight the importance of biology and geography in organ matching procedures.

Organ matching

Once a potential donor is identified, the next stage is to determine suitability for donation through a process of donor assessment (stage 3 in Figure 9.1). This consists of a thorough medical and social history, physical examination and blood testing. Physicians not only decide who should receive organs but also have a complex calculation to make on who can donate them, and the matching criteria between donor and recipient. The standards adopted and actual practices vary considerably across countries but donor eligibility criteria are based essentially on age and medical history. Expanding the donor pool is a fast-moving science, with older individuals and those with co-morbidities and infections now being accepted as donors (López-Navidad and Caballero, 2003).

Medical practices such as techniques of blood typing and tissue matching are essential in organ transplantation. Organ allocation protocols in the UK are based on matching two principal immunological characteristics between donor and recipient: blood group and genetic type (called the tissue type or human leukocyte antigen – HLA – type). There are four main blood types in human populations: O, A, B and AB. In the UK, O is the most common blood group and A, B and AB are rare. B and AB are particularly concentrated among South Asian, Chinese and Japanese communities, and these rare blood groups in the UK are also geographically concentrated (Davies, 2006). A 'same blood group' rule that matches donors and recipients is usually maintained, but increasingly debated (Rudge et al, 2007). The distribution of HLA antigens also differs between ethnic groups, and given that most organs are donated from the majority white population, it is apparent that inequalities of opportunities may emerge among groups of potential receivers.

The biological differences are not simple boundaries. In 2006, a new kidney allocation scheme was introduced aiming to prioritise 'difficult-to-match' patients in the UK. The South Asian populations were potentially disadvantaged under the previous allocation scheme because they share fewer HLA antigens with the donor population than Caucasians. The effect of the new calculations – designed to reduce the importance of HLA matching – in addressing inequalities will take several years to be assessed (Perera and Mamode, 2011). Advances in anti-rejection drugs have reduced inequalities in transplantation, and countries such as the UK strive for fairness in access to organs in their organ matching policies and guidelines. Medical practices, however, construct categories (blood type, tissue type and others) marked by differences in biology and ethnicity, which facilitate different levels of access to donated organs. An allocation policy that emphasises strict blood and HLA matching criteria can result in unequal access for minority groups.

Organ allocation

The spatial organisation of organ transplantation has potential implications for black and minority ethnic groups (Davies, 2006). Time constraints restrict donation procedures. Organs that cannot be stored using cryogenicisation have to be transplanted promptly after removal for them to retain their functional qualities. This period is variable (approximately 40 hours for a kidney and four hours for a heart) but, as a general rule, the shorter the amount of time, the better the outcomes. Other body parts such as corneas and other tissues can be stored, allowing for lapse between removal and transplantation. This complexity increases depending on the type of deceased donation. If the patient is confirmed brain dead, donation after brain death (DBD) could be organised. If the patient is not yet brain dead but his or her injuries are non-survivable, donation after circulatory death (DCD) will be under consideration.

It has been argued that DCD is a procedure that faces more hazards than DBD in preserving some organs, and DCD organs need to be transplanted locally to reduce time from extraction to transplantation. The whole process – from allocation to removal to implantation into the multiple recipients – often takes less than a few hours and this geographical element of redistribution is essential. There is a complex relationship between local and national scales in the geography of organ transplantation, but in a nutshell: geographical distribution may indirectly promote inequality (the fewer donors in one area, the fewer organs are allocated for that area). Not only is it logistically easier to transplant organs locally, but organs that are not used locally are felt to be 'stolen' from local transplant units (Roudot-Thoraval et al, 2003, p 1388). Furthermore, institutions operate under the rule that the effort of achieving consent and retrieving organs should be 'rewarded' by the local use of the organ (Rudge et al, 2003, p 1398).

Significant variation exists in demand for, access to and waiting times for organs between ethnic groups in the UK (Roderick et al, 2011). There are currently a disproportionately greater number of people from minority ethnic backgrounds waiting for transplants. Mostly they are waiting for kidney transplants, but there are also long waiting lists for heart, lung and liver transplants (Randhawa, 2011). The biological and geographical examples above demonstrate how national macro-structures can fail to resolve health service differentiations of outcomes for organ transplantation (Rudge et al, 2007; Randhawa, 2011). The current application of blood and tissue matching seems to contain inequalities, which may well be 'overlooked because they appear to reside in static biology' (Davies, 2006, p 265). We should also not forget the role that healthcare professionals play in asking for consent, and how this may be influenced by perceived and enacted preconceptions based on ethnicity (Perera and Mamode, 2011).

Nudging is directly addressed at the individual and therefore can implicitly overlook macro-structures that embed health systems. This is certainly the case for organ donation. Emphasis on individual donor behaviour may detract from other concerns within the procurement process that have little to do with altruism or with whether all citizens are going to tick the right box when/if they are applying for a driving licence. In nudge theory, regulators aim to nudge people towards behaviour based on the regulators' preferences and expectations. In the case of donation, prioritising nudge strategies as currently conceived may not be enough to meet challenges posed by complexities within health systems and in the social settings in which crucial subsequent decisions are taken. Neither do simple models for nudge programmes focused on individuals outside their social contexts seem likely to encompass in a satisfactory way the issues that arise around equality of access to healthcare. It might be argued that increasing donation rates from specific underrepresented groups is one important element here, but this is likely to lie outside the reach of nudge tactics, and perhaps would require direct collaborative activities and engagements with communities and service users. Such alternative ways forward might require some preparedness to relinquish the 'top-down' models of individual 'behaviour change' and persuasion that paternalism and behaviourism can imply.

Conclusion

Emphasis on personal responsibility for health overlooks egalitarian considerations central to democratic equality (Daniels, 2008). In this chapter, UK coalition government health policies have been analysed, with a focus on health responsibilities and nudges. The discussion addressed the broader question of what health responsibilities are and how these are represented in the UK NHS Constitution, and referred to public health behavioural strategies linked to libertarian paternalism theories.

The effects and implications from behavioural interventions through the nudges for organ donation lie within the complexity of the entire donation and transplantation system. To rely exclusively on interventions dealing with only one phase of the multiple processes ignores:

- the large number of agents involved in the system;
- the connections among them;
- the institutional arrangements required to implement the practices effectively;
- the cultural, legal and ethical forces that shape environments and individual reactions.

To conclude, Box 9.3 highlights some of the key issues touched upon in this chapter.

Box 9.3: Nudge theories and health responsibilities

- Individual health responsibilities for patients and members of the public have the potential to undermine disadvantaged groups.
- In the UK, the three main political parties have found some common ground in behavioural theories based on choice architecture ('nudges').
- Nudges are directly addressed at the individual and they can implicitly overlook health systems' macro-structures.
- The death-to-donation-to-transplantation process is complex and socially constructed. Nudges for organ donation overlook this complexity, are based on an oversimplification of human behaviour and have not as yet confronted some relevant inequality considerations.

TEN

Nudged into employment: lone parents and welfare reform

Laura Davies

Introduction

With reference to the specific impact on lone parents, this chapter examines the retrenchment of the notion of welfare as an entitlement that has occurred alongside an increased emphasis on the contractual nature of the relationship between citizen and state. Lone parents have received some financial assistance and been permitted to remain outside of the labour market to focus on the care of their children since the enactment of the National Assistance Act 1948. Changes in entitlement to Income Support for lone parents under the New Labour government in 2008 represented the first time that the eligibility of lone parents to this financial assistance was restricted (Haux, 2010, p 1). The UK coalition government has further tightened the conditionality rules for lone parents.

This chapter discusses these reforms alongside the increasing influence of behavioural economics, as coalition government policy making continues to focus on exploring the ways in which conditionality can be harnessed to influence both economic and social policies (Standing, 2011a, p 27). This engagement with behavioural economic theory, rather than the following of neoclassical economic models, appears to be underpinned by the belief that this 'new economics' can effect sustained changes in behaviour (NEF, 2005). These concepts remain intertwined with a paternalistic approach in which an engagement with the paid labour market is conceptualised as a civic duty while also being good for individuals and their families, lifting them out of poverty while positively affecting wider indicators of health and wellbeing (Waddell and Burton, 2006). The chapter considers how this may impact on the provision of care for children as lone parents attempt to balance their responsibilities as the sole adult in the household.

New Labour's policies on work and the family

As Churchill (2011, 2012) has argued, one of the primary functions of social policy is not to respond directly to needs, but to promote particular sets of values while attempting to encourage parents, families and the state to engage with their social roles and responsibilities. A key aim of the New Labour government's modernisation project was to change social behaviour by using legislation to 'sustain and induce particular types of partnership and parenting and to discourage other, less favoured, forms' (Barlow et al, 2002, p 110). Changes in family policy since the late 1990s have thus been focused on encouraging an engagement with the paid labour market, alongside a shift in the private/public distinction of family and parenting. Prior to its election success in 1997, New Labour had begun to develop policy proposals intended to persuade voters that, in a departure from the 'old Labour' promotion of unconditional welfare rights (Churchill, 2011), the party would reward hard work, and endeavour to discourage citizens from remaining on out-of-work benefits (Page, 2009). By focusing on employment as the central tool for addressing poverty, the New Labour approach began to reflect more closely the neoliberal ideology more traditionally associated with the Conservative approach to welfare policy making. Worklessness was positioned as a form of exclusion from mainstream society: those without work were seen to be idle and those using welfare benefits to support parenting were increasingly seen as 'workshy and even immoral' (Barlow et al, 2002, p 110). There would be 'no rights without responsibilities' (Giddens, 1998, p 65) as an engagement with the paid labour market became a key responsibility of all good citizens, regardless of their responsibilities for the care of children.

Placing employment as the central duty of active citizenship and 'reforming welfare around the work ethic' (Lister, 1999, p 234) led to a shift in focus in which lone parents were regarded as potential workers rather than being exempt from work requirements due to their active involvement in the daily work of caring for their children. A raft of policy measures, including the establishment of a national minimum wage in 1999 and the expansion of tax credit schemes, sought to increase the profitability of paid work at the household level and remove some of the financial difficulties of making the transition from welfare benefits to paid work. Other policy measures such as the New Deal for Lone Parents, initially launched in 1997, were explicitly designed to provide guidance to lone parents and encourage them to (re)enter the paid labour market (Finch et al, 1999). These New Deals represented a key element of welfare reforms that had begun to move in the direction of welfare-to-work in the late 1990s, as the Conservative government of the time developed Family Credit schemes, replacing the Family Income Supplement that had been in place since 1971. New Labour sought to encourage desired labour market behaviours through restructuring the welfare state around paid work, a key element of which was to change cultures among recipients and administrators of welfare and remove 'passivity' from the old system (DSS, 1998, pp 23-4; Stepney et al, 1999). Later proposals focused on the desirability of promoting inclusion and breaking the cycle of disadvantage through increasing engagement with paid work (DSS, 1999). Paid work was seen as a central tool to address the multidimensional nature of social exclusion in which poverty and low income were considered to be only a part of a range of factors contributing to the problems of exclusion (SEU, 1998).

By 2007, the Labour-commissioned Freud report examining the future of welfare-to-work was recommending substantial changes in conditionality and support for those in receipt of welfare, along with the opening up of related areas of work to contractors in the private sector, and also proposing the introduction of a single system of working-age benefits (Freud, 2007). Freud found that 600,000 lone parents had been in receipt of Income Support, a benefit with only very limited work requirements, for over a year, and identified them as one of the key groups exhibiting welfare dependency and requiring support to return to the labour market (Freud, 2007: 4). The Freud report was followed a year later by a report to the Department for Work and Pensions in which Gregg (2008) set out a 'vision' for conditionality that was heavily influenced by his view that the welfare state circa 1994 did not adequately meet the criteria of being 'progressive, efficient and coherent' (Gregg, 2008, p 5).

Recommendations made within that report were then echoed and supported in further Green Papers (DWP, 2008a, 2008b) and, by the end of 2008, Labour's welfare reform for lone parents was well under way. Although the employment-focused approach to supporting lone parents had been part of New Labour's welfare reform discourse from the beginning of its first term (Blair, 1997), the removal of automatic lone parent eligibility to welfare represented a significant departure from the previous policy framework that had offered some support to lone parents who wished to remain at home to care for their children. The phased reduction in age of the youngest resident child required to remain eligible for Income Support began with the reduction of the age of the qualifying child from 16 to 12 in October 2008. By

October 2010, only lone parents with a child under the age of seven were eligible to remain in the Income Support claimant group (DWP, 2007, p 14). Lone parents of older children who were not assessed as being eligible for disability-related benefits, for which tightening of eligibility was also occurring, were transferred to Jobseeker's Allowance and required to engage with its job search requirements under the Welfare Reform Act 2009.

Continuity and change after the 2010 General Election

The 13-year New Labour administration came to an end in 2010, and a UK Conservative and Liberal Democrat coalition government was formed. Although the Liberal Democrats had not focused on welfare reform in their election campaigning, in the weeks preceding the election both Labour and Conservative parties had made proposals in their manifestos that envisioned a future in which welfare-to-work would be the cornerstone of welfare reform (Conservative Party, 2010b; Labour Party, 2010). The campaign message from Labour on welfare reform was clear: 'tough choices' needed to be made to 'increase fairness and work incentives' (Labour Party, 2010, p 0:6) while 'all those who can work will be required to do so' (p 2:2). Responsibility would be 'the cornerstone of our welfare state' (p 2:3) and Labour pledged to 'consult on further reforms to simplify the benefits system and make sure it gives people the right incentives and personal support to get into work and progress in their jobs' (p 2:3) if the Party succeeded at the election. The Labour Party also proposed to continue to investigate Freud's (2007) recommendation to introduce a single working-age benefit to avoid the need to move between different benefits because of changes in circumstances (DWP, 2008a).

Conservative Party proposals included plans for a single Work Programme to include all people of working age not in paid work, thereby abolishing the longstanding distinction between claimant groups of unemployed people and those exempt from work requirements such as disabled people, those with long-term ill-health and lone parents. Conservative proposals included plans to enforce engagement with community work programmes for long-term benefit claimants, who would lose the right to claim out-of-work benefits if they did not agree to do so. Sanctions for non-compliance with conditionality would be severe, with a refusal to accept 'reasonable job offers' leading to the forfeit of benefits for up to three years (Conservative Party, 2010b, p 16). Of particular significance for lone parents was the proposal to end the 'couple penalty' in the tax credit system, intended to signal that 'we value couples and the commitment that people make when they get married' (Conservative Party, 2010b, p 41). This moralising approach is in line with the Conservative Party view on the 'disastrous' rise in family breakdown (Conservative Party, 2008, p 9).

Although the specifics of the approaches bore some differences, both parties were in agreement that the attachment of tightening conditionality to claims for out-of-work benefits and an increasing emphasis on (re)engaging claimants with the paid labour market were central to the future of welfare policies.

After the 2010 General Election, and subsequent formation of a Conservative/Liberal Democrat coalition government, the broad direction of welfare reform remained unchanged. The focus on welfare-to-work remained, with:

- the creation of a single welfare-to-work programme;
- the removal of the 12-month waiting period for referral to the welfare-to-work programme for those with the most significant 'barriers to work';
- a strengthened commitment to welfare conditionality (HM Government, 2010b).

For lone parents, further tightening of eligibility rules was set out in the Welfare Reform Bill 2011 (subsequently the Act of 2012), with the proposal to restrict the 'no work-related requirements' category to those with a child under the age of one. Lone parents of children between one and three years of age would be expected to take part in work-focused interviews and, as children grew older, to take part in 'work preparation' as part of their contract with the state.

Austerity: the impact on families

These reforms sit alongside an extensive programme of spending cuts as part of austerity plans to deal with the deficit. The latter include:

- reductions in entitlements to tax credits for higher earners;
- the removal of the 'baby element' in Child Tax Credit (a higher rate paid for a child under a year old);
- the pegging of tax credit and benefit levels to the Consumer Price Index rather than the Retail Price Index.

In August 2011 the Consumer Price Index stood at 4.5% and the Retail Price Index at 5.2% (ONS, 2011). Some small concessions were made with an increase of £30 in the child element of Child Tax Credit in 2011, with a further £50 increase in 2012. Other changes in family policy include restricting Sure Start maternity grants, the abolition of the Health in Pregnancy grant and other wider changes likely to impact on families such as the establishment of a ceiling for the value of Housing Benefit claims (HM Treasury, 2010a). The Spending Review (HM Treasury, 2010b) went on to freeze the basic and 30-hour elements of Working Tax Credit for three years from 2011–12 and reduced the maximum Childcare Tax Credit payable to cover only 70% (down from 80%) of childcare costs from April 2011. The cost of this change at the family level is likely to be accentuated by the disconnection between wage rates and childcare costs. Daycare Trust (2011) research indicates that typical childcare costs have risen faster than the average wage, with the average cost of a nursery place for a child over the age of two increasing by 4.8% between 2010 and 2011, while the wage growth rate for the same period was just 2.1%. It seems likely that for those on low incomes these changes may be particularly difficult to manage. Child Benefit, previously a universal benefit, ceased to be payable to households with a higher-rate taxpayer in January 2013 (HM Treasury, 2010b). For lone parents, these changes are not insignificant, with analysis from the Institute for Fiscal Studies indicating that the cumulative impact of the changes set out since the General Election mean that lone parents are one of the groups disproportionately affected by budgetary changes under the coalition government (Browne and Levell, 2010). The benefit cap, a ceiling on the total amount that a household can receive in welfare payments, will also impact on lone parents: 50% of the 56,000 affected households are headed by a lone parent (DWP, 2012f). The focus on moving lone parents into paid work is again evident, as the cap ceases to apply when the claimant (or other resident adult) moves into paid work and becomes entitled to Working Tax Credit (DWP, 2012g).

Taken together, the impact of spending cuts and welfare reforms are anticipated to be 'cumulative, abrupt and substantial ... the reforms also include a far-reaching restructuring of state services, involving significant transfers of responsibility from the state to the private sector and the citizen' (Taylor-Gooby and Stoker, 2010, p 4).

The contractual nature of relationships between citizens and the state

The notion of welfare contractualism is not a new one, with elements of a conditional approach evident throughout the 20th century (Dean, 2007). What is significant is the way in which the approach to supporting lone parents has shifted in recent years, with this group being reconceptualised as unemployed and having a duty to provide for their own financial needs. The shift from a breadwinner to an adult worker model appears to have led to a decline in support for welfare benefits to enable lone parents to care full time for their children at home. While they retain the right to stake a claim for welfare if not in work, active labour market policies require that lone parents with children over the qualifying age engage with the Jobseeker's Allowance regime and its attendant job search requirements. The welfare system is thus recast as one that seeks to provide temporary assistance during periods of unemployment with, regardless of responsibilities for the care of children, an assumption of employment for all (Millar and Ridge, 2008). All mothers, whether partnered or not, are now regarded as potential workers (McDowell, 2005). These changes appear to have some popular support, with a recent *YouGov* poll for *Prospect* indicating that 44% of respondents would prefer tax rates to fall and unmarried single parents to receive less support, with only 6% supportive of higher tax contributions and greater support for this group (Kellner, 2012, p 32). The same poll also found that 69% of respondents felt that 'the welfare system had created a culture of dependency. People should take more responsibility for their own lives' (Kellner, 2012, p 32), indicating a level of support for welfare reforms based around increasing conditionality and making work pay.

Previously, the contributions made by parents as the carers for their children were recognised in the welfare system, with lone mothers eligible for support to enable them to care for their children (Daly, 2011, p 10). These entitlements were based on some of the gendered presumptions inherent in the breadwinner model, which exonerated mothers from an obligation to seek paid work, and have now been superseded by the adult worker model in which all working-age adults are seen to have a duty to engage with the paid labour market (Lewis, 2002). Lone mothers are increasingly regarded as responsible for both breadwinning and caring, whereas the previously maternalist model had recognised that their care responsibilities impacted on their ability to engage with paid work (Orloff, 2006) and offered some out-of-work financial support. The 'contract' between citizen and state is now defined by the citizen's status as employed or unemployed, with a duty to seek and remain in work a central responsibility. Behaving responsibly, then, is primarily about having a job. What was once described as a 'creeping conditionality' (Dwyer, 2004) is now a much more tightly defined contractual relationship based on an individualised model of responsibility (Freedland and King, 2005).This focus on unemployment as a supply-side rather than demand-side phenomenon underpins welfare and employment policies that seek to tackle worklessness through an uprating of individual skills and increasing employability (Driver, 2004; Theodore, 2007), and places the responsibility for unemployment firmly at the feet of unemployed people themselves. The additional assumption that low pay is the result of low skills also underpins much of the focus on employment as a supply-side problem and ignores the realities of labour market opportunities (Lawton, 2009a, 2009b).

What does this mean for lone parents?

Part of the process of reconfiguring lone parents as potential workers involved the New Labour government seeking to reshape the boundaries of the family, intervening in the practices of family life and positioning the family as a public rather than a private concern (Gillies, 2008).This approach, in which the state attempts to influence behaviour in the private heart of the family, has continued across the political spectrum with cross-party support for the focus on early intervention. Early intervention seeks to influence and change parental and familial behaviours that are deemed to be negative, and is seen as a central instrument for tackling a wide range of problems connected to poverty, intergenerational deprivation and poor childhood outcomes (Field, 2010; Allen, 2011).

Although these interventions are framed by a dialogue that emphasises support for parenting, there is an underpinning assumption that a central responsibility of good parenting lies in making financial provision for children. Lone parents as well as partnered parents are expected to engage with paid work as a key duty to both their family and the wider community.This is enacted in a policy model that increasingly presents the presence of children as a barrier to employment rather than as a responsibility that parents need (and indeed are compelled) to attend to.The caring and domestic labour of family life, the 'work outside the work' (Breitkreuz et al, 2010), is not valued, due to the difficulties in measuring the economic value of it within the framework of an adult worker model that fails to account for the economic and social value of care (Lewis, 2002). A result of this is that parents who are not in paid work are defined in policy terms as economically inactive rather than recognised as performing a worthwhile service raising the next generation (Grabham and Smith, 2010, p 86).

Further weight is given to the approach by arguments which suggest that parental employment is an indicator of positive outcomes for children and that any negative impacts of maternal employment on the child are 'small [and] ... insignificant' (Field, 2010, p 49) if the mother returns to work when the child is 18 months or older, and that positive effects in later childhood 'counterbalance the effects in very early years' (Field, 2010, p 49). Echoing the earlier work of New Labour's Social Exclusion Unit (SEU, 1998), Black (2008, p 104) argues that '[c]hildren who grow up in low-income or workless households are also more likely to suffer worse health themselves, be workless and live in poverty when they become adults'.

Alongside this presentation of paid work as the duty of the good parent and active citizen, employment is also presented as a duty to oneself, supported by a discourse which suggests that there is an inherent goodness in an engagement with the paid labour market. In addition to the financial rewards of an engagement with the paid labour market, it is deemed to bring additional benefits from good health (Black, 2008) to self-worth, social inclusion, a sense of usefulness and economic participation (Bowring, 2000; Waddell and Burton, 2006). These arguments are invoked to justify a policy discourse that seeks to encourage parents to adapt their labour market behaviour by focusing on the inherent goodness of an engagement with paid work (see Patrick, this volume). However, while these arguments appear to be powerful, it seems likely that at least some of the benefits associated with paid work, such as status, social interaction and participation in the norms of society (Perkins, 2007, p 17), are linked to an increased income, rather than an engagement with employment in and of itself. Economic and psychological debates around wellbeing also suggest that wellbeing is achieved when individuals are able to act autonomously and move out of welfare dependency (Taylor, 2011), a process that is much more complex in the context of insecure and low-paid employment (see for example Shildrick et al, 2010).

Balancing paid work with family life: challenges for lone parents

Those arguments that advocate the goodness and 'positivity' of an engagement with paid work for the individual and family omit the reality that labour market involvement can present significant and complex challenges to lone parents. Research has found that employment with 'family-unfriendly' hours and problems in accessing childcare could act as an impetus to leave paid work (Shildrick et al, 2010), and the lone parent charity Gingerbread has also published research (Peacey, 2009) indicating that these concerns do not always diminish as children grow older: being available for children during their teenage years remains a central parental duty. It is known that children who are closely supervised are less likely to become engaged in risk-taking behaviours (JRF, 2005), and that adult supervision helps children to develop self-control and acceptable behaviours (Boutwell and Beaver, 2010; Lexmond et al, 2011). Supervision was presented as an important part of responsible parenting in the Prime Minister's response to the riots that took place in the summer of 2011 (Cameron, 2011c).

Some lone parents report that their own circumstances, in particular their mental and physical health, lack of local support networks or care responsibilities for people other than their children, could also act as barriers to paid work (Peacey, 2009). Recognition of these kinds of challenges and an appreciation of the complexity of family dynamics remain absent in the development of the work-focused policy reforms of the coalition government. Additionally, a number of research reports from Millar and Ridge (Ridge, 2007; Millar, 2008; Millar and Ridge, 2008) have challenged the claims underpinning welfare reforms that the solution to lone parent family poverty lies in paid work. Their research found that the financial gains achieved when lone parents moved into the paid labour market were often limited, particularly for those moving into low-paid or precarious employment. This was especially the case when the gains were placed in the context of the wider practical impacts of lone mothers engaging in paid employment outside the home, such as less time available for children or the need for children to take on additional household responsibilities. There is also evidence to suggest that lone mothers entering typically low-paid and part-time work do not escape poverty through wages alone (Gardiner and Millar, 2006), with child maintenance, tax credits and other in-work benefits needed to move incomes above the poverty line (Ridge and Millar, 2011). Ongoing research continues to affirm these findings (Ridge and Millar, 2011), with the poverty rate for lone parents standing at 19% even when they are in full-time work (Gingerbread, 2012). This presents a key challenge to the 'work first' approach for those with caring responsibilities and suggests that the approach may be more accurately regarded as a set of policies targeted at changing labour market behaviour than tackling family poverty.

Individualising social risks

New Labour's Social Exclusion Unit (SEU, 1998) identified a lack of aspiration and of motivation as key factors influencing an individual's risk of social exclusion. This rhetoric continues to be echoed today by the leaders of the three main UK political parties, who have all argued that long-term unemployment is a problem associated with a lack of individual responsibility (Cameron, 2011b; Clegg, 2011; Miliband, 2011). The assumptions inherent in an adult worker model which suggest that labour market participation is an expression of individual choice (Daly, 2011, pp 4-5) have influenced the new welfare reform discourse in which unemployment is also perceived as a 'choice', with the individual seen to be responsible for their own status as employed or unemployed (Page, 2009). This shifts attention from structural causes of unemployment in which unemployed people are considered to be struggling with their involuntary exclusion from the labour market towards a rhetoric that focuses on the problems of welfare dependency, scrounging and voluntary unemployment (Standing, 2002, p 156). While the classic post-war approach to welfare was based on the provision of welfare benefits as 'partial compensation' for unemployment that was 'an identified disservice caused by society' (Titmuss, 1967/2000, p 44), the movement is now firmly in the direction of one that focuses on an individual lack of motivation or employability (Crisp, 2008), casting worklessness as an individualised problem (Ferge, 1997). Central to a behavioural approach to policy making is the belief that not only should individuals be steered towards making the right choices, but that they are also fundamentally responsible for their own condition. This focus on individual responsibility as a justification for behavioural approaches is problematic, as it individualises social risks (Ferge, 1997) while at the same time suggesting that individuals are not able to make their own decisions about how to behave.

This shift informs more punitive approaches to welfare reform alongside greater political support for policies that seek to change the behaviour of unemployed people. The shift from a rights-based model of welfare contributes to the development of behavioural approaches by making desert something that can be evaluated according to obedience to moral norms (Dean, 2007, p 4). Increasingly, the welfare debate has returned to discussions about the 'deserving' and 'undeserving' poor, perverse incentives and the belief that social behaviour and social responsibility are skewed by the presence of the welfare state (see for example Byrne, 2012). While these key welfare debates have never completely disappeared (Bagguley and Mann, 1992), there has been a resurgence of these issues in popular welfare debates with welfare-to-work policy development clearly shaped by a shift in attitudes to unemployed people. Reducing welfare dependency is the key focus of welfare-to-work policies (Bryson, 2003), with dependency assumed to be a de facto problem. Rather than a rights–based model in which welfare is offered as a safety net in order to mitigate against the risks of a lack of supply of jobs, the perspective of welfare-to-work shifts the focus towards the labour market itself as a source of protection from income insecurity (Breitkreuz et al, 2010).

This part of the chapter is now concluded by summarising some key points in Box 10.1. There is then a discussion of nudge issues, followed by general conclusions.

Box 10.1: 'Welfare-to-work' and lone parents

- Welfare-to-work is the preferred policy prescription of both the Conservatives and New Labour, representing a striking area of agreement across a traditionally contested area of policy making.
- Conditional approaches to welfare informed by neoliberalism increasingly regard unemployment and poverty as the failure of the individual either to manage risk effectively or to behave responsibly.
- The influence of behavioural economics on welfare reforms is problematic because it assumes that, with encouragement or compulsion, people can be steered to make the 'right' choices, but does not account for demand-side issues such as job availability, sustainability and retention.
- For lone parents, a work-focused welfare regime presents particular challenges, as the system fails to properly account for the complex practical challenges they may face when attempting to combine paid work with the care of their children.
- Welfare reforms are based on a narrow conception of 'work' as only being about an engagement with the paid labour market. This neglects the social value of parenting as a type of work that is unpaid, yet a necessary and important social contribution.

Nudged into employment?

A key indicator of the extent to which policy now seeks to influence behaviour is the establishment of the Behavioural Insights Team in the Cabinet Office (also known as the 'Nudge Unit'), established to utilise the perspectives of the behavioural sciences in public policy making. Neoclassical economic theory is based on the assumption that people carry out a full rational assessment of their options before making decisions. Behavioural economics takes account of social and psychological factors and, in particular, recognises that habit is an important behavioural influence. So, encouraging people to change their habits via a selection of carrots and sticks is seen to be the first step in effecting behavioural change (NEF, 2005). Creating a 'choice architecture' (Thaler et al, 2010), in which people are steered to make decisions in a favoured direction, is seen as a better approach than classically paternalistic ones.

The central argument of nudge lies in 'libertarian paternalism' (see Wells, 2010), a position that appears to be oxymoronic (see also Chapter Nine, this volume). Specific to this approach is a focus not on enforcing and compelling certain desirable or undesirable behaviours but on providing encouragement (nudges) to ensure that the desired behaviour is (apparently) freely chosen by individuals. The retention of choice is felt to be necessary in order to avoid an overtly directive tendency from developing. When applied to welfare reform, there are links with the approach advocated by Mead (1997, p 61) who suggested that poor people need to be encouraged into paid work through a combination of 'help and hassle'. In effect, the application of behavioural approaches to welfare conditionality requires the articulation of a system in which choices are increasingly constrained, thus steering welfare claimants firmly in the direction of the (government's) desired choice.

The recent welfare reforms discussed in this chapter seek to steer claimants into paid work via increasing the conditionality attached to their claims. A central element of this is to apply sanctions for non-compliance, with the requirement to seek work in addition to (for example) the requirement to attend the Jobcentre regularly and engage with training if this is deemed necessary by an advisor. The sanctions applied for non-compliance with conditionality requirements are financial and therefore particularly difficult for those on already very low incomes to absorb. Data indicate that in the year up to and including September 2011, 66,500 sanctions were applied to lone parents on the Income Support regime. The sanction in these cases was a reduction in benefit equivalent to 20% of the single adult rate of Income Support for a person over the age of 25. In the year 2010/11 this was a sanction of £13.09 from the personal allowance rate of £65.45 (DWP, 2012h). These lone parents, as Income Support recipients, are some of the claimants to whom the lowest level of conditionality is attached. Proposals for the Universal Credit regime suggest much harsher penalties for non-compliance, such as the cessation of 100% of payments for a period of at least three months for failing to accept a reasonable job offer, failure to apply for a job or failure to attend Mandatory Work Activity. This sanction could be extended for a longer period in the case of repeat 'offences'; and, for claimants in the 'high conditionality' group, which includes most Jobseeker's Allowance claimants, a third failure to comply can result in a sanction of 100% of Jobseeker's Allowance fixed for three years (DWP, 2010a). Full conditionality is to be the default option for lone parents with children over the age of five, although lone parents with children aged between five and 12 will be permitted to seek work that is compatible with school hours (DWP, 2011b). Lone parents will not be exempt from sanctions and these will apply 'where necessary' (DWP, 2010a, pp 28-9).

Conclusions

Conditionality is linked to behavioural economics by the idea that people need to be steered towards making the 'right' choices, and that without some element of compulsion people will not do so. The importance of making a commitment towards particular behaviour can be regarded as one of the key arguments in favour of making welfare contractual. Behavioural conditionality, broadly interpreted, refers to those policy instruments whereby access to benefit or service provision is dependent on the recipient behaving in a particular way or adhering to a predefined rule or rules (Standing, 2011a, p 27). This chapter has discussed how, for New Labour, the focus on lone parents was influenced by a belief that work was the best form of welfare (Blair, 1997; Harman, 1997), alongside the drive to tackle intergenerational deprivation (Deacon, 2002). The coalition government has demonstrated a remarkably similar approach to welfare reform to that of New Labour, in which welfare for lone parents is seen to be best provided by 'incentivising' paid work through increasing welfare conditionality and work-related activity requirements.

Sanctions for non-compliance illuminate starkly the extent and impact of the behavioural approach proposed by the Universal Credit system, and the lack of choice that parents (as well as other claimant groups) will have in making decisions about their engagement with the paid labour market. The Universal Credit approach has been specifically designed to produce 'positive behavioural effects' (DWP, 2010b, p 2) in enforcing an engagement with paid work. For lone parents, a key element will be enacted via the widening of the financial gap between those lone parents who are in paid work and those who are not (Browne, 2012, p 6), as well as through mandating welfare claimants to undertake work and/or training through the Work Programme. Illuminating how clearly welfare reform is focused on effecting behavioural change, Prime Minister David Cameron (2011d) has argued that the central purpose of the Welfare Reform Bill is 'not an exercise in accounting. It's about changing our culture'. Secretary of State for Work and Pensions, Iain Duncan Smith (2011), has suggested that the reforms are about 'changing lives', while Labour Party leader Ed Miliband has suggested that the key challenge of reforming welfare and instilling a greater sense of responsibility lies in changing 'the ethic of our society' (Miliband, 2011). The neoliberal approach underpinning these increasingly conditional approaches to welfare regards poverty as a failure to either manage risk or behave responsibly (Dean, 2007). However, changing lives and cultures in the current economic climate means that it is also necessary to address some demand-side issues, by improving the availability of decent work (Women's Budget Group, 2010), while also improving employment sustainability and job retention (Bennett and Millar, 2005). Some have argued that precarious and insecure employment (TUC, 2008; Standing, 2011a, 2011b) may become a key feature of future labour markets (Clayton and Brinkley, 2011). For lone parents facing complex practical challenges (Ridge, 2007; Millar, 2008; Millar and Ridge, 2008; Peacey, 2009) as jobseekers in a highly uncertain labour market (Browne, 2012, p 3), welfare reforms based on sanctions rather than support seem to be a particularly problematic policy response.

ELEVEN

Welfare reform and drug policy: coalition, continuity and change

Mark Monaghan

Introduction

During the past two decades, it has become accepted wisdom across the political divide that the best way to solve the problem of crime is to tackle the problem of drug use, or more accurately, certain kinds of drug use (and drug users): those widely referred to as 'problematic'. Problematic drug use equates mainly to the relatively small numbers of drug users who are current users of heroin and crack cocaine – the two illegal substances that are seen to be the most harmful (Nutt et al, 2007, 2010) and linked to criminality. Drug-related crime has come to be viewed as the prime scourge for the wellbeing of families and communities (Hunt and Stevens, 2004). In response, the criminal justice system has consolidated control over UK[1] drug policy, which has entered, according to Stimson (2000), a 'crime phase'. It was not always thus. As Hunt and Stevens (2004) note, the crime phase is a transition from the health phase of drug policy whereby drug harms were primarily a matter of individual and public health.

A central premise of the drug strategies developed by successive governments over recent years is that so-called problematic drug users (PDUs) are responsible for large amounts of criminal activity in society. The main thrust of policy developments has been that if drug users could be treated either voluntarily or through compulsion then crime rates would decline. This represents a line of continuity over recent years in national drug policy formulation. Alongside this there have, however, been a number of recognisable changes, which relate primarily to the methods and means proposed for tackling the problem of drug-related crime. This chapter charts development, looking at what this means for current drug policy. As this is so, it is organised in the following way. The first section takes a critical look at the drugs–crime link that underpins contemporary drug policy, focusing on the political background to its realisation and the policies developed thereon. Moving on, discussion turns to the early drug strategy of New Labour and its crime-driven, but treatment-led policy and its accompanying promotion of methadone maintenance treatment. After this, a closer look at contemporary drug policy from New Labour to the coalition government is undertaken, paying close attention to how changes in drug policy are linked to broader changes in contemporary social policies, which in turn need to be considered alongside criminal justice policies to get a rounded view of the contemporary direction of UK drug policy. The changes in question here relate to a renewed emphasis on 'recovery' in drug treatment. They started in the later years of the New Labour government (1997–2010) and have received new impetus under the current coalition government. Broadly speaking, there has been a change of emphasis over how best to solve the issue of drug-related crime, and underpinning this is the re-emergence of 'moralising' rhetoric, which has at its heart the desire to specifically change the behaviour of populations identified as being 'problematic'. No longer is criminal law seen to be the main lever by which this is achieved, as the welfare system is playing an increasingly central role.

The politics and policy of the drugs–crime link

Since the mid-1990s, one consistent theme underpinning UK drug policy has been that a hard core of persistent PDUs are responsible for a significant proportion of criminal activity. Prior to this, in light of the heroin 'epidemic' of the 1980s, UK drug policy had been heavily influenced by the view that certain kinds of drug use, particularly those involving intravenous administration, had the potential to contribute to the vigorous proliferation of life-threatening viral infections such as HIV/AIDS. In policy terms, a tipping point was a report published by the Advisory Council on the Misuse of Drugs (ACMD, 1988), which stressed that the threat of HIV/AIDS was a more pressing social problem than heroin use itself and that a policy shift was necessary to avert a public health crisis. A pivotal feature of this policy change was the necessity to create and promote a culture of controlled and safe use of heroin under the aegis of 'harm reduction'. In this context, harm reduction was based on principles of containing, rather than eradicating, the problems associated with mainly heroin. Needle/syringe exchange programmes were developed to this end and the roll-out of opioid substitute treatment programmes became more widespread.

Much significance is placed on this development by drugs scholars, some praising the then Prime Minister Margaret Thatcher for her pragmatism. It is interesting to note, however, that in her memoirs of her time in office (Thatcher, 1993), the drugs issue barely receives a mention and this particular episode goes unexplained. The pragmatic change must, however, be seen in context. Farrall and Hay (2010) demonstrate how the criminal justice policies of the first Thatcher government were not of the same ilk as under later administrations. Hough (2011, p 216), furthermore, points out how the policies of various 'One Nation' Home Secretaries in the Thatcher administrations (1979–90) – William Whitelaw, Leon Brittan and Douglas Hurd – were not immediately associated with 'social Conservativism', and that the flagship Criminal Justice Act 1991 was 'the most explicitly decarceral of the Criminal Justice Acts of this period, placing a series of hurdles in front of sentencers that they had to surmount before they could pass prison sentences'. It can be said that the turn to harm reduction at this time was understandable in light of the general direction of criminal justice policy making.

It was not long, however, before such policies were abandoned as an era of what Ryan (1999) has referred to as 'authoritarian populism' emerged whereby criminal justice and penal policy arguably became more draconian. In the early years of John Major's premiership (with Michael Howard in the Home Office), there was a 'return to justice'. Crime rates, as indicated by both the official statistics compiled by the Home Office and the British Crime Survey, had risen to an all-time high and drug users became the 'suitable enemy' (South, 1999) on which to pass the blame. In a speech at the 1993 Conservative Party conference, Michael Howard outlined a number of 'law and order' measures to control crime, which, according to Hughes and Anthony (2006, p 80), 'included substantial revisions' to current policy and practice working with drug users. These were consolidated in the 1995 Drug Strategy *Tackling drugs together* (DH, 1995), which placed significant stock in the potential of 'joint working' of health and criminal justice professionals (among others) through the creation of drug action teams to address the drug problem, but which very much prioritised measures aimed at curbing drug supply, traditionally the domain of criminal justice rather than of those more health-oriented aims of reducing the demand for illicit drugs.

Also around this time, the notion that 'prison works' gained currency and the prison population began to bulge somewhat ironically as the crime rates began to fall. This was a time of significant expansion in prison building and a clamour for longer sentences for serious crimes alongside a more 'punitive edge' to non-custodial sentences (Ryan, 1999, p 8). For Feeley and Simon (2003, p 439), the swelling prison population was part of the 'new penology', whereby the prison was no longer seen as a 'special institution capable of making a difference in the individuals who pass through it'. It was instead part of a combination of intertwined correctional and custodial networks, which govern to control the behaviour of those identified as a risk to society. Here, PDUs sat alongside suspected terrorists, drug traffickers, paedophiles and knife- or gun-using youths.

Other epithets have been assigned to policy development in this era such as 'populist punitiveness' (Bottoms, 1995) and 'totemic toughness' (Stevens, 2011a). The Conservative government's shift was in part a direct response to the repositioning of the Labour Party in terms of its law and order policies. In January 1993, the then shadow Home Secretary Tony Blair famously declared that New Labour would get 'tough on crime and tough on the causes of crime' with a predilection towards the latter. In 1994 Blair calculated that half of the cost of all property thefts, some £2 billion, could be attributable to drug users (Blair, 1994). This consolidated the view that prolonged use of substances such as heroin and crack cocaine was linked to frequent offending. This set the tone for the New Labour approach to drugs and crime when in government. For example, in a speech some years later, Blair (2001) commented:

> The bulk of crime is committed by a hard core of persistent offenders, around 100,000 in all.... These persistent offenders share a remarkably similar profile. Half are under 21. Nearly two-thirds are hard drug users. More than a third were in care as children. Half have no education at all. More than three-quarters were unemployed when they were offending.

Although the drugs–crime link underpinned much of the law and order policies of the two largest political parties throughout the 1990s and into the new millennium, the exact nature of the relationship between drugs and crime is difficult to ascertain. The drugs–crime nexus is, however, one of the most researched areas of drug policy (see for example MacGregor, 2000; Bennett and Holloway, 2005, 2009; Duke, 2006; Seddon, 2006). The notion that most acquisitive crime (crimes committed for some sort of financial gain such as shoplifting, burglary and robbery) or 'volume' crime (that which consumes large amounts of police time) is somehow drug related is often taken to be self-explanatory. The suggestion of a causal connection has been given additional impetus over recent years with the rising profile of gang crime and the perception that many so-called 'gangsters' are embroiled in retail-level drugs markets (Kintrea et al, 2011; Pitts, 2011).

There are doubts, however, about the direction of causality. Various examples could be given as illustration, but as Bennett and Holloway (2009) note, research on drug use and prostitution is useful for highlighting some of the complexities of assigning causality. Drawing on the work of Maher and Curtis (1992) and Feucht (1993), they found that for some women prostitution was a means of financing drug taking, yet for others drug taking had more therapeutic aspects serving to desensitise them to their situation or helping to reduce their inhibitions, thus putting their clients at ease. When looking at other transgressions, such as robbery and theft, research has also proved inconclusive as to which activity occurs first. For certain offenders, the initiation into criminal activity may pre-date the first episodes of drug taking, and for others 'successful' episodes of criminality may be celebrated with drug consumption rather than drug addiction being the raison d'être. Hough (1995) makes a distinction between drug-driven and drug-related crime to demonstrate this point. The former is crime specifically committed to fund the purchase of drugs. The latter, meanwhile, is where the proceeds of the offence happen to be spent on drugs.

A question remains over the evidence for the drugs–crime link. We have witnessed from politicians – and Blair was by no means alone – the repeated 'killer facts' that 'drug use causes crime' and drug use costs society billions of pounds a year. The NEW-ADAM (New England and Wales Arrestee Drug Abuse Monitoring) found that 65% of sampled arrestees had traces of drugs in their urine. The figures showed that the most common drug was cannabis, with 24% testing positive for heroin and 15% for cocaine (Stevens, 2007, p 81). This is often taken as proof of the drugs–crime link. Economic analysis conducted by Godfrey et al (2002) estimated that Class A drug users in England and Wales caused between £9 billion and £16 billion of social costs through their criminal activities in the year 2000. These costs were mainly to healthcare services, the benefits system and the criminal justice system.

As argued elsewhere (Monaghan, 2012), this research is not without its problems. The NEW-ADAM findings came with repeated warnings from the authors themselves (Holloway and Bennett, 2004) that because of shortcomings over the methodology, they should not be used for the purpose of claiming a drugs–crime link. Stevens (2007, p 81) meanwhile has provided a detailed critique of the economic analysis underpinning the drugs–crime connection, claiming that the figures are reached by 'estimating the costs of recent crimes reported by drug users entering treatment in the National Treatment Outreach Research Study (NTORS)' and 'multiplying them by the estimated number of problem drug users'. Problem drug users are identified by Godfrey et al, (2002, p 9) as 'those whose drug use is no longer controlled or undertaken for recreational purposes and where drugs have become a more essential element of an individual's life.' It is this category that is thought to generate the most costs to the public purse. Stevens maintains, however, that drug users are more likely than non-drug users to be arrested and, therefore, studies of arrestees – on which government drug policies are based – are an exercise in what Young (2004) has termed 'voodoo criminology'. This is because such explanations also fail to account for the fact that a drug user's offending peaks just prior to the point of arrest as this coincides with the moment when help-seeking behaviour is most acute and when one's lifestyle is most chaotic. Behaviour at the point of arrest is not representative of a drug user's routine activities.

A growing body of evidence also shows that so-called 'harder' drugs can often be used in relatively unproblematic and controlled ways (Shewan and Dalgarno, 2005). Research from a 'hidden' sample of drug users – that is, those who have not been accessed via criminal justice or treatment agencies – has demonstrated that heroin use is not necessarily followed by criminal activity (Warburton et al, 2005). Nor does criminality necessarily precede use, save for the actual purchasing and thus possession of drugs. In short, the evidence of a causal link between drug use and criminality is inconclusive. Seddon (2006) has attempted to move the debate beyond a narrow causal discussion of drug-related crime. While accepting that there is a correlation, he demonstrates how both problematic, chaotic drug use and significant amounts of criminality are linked to social disadvantage. The nature and extent of each is contingent on other factors such as (lack of) opportunities in the local formal economy, which are counterbalanced by opportunities afforded to certain groups in the informal economy. For Seddon, these nuances are often overlooked in public debates, which have tended to see the drugs–crime link as a historically 'natural' phenomenon, and that the poorer members of society are somehow more predisposed to drug taking and criminality out of either fecklessness or greed. Politicians and policy makers have, however, generally chosen to ignore these structural explanations of drug use and criminality. That said, there has, over recent years, been incremental change in the way governments have attempted to regulate the behaviours of PDUs and these are linked to changes underpinning many social policy developments of recent years. It is this to which we now turn.

New Labour's early drug policy

The early New Labour approach to drug control was a continuation of its stance outlined while in opposition. The direction of policy was outlined in the four main priorities of its 1998 strategy *Tackling drugs to build a better Britain* (Cabinet Office, 1998 [updated in 2002]). These were:

* to help young people resist drug misuse;
* to protect communities;
* to invest in treatment for people to live healthy and crime-free lives;
* to stifle the availability of illegal drugs on the streets.

The passing of the Crime and Disorder Act 1998 – which introduced the flagship Drug Treatment and Testing Order (DTTO) – was also a key moment. The DTTO invested the courts with powers to sentence persistent offenders to a period of drug treatment on the agreement of the offender. The alternative was a custodial sentence. This became known as 'coercive' or 'quasi-compulsory treatment' (QCT).

The DTTO featured heavily in New Labour's initial drug strategy, which placed significant emphasis on increasing the total number of people in drug treatment. However, as Stevens (2011a, p 71) demonstrates, the DTTO itself was rarely used. It was, however, the first time drug-dependent individuals could be sentenced to treatment by the courts. It was replaced in 2005 by the Drug Rehabilitation Requirement (DRR), although the two policies were very much of the same lineage, acting as alternatives to imprisonment in the first instance (see McSweeney et al, 2007). Regardless, the policy direction at the time is aptly illustrated by the National Treatment Agency's written memorandum to the 2002 Home Affairs Select Committee inquiry into UK drug policy (Home Affairs Committee, 2002), in which it commented:

> UK drug policy is crime-driven and treatment-led. Crime-driven in that the perceived link between dependent drug use and acquisitive crime underpins the Government's decision to dramatically increase expenditure on drug treatment. Treatment-led in that effective treatment is seen as the appropriate response not only to the individual and public health problems associated with drug misuse but also to drug-related crime.

The notion of drug policy being crime driven but treatment led, through QCT, suggests a fusion of erstwhile separate philosophies of punishment and rehabilitation. Coercive treatment measures empowered the state to employ various means to 'track down drug users and lock them up' if they did not comply with the conditions of the order, which generally meant undergoing a period of drug treatment (Hunt and Stevens, 2004, p 355). Critical commentary on QCT abounds (see Stevens et al, 2005; Duke, 2006; Seddon, 2006; Webster, 2007). Seddon (2006), for instance, comments on the ethical implications of coercing people into treatment, particularly if these services are delivered in part by the NHS, as this calls into question principles of patient consent, volition and confidentiality, which are the foundation stones on which treatment services have traditionally operated.

A defining feature of drug treatment at this time was the use of methadone maintenance, which formed a central part of state-sponsored drug treatment within the community and within the prison system. Methadone is a kind of opioid substitution and is one of the most widely evaluated interventions in health (Farrell et al, 1995). There are some gaps in the evidence base with regard to how users themselves experience the process of treatment, but these are starting to be filled (see for example Bauld et al, 2010, 2012; De Maeyer et al, 2011; Harris and McElrath, 2012). A recent overview of UK drug policy by the present author (Monaghan, 2012) demonstrated that, ultimately, where methadone is concerned, most of the debate has revolved around the intensely complex issue of the efficacy of methadone treatment as an aspect of quasi-coercive treatment. On the one hand, there is evidence to suggest that methadone maintenance treatment can help to reduce the criminality associated with heroin use and can lead to positive health gains. A recent report by the National Treatment Agency (2009) suggests that heroin users who are prescribed methadone reduce their offending by up to a half while engaged in treatment. Webster (2007) also demonstrates how methadone can help to reduce heroin consumption in the short term and is a vital step towards abstinence in the long term if that is the end goal required by the participant in the programme. On the other hand, such findings are questioned by claims that methadone treatment simply replaces one drug dependency with another (McIntosh and McKeganey, 2002; Gyngell, 2007), and that very few people emerge from methadone programmes drug free.

Elsewhere, Stevens and colleagues (2006) highlight how the successes of drug treatment including methadone programmes are contingent on various factors, including the motivations of the offender, which, in turn, hinge on factors such as:

- whether legal pressure is applied to treatment;
- the length of the treatment episode;
- medical status;
- employment/support status;
- levels of drug/alcohol use;
- family and social relationships;
- psychiatric status.

Whatever the true picture, it is clear that from around the middle of the last decade there was an increasingly polarised academic debate over the efficacy of methadone maintenance treatment – a point also raised by the United Kingdom Drug Policy Commission (UKDPC) report into 'recovery' from drug dependency (UKDPC, 2008) – and that this occurred alongside increasing disenchantment in policy-making circles over its efficacy. The loss of confidence within government over methadone treatment manifested itself in a change of emphasis in drug policy where the focus on recovery was brought to the fore and became conjoined to the issue of employability and welfare reform.

Enter the coalition government: work, employment and behaviour change for 'recovery'

It is a key assertion of this chapter that a broad political consensus exists which maintains that a large proportion of criminality in society is drug-related and that communities need to be protected from this. Whereas in the early days of New Labour the treatment sector was rapidly expanded as this was seen as the best means of tackling the problem, more recently there has been a change of emphasis. In effect, it can be argued that from 2008 the 'containment' policy advocated over preceding years began to be rolled back as the later New Labour strategy – *Drugs: Protecting families and communities* (Home Office, 2008) – advocated a more explicit attempt to foster behavioural change among PDUs, signalling a desire to help them move towards recovery.

The contrast between the early and later New Labour drug strategies that has been demonstrated elsewhere (see Monaghan, 2012) can be brought into focus with the following passage from the 2008 strategy, which reveals an explicit commitment to abstinence in the long-term: 'The Home Office, Ministry of Justice, prosecutors, police and partners will continue to present drug-misusing offenders with tough choices to change their behaviour or face the consequences' (Home Office, 2008, p 16). Later in the same document, the message is reinforced but a short-term commitment to maintenance is also indicated as it states: 'The goal of all treatment is for drug users to achieve abstinence from their drug – or drugs – of dependency. For some, this can be achieved immediately, but many others will need a period of drug-assisted treatment with prescribed medication first' (Home Office, 2008, p 28).

This movement towards abstinence was linked to broader themes and developments in the later New Labour government's approach to social policy, which Harrison (2010) suggests was underpinned by a 'new behaviourism' in the form of a specific desire to bring about change in the behaviour of problematic populations. This was usually achieved through a combination of incentives and increased surveillance, or as Wincup (2011) suggests, by a series of carrots and sticks. Breaking with previous strategies, the surveillance of drug users was increasingly achieved through the benefits system *and* the criminal justice system as concern was raised in government over the estimated 267,000 PDUs accessing the main welfare benefits in England. This figure equated to approximately 7% of all benefit claimants and four fifths of all PDUs (Hay and Bauld, 2008). More specifically, more closely monitored are the estimated 100,000 PDUs believed to be claiming out-of-work benefits (DWP, 2008b) but not engaging with drug treatment services (Monaghan and Wincup, 2013).

With a desire to see 'no one written off', under proposals first outlined by a Department for Work and Pensions' Green Paper published shortly after the 2008 Drug Strategy (DWP, 2008b), a series of carrots and sticks were promoted to enable dependent drug users to avoid the 'sin' of 'worklessness' and to work towards recovery. The carrots amounted to additional support for PDUs undergoing treatment to prepare them for work. Alongside this was a stick of having benefits withdrawn if PDUs did not take steps to address their drug dependence. Indeed, it was hoped that via the intended introduction of the Welfare Reform Drug Recovery Pilots in October 2010, a condition of claiming out-of-work benefits would be that PDUs would have to undergo mandatory drug treatment (see Wincup, 2011). As it transpired, the Recovery Pilots were defeated in the House of Lords and the plans were subsequently scrapped as the UK coalition government came to power in May 2010.

The coalition approach to drug policy outlined in the 2010 Drug Strategy (Home Office, 2010a) was very much a continuation of that of the previous government. Other statements regarding drugs from the coalition, however, seemed to favour abstinence as the chosen policy goal. The *Programme for government* included a statement that its sentencing proposals would work towards helping 'offenders come off drugs' (HM Government, 2010b, p 21), and the Ministry of Justice (2010) Green Paper seemed to equate recovery with abstinence. In this sense, they were perhaps influenced by findings from the Centre for Social Justice Think Tank (Gyngell, 2007), which suggested that the most effective means to work towards abstinence was not through the 'madness of methadone', but through increasing the provision of residential rehabilitation programmes.

There has since been some backtracking on residential rehabilitation, not least because it was unclear how this was to be funded. Stevens (2011b) highlights that on average it costs around £26,000 per person per year to undergo residential rehabilitation treatment in comparison to the £2,020 it costs to run a methadone maintenance programme over the same duration. However, reinforcing the commitment to residential rehabilitation, the proposals outlined in the welfare reforms taking place under the aegis of Universal Credit (see below) show how the only PDUs who are deemed to have a reduced capacity to work are those attending residential rehabilitation, currently around 2% of people in adult drug treatment (National Treatment Agency, 2012).

There are further issues to be resolved. As it stands, drug treatment is funded through the Department of Health and Home Office via the 'pooled treatment budget', which is distributed to drug action teams who coordinate treatment provision at the local level. The sums distributed are proportional to the demand for services, which is monitored by the National Treatment Agency. The UKDPC (2012) notes that under conditions of austerity and with a drive towards localism, uncertainty about such funding arrangements remains, not least because under the Health and Social Care Act 2012, a new public health system will be created, which will oversee the commissioning of services. The context for these changes will be that they have to occur in line with £20 billion worth of savings to the NHS by 2014. Second, reforms to policing mean that the elected Police and Crime Commissioners will control significant budgets that currently incorporate the money ringfenced for drug intervention programmes. At the time of writing (November 2012), little has been said about what the outcome of this will be and whether the current funding arrangements and organisation of drug treatment will remain.[2]

Ultimately, the UK coalition's drug policy is premised on building recovery through decreasing the number of drug-dependent benefit claimants and increasing the number of PDUs in paid work through participation in the Work Programme. In facilitating this, the benefits system offers tailored conditionality for those already engaged in drug treatment and rigorous enforcement of 'normal' conditions for those not participating. These normal conditions include the commitment of the claimant to participate in work-related activity, but not necessarily to undergo drug treatment. Thus, under current rules, treatment for PDUs is not mandatory. However, in May 2012, press reports suggested that Iain Duncan Smith, the Work and Pensions Secretary, was attempting to shift policy in this direction by suggesting that treatment should be mandatory for any PDUs wishing to access benefits under the Universal Credit system. At the time of writing (November 2012), this specific policy has not been adopted, but stringent conditionality applies nonetheless (Monaghan and Wincup, 2013). Consequently, PDUs claiming benefits cannot be sanctioned for failing to participate in drug treatment per se, but they can be if they fail to engage in mandatory work-related activities unless they are deemed to have a reduced capacity for work, for example through engaging in residential rehabilitation, or if they have a significant 'disability', illness or caring responsibilities; and even then it is possible that some conditionality relating to work may be applied (see Patrick, this volume).

Central to the 'work first' strategy of the coalition are attempts to improve the life chances of PDUs through the development of recovery capital. Apparently influenced by the work of Pierre Bourdieu, this comprises four main dimensions:

- social (building and maintaining relationships);
- physical (securing resources such as money and accommodation);
- human (developing new skills and keeping a healthy lifestyle);
- cultural (fostering the values, beliefs and attitudes that will aid recovery such as a work ethic).

It has been noted how these reforms are likely to promote certain kinds of capital while undermining others. For instance, compelling people into work is not always compatible with the rebuilding of relationships such as when a PDU is trying to establish a role as a primary carer to a minor (Monaghan and Wincup, 2013).

Other aspects of welfare reform may also serve to undermine certain aspects of recovery capital of individuals. Stevens (2011b) raises concern over how the rolling back of Housing Benefit as part of what was the Welfare Reform Bill will be detrimental to the pursuance of physical capital for PDUs. He suggests that for drug users to obtain the said capital then investment in specific services is the order of the day, not least those that provide access to good-quality, affordable housing.

Similarly, a report by the UKDPC (2008, p 27) noted that one of the key challenges of getting PDUs who are at some distance from gaining employment ready for the labour market is to provide 'stable and supportive accommodation', and to invest in allied services. This is because, as it notes, a lack of appropriate accommodation can lead to relapse on the grounds that it is difficult to maintain progress in a setting such as a hostel where many of the other residents use alcohol and drugs. It is a spiral of difficulty.

Before this chapter moves to an overall conclusion, Box 11.1 summarises for readers some key points from the analysis.

Box 11.1: Key points of current drug policy and welfare reform

- Despite the paucity of evidence, drug strategies developed by successive governments over recent years have settled on the claim that problematic drug users (PDUs) are responsible for large amounts of criminal activity in society.

- Under its crime-driven but treatment-led policies, New Labour promoted the use of quasi-compulsory (or coercive) treatment to tackle the problem of drug-related crime. Coercive treatment was designed to keep PDUs out of the criminal justice system by making drug treatment and testing a key aspect of any sentence for specific offences.

- Methadone maintenance treatment was a central aspect of the coercive treatment strategy, but this fell out of favour towards the end of the New Labour administration and under the 'recovery' agenda advocated by the UK coalition government.

- For the UK coalition government, drug policy has moved away from a primary concern with drug-related crime towards a focus on building recovery through decreasing the number of drug-dependent benefit claimants and increasing the number of PDUs in paid work. The 'work first' policies of the UK coalition may hinder rather than aid recovery by placing unrealistic demands on PDUs.

Conclusion

At the end of the 20th century, and into the 21st, successive strategies left unquestioned the assumption that increasing the numbers of drug users entering treatment – through voluntary means or not – would successfully drive down crime rates. This was in spite of the fact that the evidence base was equivocal about the efficacy of such a strategy. It is the central contention of this chapter that clear points of departure can also be witnessed between early New Labour approaches and those of the later New Labour government and that of the coalition. Thus, although contemporary drug policy is still underpinned by the drugs–crime nexus, since around 2008 there has been a notable change in rhetoric typified by a steady disillusionment with methadone maintenance treatment and a desire to solve the drug problem by promoting the goal of 'recovery'. Recent changes in UK drug policy can, therefore, be understood alongside broader changes in contemporary social policies, which have become entwined with the criminal justice response to the drugs issue.

A key tenet of the so-called 'recovery revolution' has been to promote the outcome of paid work for problematic drug users. This 'work first' strategy is part and parcel of the recent welfare reforms being implemented by the coalition under the auspices of the Work Programme and the roll-out of Universal Credit. In essence these policies are a continuation of others set in place by New Labour whereby labour market activation was the key strategy for reducing the welfare bill, particularly by restricting payments for those deemed unworthy of full support. Such policies have been pursued despite warnings that ultimately they may be self-defeating:

> Since many of the 'working poor' are not making a decent wage, it is amazing how they survive in the face of being 'nickel and dimed'.... For example, when a server in a fast-food restaurant works for a pay check [sic] that precludes him or her from eating properly so that the customer can eat more cheaply, this person will experience alienation, social exclusion, and relative deprivation, which are major correlates of crimes committed by disenfranchised people. (De Keseredy, 2011, pp 90-1)

Changes first outlined by New Labour and then the coalition are underpinned by a belief that if individuals wish to receive benefits then they have to take the responsibility to appreciably amend their ways. For PDUs this means that benefits are increasingly contingent on engaging with drug treatment programmes and demonstrating a commitment to move beyond maintenance towards recovery. Yet the potential for recovery may be hindered by the focus on paid work, which in reality means low-paid jobs due to the patchy employment history and general low skill levels of many PDUs. In this sense, a fourth 'c' could be added to the title of this chapter, as welfare reform and drug policy involve the coalition, continuity, change and contradiction.

TWELVE

Regulating social housing: expectations for behaviour of tenants

Jenny McNeill

Introduction

Social housing has continued to be a site for regulation of behaviours under the previous and present UK governments. Since the Conservative/Liberal Democrat coalition came to power in 2010 there have been a number of changes affecting access to and maintenance of tenancies in social housing. Notably, there have been deep cuts in public sector funding, changes to welfare benefits including the move towards a Universal Credit system, and the introduction of the Localism Act 2011 with changes to security of social housing tenancies and local authority treatment of homelessness claims. Under New Labour, Anti-Social Behaviour Orders (ASBOs) were a key apparatus for controlling behaviours deemed 'unacceptable' in neighbourhoods, and, while such approaches were not abandoned under the coalition government, ideas of a 'Big Society' suggest ways of self-regulation of behaviours but also decentralisation in monitoring behaviours of tenants (and potential tenants) through the strengthening of powers for registered social landlords (RSLs). This chapter examines the barriers to accessing social housing in an overstretched housing market, as well as the pressures for certain groups to behave in 'acceptable' ways to sustain increasingly conditional tenancies, including 'vulnerable' groups such as young people, formerly homeless people and those with complex needs. A discussion is included on the selection process for social housing and on exclusionary policies as well as the ongoing surveillance of tenants and their families. The consequences of 'non-compliance' in social housing contracts are also discussed. Social housing is explored in the context of its relationship to employment and the continued drive to get people into work, ideas of empowering communities and, linked with this, notions of citizenship based on Big Society values.

The backdrop of housing policy

The complex interaction between current housing policy, changes in welfare regulations and the economic downturn make this period of time in the UK an interesting juncture for analysis. This chapter presents a general overview of contemporary social housing in the UK and issues in accessing social housing. This moves towards a discussion of the barriers to social housing and ways in which allocations policies exclude certain groups. A more detailed analysis follows on how behaviours of tenants and would-be tenants in social housing are regulated, controlled, empowered or liberated. This includes a critical analysis of the ongoing concern of both previous and successive governments to:

* activate people to work;
* move away from (limited) social housing;
* behave in an appropriate manner;
* actively participate in community in 'meaningful' ways.

Social housing has traditionally been targeted as requiring intervention, and this chapter explores how access to social housing has been restricted and behaviours of tenants monitored and controlled, through housing allocation policies, welfare reform and the use of ASBOs. Social housing was viewed as a site for intervention to tackle social exclusion under New Labour's Social Exclusion Unit and, from 2006, the Social Exclusion Task Force. The concern with tackling the problem of social exclusion in social housing has continued to be an interest during the coalition government period. However, despite housing and neighbourhood regeneration policies actively pursued over the last decade, some research suggests that the impact on reducing social exclusion has been minimal (Tunstall, 2011).

While it touches on New Labour approaches to social housing and welfare, this chapter focuses especially on new developments for social housing under the coalition government, and the potential impacts for tenants and potential tenants. More extensive historical overviews of social housing in the UK can be found elsewhere (see Cole and Furbey, 1994; Lund, 2011). The present chapter looks in particular at changes implemented under the Welfare Reform Act 2009 and the Localism Act 2011 and what these mean for social housing tenants. The key message is that policy interventions reflect ideas of citizenship based on contractual agreements between citizens and governing bodies. Rights and responsibilities in social housing continue to be closely bound together, and social welfare in this policy domain remains a powerful means of social control.

Controlling access to and security of housing tenures

In recent decades social housing has conventionally been seen as housing for the poorest and most vulnerable people in society, and certain households have consistently been found to be overrepresented there, including lone parents, older people, minority ethnic households and economically inactive groups (see Hills, 2007; Shelter, 2012a). One main purpose of social housing, owned and run by local authorities and housing associations, is that dwellings are affordable to low-income households compared with higher-rented private sector accommodation. Approximately eight million people live in social housing in England, and the Localism Act 2011 details reforms to allocations, housing tenure, and homelessness legislation, and regulation to change social housing (DCLG, 2011b). Access to social housing often involves lengthy waiting periods and is based on certain needs-based criteria; social landlords draw up factors for determining preference in social housing allocations. A 'points-based' system has often applied to allocations, and policies that determine who is entitled and who is *not* entitled to social housing generate much debate. By law, certain groups are given 'reasonable preference' to social housing if they:

- are legally classed as homeless;
- are in inadequate or inappropriate housing (as with overcrowding);
- need to move for medical or welfare reasons; or
- need to move to gain access to other support, without which there would be hardship (Shelter, 2012a).

A 'choice-based' lettings system, which allows potential tenants to bid for appropriate accommodation, was introduced, but a points system to judge 'need' frequently determines who secures social housing (see Van Ham and Manley, 2012, for a historical overview). Under the Localism Act 2011 (section 145), local authorities now have greater control over who joins the waiting list for social housing based on needs (thereby reducing false expectations of those 'without need' of social housing). Some research has also pointed to the potential for choice-based lettings to create and sustain segregation of neighbourhoods, although possible positive effects have also been noted for minority groups (see Law, 2007; Van Ham and Manley, 2012, for discussion). In this way there can be regulation of social housing, but also some shaping of neighbourhoods through the social housing allocations process.

A salient policy development under the coalition government has been the introduction of the Localism Act 2011. The localism agenda has been promoted under the new government as a means of enhancing power and accountability at a local level. This local-level control has implications for the allocations of social housing. In terms of dealing with homelessness applications, for example, the Localism Act (section 148) outlined new powers for local authorities to offer private rented accommodation, without the option for homeless households to refuse. Thus, the Localism Act gives powers to local authorities in handling homelessness to make greater use of the private rented sector and protect limited supplies of social housing. However, with local authorities able to discharge their duties of rehousing through greater use of private sector accommodation, there are concerns that local authorities may choose to do very little to take action to address single homelessness (see Jones and Pleace, 2010).

In addition, some homeless people are perceived as 'difficult' or 'risky' tenants, bringing substantial housing management costs to providers (Pleace et al, 2011). Furthermore, some RSLs are reluctant to offer tenancies to those with poor rent payment histories, past 'nuisance' behaviour or complex support needs (Pleace et al, 2011). Rent arrears can provide a stubborn barrier for rehousing of some social housing tenants, which precludes access to another social housing tenancy. Debts, including rent arrears, can also be an obstacle for gaining access to the private rented sector, and act as a disincentive for some homeless and vulnerable housed people to find paid work (McNeill, 2011).

The allocations system has been examined in terms of exclusion from social housing for particular people and especially migrant groups (see Robinson, 2010). The introduction of the Housing Act 1996 signalled new limitations in accessing social housing for people with refugee status, asylum seekers granted leave to remain and those with settled status in the UK (see Rutter and Latorre, 2009, for further discussion). The majority of recent migrants face restricted access to social housing based on their immigration status, legal rights and financial resources, so must rely on private rented accommodation (Shelter, 2008a). However, encouraging low-income migrants to move to the private rented sector leaves them in insecure housing situations with few housing rights (O'Hara, 2008). A number of studies have found racist discrimination in social housing policies and practice, including limitations in access to quality homes and extended periods of time in temporary accommodation for some black and minority ethnic groups (see Rutter and Latorre, 2009).

As well as changes over access to social housing, increased control has been given to local authorities in the length of tenancies they may now offer. The Localism Act 2011 means that social landlords have greater 'flexibility' to grant tenancies for a fixed period of time, with the minimum of two years in exceptional circumstances, and five years more typically, but with no upper limit of length of tenancy. However, the determination of 'exceptional' circumstances will lie with local authorities. In this way, housing policies have been developed to change the behaviour of tenants towards seeing social housing as short term with a view to moving on. With short supply of social housing stock, the coalition government emphasises that there is an economic cost for allowing tenants to stay in these homes (especially if 'underoccupied') when their personal situations change, including household composition, income levels or relocation of work. From the government's perspective, the move to shortening tenures is aimed at promoting social mobility.

However, the move away from secure tenancies towards flexible tenancies of a minimum fixed term of two years has raised concerns for the impact on social capital and individuals' and groups' attachments to community (Shelter, 2012b). With the shift away from 'homes for life' to fixed-term tenancies, individuals may become displaced from supportive social networks and opportunities for paid work. Moreover, ideas for ending lifelong tenancies and offering short-term tenancies of five years or less have met with criticism that social housing tenants will be disincentivised to find work for fear of losing their homes. Limiting tenure length in social housing has also heightened concerns about contributing to or exacerbating homelessness (see Shelter, 2012b).

Recent proposals to ensure that social housing is maintained for low-income households have suggested 'pay to stay' plans, where rent increases for high earners in social housing encourage social mobility (see Wintour, *The Guardian*, 19 May 2012). While not yet implemented, this proposal suggests that social housing policy should be closely connected to employment, but also that social housing no longer represents a home for life. However, some critics have suggested that this policy proposal would be of 'limited value', affecting only a small minority of social housing tenants, and create a bureaucratic encumbrance for social landlords who would need to examine the incomes of tenants (Shelter, 2012b). Ideas encouraging social landlords to probe tenants' incomes show further evidence of how social housing is increasingly linked with employment.

With austerity cuts in public expenditure, housing allocations have been tightened by many local authorities. Coalition reforms in welfare and housing may be seen as an extension of the previous 'rights and responsibilities' agenda under New Labour. There are certain duties of social housing tenants, but not always balanced with rights to housing. A number of specific New Labour developments, such as the 'Respect' agenda, reflected ideas of the 'balancing' of rights and responsibilities, and under the coalition there are both extensions to rights to social housing for certain groups (such as ex-service personnel) and also limitations on rights to secure, long-term tenancies for others. There are ongoing responsibilities placed on social housing tenants to behave in certain ways. The Localism Act means that local authorities now have greater control in determining who accesses social housing (with changes to waiting list selection) and the period of time for which tenants secure social housing.

Employment, welfare and social housing

The linking of social housing and employment is not new, but has been given increasing emphasis in recent periods. This section will first discuss New Labour and the coalition's drive to get people into work and its links with social housing. Coverage will then move on to recent changes in welfare reform and the localism agenda that attempt to influence behaviours of many social housing tenants. Reference is made to changes in work-to-welfare schemes, the introduction of the Universal Credit system and changes to Housing Benefit legislation, with the extension of single room rates for people under 35 years old and the new 'under occupancy' rules.

The use of welfare systems to control and influence citizens to behave in certain ways has a 'long history' (Dwyer, 2008). A number of changes were introduced under New Labour that strengthened conditionality in welfare, and as under New Labour, welfare reform is also at the core of the coalition's plans to tackle worklessness (Finn, 2011). The foci of coalition reforms have been to 'reduce social security spending, increase local control over housing and affect behaviour in seeking work and in housing and mobility' (Murie, 2012b, p 56). An 'overrepresentation' of working-age people who are unemployed living in social housing drives government policies to implement initiatives to get tenants into work. The expectation on unemployed tenants to seek and sustain paid work has remained a primary focus for government interventions, and a raft of initiatives that link social housing and employment have been developed (see Hills, 2007). Within homelessness policy the

Transitional Spaces programme, for example, prioritised 'work-ready' people into the private rented sector. Thus, the Transitional Spaces project can be seen as an incentivising approach to accessing housing through engagement in work-related schemes. Moreover, the Hostels Capital Improvement Programme, succeeded by the Places of Change Programme in 2008 under New Labour, encouraged the take-up of work-related opportunities for people living in homeless hostels as a means of breaking the cycle of homelessness and moving into resettlement. However, these programme priorities may be at odds with the priorities of some homeless groups deemed multiply excluded who face the greatest barriers to the paid labour market (OSW, 2006; Bowpitt et al, 2011; McNeill, 2011). Furthermore, initiatives such as the Places for Change programme do not tackle the problem of a lack of affordable housing for homeless people (Broadway and Resource Information Service, 2006). Certainly, there are difficulties in combining access to housing and employment for some groups facing stubborn barriers to paid employment but also to resettlement.

As with New Labour, coalition welfare-to-work programmes continue to use 'carrot' (incentivising) and 'stick' (sanction) approaches to work-related benefits. These extend New Labour's activation policies with the coalition's introduction of a single Work Programme and the Universal Credit system that has been rolled out since October 2013 (see Finn, 2011). Universal Credit replaces many of the existing welfare benefits for working-age claimants and incorporates housing costs. The introduction of the Universal Credit system is expected to create further difficulties for low-income households (Pawson and Wilcox, 2012). While some low-income households in low-paid work are expected to be, on average, slightly better off in terms of the amount of benefits they will receive (Pawson, 2011), other groups may fare less well, including lone parents (IFS, 2011). Cuts in welfare benefits will make it difficult for low-income households to maintain their homes or move on to affordable accommodation, but the impact of the new Universal Credit system on activating individuals to seek paid work is yet to be known. However, critics have in the past argued that sanctions and incentives approaches fail to recognise the diverse challenges facing particular groups in securing paid work (Flint, 2009), and thus may do little to help those 'hardest to help' into employment. 'Carrot and stick' approaches that tie together welfare and the take-up of paid employment have met with further criticism.

In welfare-to-work schemes, conditions and sanctions have meant that some individuals have been moved from disability-related benefits to jobseeking-related benefits or have been unable to fulfil onerous job search obligations, with many of these changes disproportionately affecting disabled people and people with complex support needs (see also Chapter Two, this volume). The complexities of the benefits system arguably create a disincentive for some groups, including homeless people looking to move into long-term accommodation and requiring Housing Benefit assistance, and present barriers for some homeless people seeking employment (Singh, 2005). Not only is the system complicated, but delays in the processing of Housing Benefit claims are also a major problem, and one that could lead to an individual's eviction from a property for non-payment of rent (Blake et al, 2008).

The Hills (2008) report estimated that a third of people out of work live in social housing, and highlighted a number of barriers in securing work that connect with deprivation in concentrated social housing areas, such as:

- lack of employment opportunities;
- discrimination from employers;
- inadequate childcare;
- poor transportation.

However, the report also acknowledges that rather than a disincentive to work, social housing offers a stable home from which people can move towards employment. Under successive governments there has been a salient shift in landlord functions: social housing landlords' roles have traditionally included collecting rent and maintaining properties but there has been an increased emphasis on encouraging tenants to seek employment. With tighter allocations policies for social housing there may be a move towards favouring those in or actively seeking paid work or other 'socially meaningful' activities such as volunteering, as seen in homelessness policies that increasingly link housing and employment (see Dobson and McNeill, 2011). Proposals for greater conditionality on unemployed tenants being expected to seek paid work have entered political debates before. The former Minister for Employment and Welfare Reform, Caroline Flint, had advocated contractual agreements for new tenants of social housing to seek paid employment as part of their tenancy arrangements (Flint, 2008). Although the matter did not lead to a legal clause in tenancy agreements, housing associations have increasingly developed new services to encourage tenants to take up job-related activities. The important role that housing associations can play in getting people into employment has been highlighted under successive governments (see Housing Corporation, 2007). However, the Hills (2008) report suggested that such schemes to support unemployed people into work were not available to many tenants in social housing, suggesting that some groups continued to be excluded from employability schemes. Despite the various barriers to paid work, furthermore, government policies continued to focus on the 'culture of worklessness' among social housing tenants (Shelter, 2008b).

Many low-income households who can least afford to pay are likely to struggle maintaining their tenancies in the light of changes in Housing and Council Tax Benefits. Changes detailed in the Welfare Reform Act 2012 and the Local Government Finance Act 2012 will affect many low-income working-age households in both the social rented sector and private rented sector. In line with the localism agenda to give greater powers to local authorities, Council Tax Benefit was abolished from April 2013, and local authorities have devised and administered Council Tax Support schemes in its place, but with less funding. What this means for many former Council Tax Benefit recipients is that they now have to make a contribution towards their Council Tax bill although the amount varies in different areas. While the government plans to make savings of up to £480 million a year with the new scheme, it is also hoped that councils will create stronger incentives to get recipients into paid work.

However, the welfare reforms most directly concerning housing relate to changes in Housing Benefit legislation (Pawson, 2011). Local Housing Allowance (LHA) was introduced in Housing Benefit legislation in 2008 to determine the maximum amount of Housing Benefit that could be paid out for rent in private sector accommodation based on household size and composition and local rents. Some have pointed out that reductions in LHA rates could:

- signal increased difficulties in accessing private rented accommodation (Pawson and Wilcox, 2012);
- reduce incomes of claimants and diminish housing availability (Fenton, 2010);
- create financial hardship and rent arrears (see Frost et al, 2009; Warnes et al, 2010).

Housing Benefit cuts have sorely affected many claimants in private rented accommodation who are unable to afford the shortfall in rents. Young people without dependants face particular difficulties accessing social housing (Stone et al, 2011), and the recent change to extend the age restriction in LHA rates to 35 years from 25 years presents barriers in accessing private rented accommodation. Age-related restrictions to Housing Benefit for single young people on low incomes mean that many young people are unable to afford their own home. Young people will be pressured to stay in the parental home for longer, which may create financial hardship for their families due to non-dependent deductions if their families claim Housing Benefits and are not in receipt of certain disability-related benefits. Thus, while some unemployed young people will feel forced to turn to their families for shelter it may be costly to some benefit recipients to house them.

In line with LHA rules for household sizes, the size criteria for households have also affected those in social housing since April 2013, with reductions in Housing Benefit for working-age people in social housing deemed too big for their needs (Welfare Reform Act 2012; Housing Benefit [Amendment] Regulations 2012). While increased Discretionary Housing Allowance (DHP) funding in 2013 of £30 million is expected to plug the gaps in rent shortfalls for some households in these circumstances, there are concerns it will specifically prioritise but not ringfence certain groups such as disabled people in properties adapted for their needs (National Housing Federation, 2012). However, the challenge for many working-age single occupiers without dependent children is to obtain 'appropriately sized' accommodation in an already overstretched housing market with limited stock for one-bedroom properties. While the full impact of the new under-occupancy rules is as yet unclear, the 'bedroom tax', as it is commonly referred to, may exacerbate risks of homelessness for certain groups who may face eviction for high levels of rent arrears leading to costly homelessness applications.

Cuts to welfare benefits and the introduction of the new Universal Credit system, which incorporates Housing Benefit payments, will have impact on unemployed and low-income households. Changes to welfare may mean that social housing tenants claiming housing benefits risk losing their homes if unable to meet the shortfall in rents, and could force migration to the private rented sector. However, challenges in accessing the private sector for certain marginalised groups have also been raised (see Luby, 2008), including higher rents and rent deposits, which act as barriers. The complex interaction of benefit systems with the housing market in both social housing and private sector housing generates problems of access for some marginalised and disadvantaged groups, and poses key questions on how social housing may be regulated for those most in need.

'Punishment' and 'empowerment' in social housing

As well as expectations of unemployed social housing tenants seeking work, tenants should be 'good neighbours' and behave in certain ways that promote community. The conditions of keeping a tenancy are therefore linked with forms of citizenship that emphasise behaving in ways that suggest being a 'good neighbour', including expectations of tenants maintaining a tidy home and garden (see Saugeres, 2000). However, the duties of social tenants also extend to behaving in other socially responsible ways.

The use of ASBOs, introduced in the Crime and Disorder Act 1998, was seen as a key tool under New Labour in managing (and monitoring) behaviours of tenants and punishing behaviours deemed socially unacceptable. Support for ASBOs may have been affected by hopes that they could enable action against owner-occupiers and those in the private rented sector, alongside social housing tenants. Anti-social behaviours encompass a broad range of actions, including annoyance of neighbours by children, racist harassment and violence (see Flint, 2002). The Housing Act 1996, Part Five, introduced legislation that tied social housing closer to certain behavioural responsibilities of tenants (Dwyer, 2000, p 70). Registered social landlords now have greater powers in the regulation and surveillance of the anti-social behaviour of tenants (see Flint and Nixon, 2006; Burney, 2009; Anderson, 2011). Thus, there has been a key shift in social landlord duties, which now incorporate more fully the management of 'problem' behaviours of tenants and their families. A potential consequence of not fulfilling obligations as a 'good tenant' is eviction. In the case of anti-social behaviour, some critics have argued against the use of ASBOs in housing contexts for non-housing-related disorder, while also noting that eviction does not *actually* deal with the problems of anti-social behaviour (see Shelter, 2011).

The preoccupation with anti-social behaviour under New Labour and the coalition government is driven by beliefs that anti-social behaviour is a growing issue that destroys communities (see for example Home Office, 2003, 2012b). In this context, anti-social behaviour is something that can be controlled and that without intervention disrupts core values of the coalition's notions of Big Society. However, there may be a shift in the key regulators of intervention, with a 2010 Home Office paper advocating that empowerment of the public and voluntary sector is crucial in combating crime and anti-social behaviour. This pivotal role for 'empowering Big Society' means that individuals and communities may have greater powers in enforcing rules, with neighbourhood policing teams acting as key players in tackling problem behaviour (Home Office, 2010b, p 39). Hodgkinson and Tilley (2011, p 283) have suggested that the coalition planned to abandon the ASBO in favour of more 'proactive community-based measures'. Under Big Society discourses, interventions to control or stem anti-social behaviour may take place through other forms of control. Steps towards new tools to replace ASBOs in tackling anti-social behaviour include the proposed introduction of Injunctions to Prevent Nuisance and Annoyance (Ipnas), as outlined in the Anti-Social Behaviour, Crime and Policing Bill 2013. A Home Office (2012b) report signalled greater powers to empower communities in tackling the problem of anti-social behaviour. In line with localist ideas, anti-social behaviour is seen as a 'local' problem that 'looks and feels different in every area and to every victim' (Home Office, 2012b, p 6). However, this places greater onus on the community to deal with anti-social behaviour.

As well as empowering communities to take a bigger role in addressing problems of anti-social behaviour, government expects communities to take a bigger lead in creating change in the delivery of housing-related objectives. This has been a key message of the Localism Act, and is an extension of New Labour policies concerned with neighbourhood empowerment (see Jacobs and Manzi, 2012). The Localism Act has been proclaimed as a 'radical shift of power from the central state to local communities' (HM Government 2010a, p 2). Ideas of localism and Big Society are declared by the government as the drivers behind initiatives that might put social tenants in greater control of managing housing-related services and decision making in housing stock. In line with the legislation has been the establishment of new guidelines and regulations for RSLs, with a reduced role for central government. The Tenant Services Authority was promoting a new framework for 'co-regulation' from 2010, encouraging participation of tenants in effective delivery of housing services, and since April 2012 the Homes and Communities Agency has taken over responsibility for social housing regulation. New conditions on social landlords mean that they must meet new standards, which include tenant involvement schemes (such as tenant panels). Co-regulation means that RSLs and providers are required to 'support tenants both to shape and scrutinise service delivery and to hold boards and councillors to account' (Housing and Communities Agency, 2012, p 4). Guidance in the establishment of tenant panels has been developed, with examples of such UK groups and the ways in which they are run available to local authorities and RSLs (see Bliss and Lambert, 2012). There is so far little research into the potential impact of these changes to the social housing sector, but also, specifically, on the effectiveness of tenant panel schemes, which is critical to help understand the benefits of co-regulation for all stakeholders involved. However, research on resident involvement in one housing association in England suggests that the government's 'localist ethic implying enhanced resident influence on services ... poses a particular challenge for many large housing associations' (Pawson et al, 2012, p 26).

A recent government consultation paper highlighted how tenant-led services, which give tenants a greater say in management of social housing, would promote Big Society principles (DCLG, 2012b). 'Community' involvement includes tenant-run forums, where tenants are encouraged to take part and improve social housing and neighbourhoods and have a greater say in how neighbourhoods are run. However, the apparent shift in power to tenant groups and communities may also be interpreted as the government abandoning responsibilities and duties in social housing. Relinquishing some control in favour of empowerment of tenants may also be viewed critically as relying on alternative resources that are already overstretched, and coercing tenants to act responsibly in terms of their judgements and actions.

Ideas of a Big Society, a coalition mantra, relate to a brand of citizenship thinking that emphasises power to the community. In terms of social housing this has been translated into active participation in improving housing services and neighbourhoods. Thus, a key means of changing behaviour is to 'empower' users or recipients of services and interventions. However, research by McKee (2009) showed that while non-participation could be viewed as apathy, the picture was far from straightforward. Many people living in social housing have unequal opportunities to participate in tenant involvement groups. Inequalities in participation and access to schemes that promote tenant voices suggest that such schemes have some way to go to ensure fairness in regulation of social housing. Major concerns regarding tenant involvement include inequalities in capacity for some tenants to participate, including those with multiple complex needs or communication difficulties, or from other socially excluded groups (Shelter, 2011). Furthermore, tenant involvement groups may be unrepresentative or unapproachable in some sensitive cases where tenants are reluctant to disclose personal details to their neighbours.

However, with large cuts in public expenditure, there are other concerns that neighbourhood-level services and charitable and voluntary sector involvement will be at risk (see Durose et al, 2011). Some critics have suggested that aspects of localism policy may act as camouflage to justify government welfare spending cuts (see Jacobs and Manzi, 2012). Others have minimised the idea of Big Society altogether as 'essentially empty' and 'flawed', only serving as guidelines for communities to act responsibly, or, at worst, 'dangerous' in its vision for charities and volunteers rather than the state providing key public services (Kisby, 2010).The concerns of Big Society thinking for empowering communities to tackle anti-social behaviour in housing and effect change in the delivery of housing provision have far-reaching implications for the future of social housing. Box 12.1 summarises some of the key points on social control discussed in this chapter, and then there follows a brief conclusion.

Box 12.1: Controlling and influencing behaviours in social housing

- Social housing has long been a site for the regulation of behaviours and this continues under the coalition government.
- Access to tenancies is linked to needs-based criteria, but other factors also affect organisations' responses to households. Issues include rent payment histories, 'nuisance' behaviours, complex support needs and citizenship status.
- Links between employment and housing have taken on increased importance in governmental discourses in recent periods, with various incentives, contracts, conditionality and financial drivers to push people into paid work.
- Control of anti-social behaviour moved up the housing agenda from the mid-1990s onwards. Today it should be seen alongside coalition Big Society and localism strategies. Perhaps tenants will be further 'responsibilised' at the same time as coming under pressure from benefits changes and funding cuts.

Conclusions

Clearly there are a number of coalition housing and welfare reforms that are likely to impact on vulnerable people in social housing. The allocations process for social housing is increasingly conditional on meeting particular criteria. At the time of writing, 2013, the UK government is set to introduce new measures that will affect low-income households in social housing and potentially deter others from accessing this housing. This chapter has examined how increased conditionality in welfare, rigid allocations policies, strengthened powers for RSLs and criminalisation of behaviours affect particularly 'vulnerable' groups.This review of the use of housing policies to affect and influence behaviour has shown how certain people are excluded from social housing, and social housing tenants are increasingly expected to behave in 'acceptable' ways, such as moving on from social housing rather than viewing social housing as a home for life, seeking paid employment, and participating in ways that promote ideas of Big Society and community involvement.

The changing face of social landlords means that their roles have changed from limited ones centred on dealing with basic housing issues towards more complicated ones that encompass managing anti-social behaviour, encouraging tenants to find paid work but also working with tenants collaboratively in improving housing services. The blend of coercive and incentivising measures to change behaviours of social housing tenants is arguably not new, and this chapter has explored examples under both the previous government and current coalition government, which demonstrate continuity (rather than completely distinctive changes) of policy responses to regulating behaviours of particular groups.

Part Three
Conclusions

Part Three

THIRTEEN

Concluding thoughts: the consequences of a 'not-so-big society'

Teela Sanders

Introduction

This book has investigated a number of social policy fields, to explore aspects of social control that have been evident over the recent past and have continued into the present period of UK coalition government. One key question has concerned how far social control and behaviourist ideas are common ground across a range of welfare, education, health and care policy fields. Although policy domains have their own specific histories, environments and orientations, the chapters in this collection nonetheless demonstrate that there is indeed a broad pattern of similarities in disciplinary and behaviourist ideas and approaches across a range of territories. This concluding chapter touches briefly on these similarities while summarising some of the main findings across the social policy terrain. There is then a more general discussion, referring to trends, their implications and the Big Society. The importance of exclusion is highlighted, as a frequent adjunct and part of social control strategy and consequences. Current approaches to dependency contribute to damaging outcomes as far as the lives of low-income and vulnerable people are concerned, and it seems to be a 'not-so-big society' that is unfolding under the coalition, rather than something inclusive and supportive for social integration in difficult economic times. Simultaneously, governments' attempts to control behaviour in line with economic liberal assumptions and desires have given support to substantial reductions in both liberties and opportunities.

A review of findings

Generally, the patterns of a 'new behaviourism' that appear as an undertone for contemporary social policy individualise social problems. Difficulties for households are seen as being caused by the individual, the family or perhaps an entire community or social category that has failed to act appropriately or fulfil duties as citizens. Harrison and Hemingway in Chapter Two explored the various indicators of a behaviourist approach, describing how policies are often centred on incentivising, reclaiming, disciplining and excluding people who appear to step outside what is judged to be acceptable behaviour. The authors discussed how behaviour is judged and controlled increasingly through a range of contracts, imposed duties and expectations of conditionality, with individual behaviour monitored by a range of policing agencies. Chapter Two illustrates the continual reinvention of interventions, programmes and approaches to behaviour management, as 'vulnerability' and the perceived challenges posed by particular households are dealt with by imposing responsibilities and duties. At the heart of these interventions and initiatives there seems to be an assumption (and perhaps a growing political consensus) that the social pathologising of groups and individuals is an acceptable and positive means of achieving a stable and independent society. What has been happening to disabled people exemplifies especially clearly the pressures, disciplines and exclusions with which government is involved.

Chapter Three by Kate Brown, focusing on the concept of 'vulnerability', neatly demonstrated how 'vulnerability' and 'need' are translated into notions of 'deservingness'. It was indicated that policies related to vulnerability result in protective measures, which in turn might shade into more subtle mechanisms of social control. Classifying individuals as vulnerable may have the potential implication that they 'need to be controlled'. It seems that comparison of those perceived as vulnerable (to varying degrees) may be made with those who are 'active' and 'capable' citizens, and that the label of 'vulnerable' can sometimes mean 'risky' behaviour towards others and society at large. Those who are vulnerable therefore can become treated as those who are 'other'; under-performing individuals who are at odds with the expectations of active citizenship. Further, Brown's arguments suggest that the labelling process can have an impact on the types of services that vulnerable young people are given access to, while resource allocation on the basis of 'vulnerability' can often detract from resources being distributed more broadly across society through universal benefits. Brown's analysis indicates that a distribution to only the 'most' vulnerable can sometimes place groups of people in competition with each other to be seen as 'the most vulnerable' and deserving of state intervention. Certainly, in relation to children and young people's services, reducing or narrowing the categories of 'vulnerability' ultimately withdraws resources from some children and families who are in need.

It is in the 'welfare-to-work' programme, enhanced under the coalition, that behaviourist thinking is perhaps most stark. In Chapter Four, Ruth Patrick mapped out the details of the current Work Programme (which Patrick highlights is remarkably similar to New Labour's Flexible New Deal). Paradoxically, this seems to offer those seeking work more support in returning to work, yet does so through a series of conditions. With various costly programmes such as the Work Programme and the Youth Contract intended to reduce unemployment, initiatives have at the heart of them efforts to responsibilise adults. 'Support' back into work comes with mandatory conditions such as programmes of work placement and work experience, and a claimant commitment to reinforce the idea of a welfare contract between benefit claimant and the state. Chapter Four explained how the coalition has introduced a range of sanctions with this 'support' to return to work, to punish non-compliance, signalling that welfare is now increasingly based on work-related conditionality. Currently, the ultimate sanction is the threat of three years without benefits for those who fail to comply with job search requirements three times. As Patrick made clear in her chapter, the coalition's 'valorisation of paid work' ignores the complexities of being out of work. Government's 'uni-dimensional approach too often seems to suggest fixed groupings of hard workers and passive benefit claimaints', ignoring the point that these groups are in fact fluid categories, 'with frequent movements between work and benefits'. Patrick has set out just how a range of welfare support has been brought under the auspices of work-related conditionality, as these programmes are at the centre of disability reform and benefit support for lone parents.

Chapter Ten by Laura Davies continued the dissection of the behaviourist approaches to 'welfare-to-work', by considering what is imposed on lone parents. While traditionally an area of political disagreement across the parties, the current approach to conditional welfare under neoliberalism appears to be widely approved in the political mainstream. At the core of policy design is the theme that individuals' failures to either manage risk or behave correctly are the primary reasons for poverty or unemployment. Davies explained in her chapter how under New Labour the mantra was that 'work was the best form of welfare' for lone parents, and demonstrated that the coalition government 'has further tightened the conditionality rules for lone parents'. The chapter went on to indicate how behavioural economics may ignore the state of the markets, such as availability of jobs, the condition of employment contracts, family responsibilities, the costs of childcare and so forth. The approach that is currently taken for lone parents appears to be paternalistic. As Davies argued, an engagement with the paid labour market 'is conceptualised as a civic duty while also being good for individuals and their families, lifting them out of poverty while positively affecting wider indicators of health and wellbeing'. Chapter Ten also charted how the valorisation of work blurs any concept of what it means for lone parents to move into paid work and off benefits entirely. For many lone parents, a work-focused welfare regime seems incompatible with the demands and realities of caring for children. The steer to move lone parents (invariably mothers) into work undervalues or ignores the very difficult reality of combining paid work with childcare.

This collection has provided insight into a range of specific policy areas where the coalition government, sometimes continuing from New Labour initiatives, has been cutting back some basic human or social rights as the welfare state contracts. Chapter Five provided a review of the contemporary asylum process by Ala Sirriyeh. Echoing some of the ideas and debates aired in Chapter Three on 'vulnerability', her analysis demonstrated how 'asylum-seeking children are subject to inherently conflicting policy and practices on child welfare and asylum'. Sirriyeh showed how a range of mechanisms of social control exist throughout the asylum process through what the author aptly calls 'surveillance'. Sirriyeh here mapped out the changing 'social worth' of the asylum seeker, who is expected to be 'passive and non-instrumental' in order to earn the badge of 'vulnerability'. Through tools such as interrogative age assessments and asylum interview questioning (and it is worth noting that one of Sirriyeh's own research participants was asked 192 questions in her asylum interview as officials quizzed her on her reasons for entry), the asylum process is increasingly regulatory. In some ways looking similar to the work programmes, the asylum process is now built upon a series of conditionalities. Sirriyeh has reminded readers that there are limits on entitlements to work for asylum seekers, restricting efforts to integrate and make a living, and pushing individuals into severe financial hardship. On top of these work restrictions, asylum seekers have no choice in their housing location or type, even where overt prejudice and harassment against them are evident. Again, sanctions will be imposed on this group if non-compliance is detected. This can range from a withdrawal of financial support to detention and even deportation.

In Chapter Twelve, Jenny McNeill discussed how social housing policy is concerned with controlling and influencing behaviours, and the ever-closer relationship between social housing and employment. While social control here is not a new phenomenon brought by the coalition, housing continues to be a key mechanism through which individuals are controlled. However, McNeill noted some changes of approach being developed during the Cameron administration. In the New Labour period, Anti-Social Behaviour Orders (ASBOs) were a key apparatus for controlling behaviours in neighbourhoods. Under the coalition, commitment to control has continued, but with plans for revised tools including new orders and injunctions, alongside the aim of more fully involving communities.

While tenancies are granted on needs-based criteria, behavioural factors also affect housing decisions. McNeill explained how the selection and allocation process for social housing is based in part on a range of exclusionary policies. For instance, a household will be quizzed about rent payment histories, 'nuisance' behaviours, complex support needs and citizenship status, all of which affect housing outcomes. Furthermore, links between employment and housing have taken on increasing importance under the coalition government, as incentives, contracts and conditions nudge tenants into paid work and private housing. McNeill has summarised the current approach, noting that social housing tenants are increasingly expected to behave in 'acceptable' ways, such as 'moving on from social housing' rather than viewing these dwellings as 'a home for life', seeking paid employment and participating in ways that promote ideas of 'Big Society' and 'community involvement'. Housing policy now appears based on a 'blend of coercive and incentivising measures', bringing social landlords in as another policing agent to survey behaviour, encourage a return to work and manage anti-social behaviour.

One theme evident from this collection is that New Labour and coalition politics have not only targeted individuals to responsibilise them, but have also incorporated or facilitated behaviourist approaches within social policies designed to 'support' but also perhaps 're-engineer' or shape communities, groups and neighbourhoods. Chapters Six and Eight touched on ways in which strategies to support and engage neighbourhoods and place-based categories of people may reiterate principles of discipline, responsibility or sanctions. Andrew Wallace, in Chapter Six, discussed 'the enduring behaviourism' that has underpinned much recent communities and civic governance policy within the broader agenda of neoliberal regulation. This chapter neatly summarised a range of agendas and approaches employed in recent years across New Labour and coalition governments for working with communities. Under these governments, 'community engineering' has taken place, with values of 'voluntarism' and 'orderly citizens' at the core of community and civic policy. Through empirical examples of community interventions, Wallace described how communities have experienced direct cuts to welfare entitlements and increased welfare conditionality (particularly in relation to work), fuelled by political rhetoric about the 'broken society' and a supposed welfare dependency culture. Policies used to assist families who are considered dysfunctional and anti-social are often not voluntary, but compliance-related interventions with specific outcomes required (otherwise further welfare and/or criminal sanctions will ensue). Under New Labour the Family Intervention Programmes mobilised intense resources and personnel for families with multiple needs, and similar approaches have been presented by the coalition as the 'Troubled Families' programme. While these programmes may appear to have had some success at the time of the interventions, long-term outcomes are yet to be determined. Wallace traced how the ideas of David Cameron's Big Society as a 'vision of a more reciprocal and responsible civic culture' provide an umbrella for changes such as 'free' schools, neighbourhood planning changes and the general encouragement of greater family responsibility. Chapter Six showed that while some 'active' communities have been better off in recent periods from neighbourhood planning and funding rounds, there are areas where some communities have struggled to mobilise and hence become forgotten, with resources withdrawn or unallocated and the possibility of being labelled as 'broken'.

In Chapter Eight, Gabrielle Mastin highlighted related issues about participation, responsibilisation and empowerment. Her chapter sketched some recent history around participatory engagement, where collective forms of participation have been evident with consequences of empowerment, alongside efforts at persuading and activating individuals to engage. The history shows how the past 30 years have seen 'a reinforcement of the roles of the users of public services in their relationships with the state', almost irrespective of who holds political power in Westminster. Mastin charted how New Labour encouraged the input of the consumer voice in the development of a welfare quasi-market, with her chapter focusing especially on social care provision, and the introduction of new rights and responsibilities through community care policies, the Citizen Charter and 'direct payments'. There is a helpful synopsis of 'modernisation' changes under the New Labour government, where the quality of service provision was to be enhanced, and service users were encouraged to influence services. The personalisation of services as a core delivery mechanism is at the heart of social care policy today, as individual service-driven involvement is favoured over more collective, needs- and rights-based care provision (and systems of accountability). Mastin's chapter indicates that with the austerity cuts there may perhaps now be less inclination towards 'releasing and mobilising the consumer voice' in the manner favoured under New Labour, but instead a call to be part of the Big Society and the coalition's commitment to localism. Here government expects and urges citizens to 'participate in local consultation and involvement exercises, both individually and as members of wider collective intermediary organisations'.

It is not only in the areas of welfare and care that behaviourist approaches are shaping or influencing policy. Chapter Seven by Doug Martin has provided an overview of the relationship between schooling and regulation over previous decades, and demonstrated how education policy under the coalition government has reintroduced 'educational traditionalism'. Reviewing trends in social regulation affecting pupils from disadvantaged households since the end of the 1970s, Martin observed some 'divergent or complementary policy strands over time', but also 'a growing emphasis on trying to manage or contain behaviours'. The chapter traced how the 'social order' of schools is achieved partly through an emphasis on securing discipline and protecting schools and staff. It is the school that is increasingly brought in to manage the behaviour of 'troubled families' as the role and function of the school are increasingly considered key in maintaining social order. The chapter has also outlined how market tendencies are ever stronger in education, as fragmentation of school provision and competition are encouraged. This builds on some elements of the New Labour approach, with the coalition continuing to facilitate particularistic control of individual schools, which can lead to some disadvantaged pupils having less choice over education (as well as to specific disciplinary inclinations and expectations at school management level). The links between the youth criminal justice system and education remind the reader that the school is indeed an agent of social control, with 'disciplinary practices' forming one building block for education policy.

Ana Manzano, in Chapter Nine, has provided insight into how healthcare policies are increasingly adopting principles of behaviourism. This chapter explained how 'bio-psychosocial models of health focused thinking on disease prevention through the control of individual lifestyles'. Continuing some themes found in other parts of the book, the author traced how 'victim blaming' is apparent throughout health policy. Evident across the political spectrum, behavioural theories are used to reinforce individual health responsibilities of patients and the general public. Using the empirical case of organ donation it is demonstrated how 'nudge' theories have been introduced into responsibilising individuals about their health. This chapter provides an invaluable discussion of the complexity of the death-to-donation-to-transplantation process, highlighting how this is socially constructed through an oversimplification of individual behaviour, ignoring social inequalities. The individualising of behaviour (here applying in the context of organ donation) further ignores the macro-systems and infrastructure that have a significant bearing on individual choices and actions. The author indicates that in practising 'nudge theory', regulators aim to nudge people towards behaviour based on the regulators' preferences and expectations, and (in the case of donation) prioritising nudge strategies as currently conceived may not be enough to meet the challenges posed by complexities.

Drug policy is sometimes treated as if it stood at the periphery of social policy analysis, as it meanders through welfare, health and criminal justice policy territories. From Mark Monaghan's significant contribution to this field in Chapter Eleven, the reader can learn how policy (as in other social policy areas) is based partly on the notion of changing individual behaviour to fit a template of acceptable citizenship. At the heart of drug strategies across the past 20 years (and despite often running contrary to evidence from the majority of academic research), government has linked problematic drug use directly to significant amounts of criminal activity, and asserted that strategies to tackle drugs should focus on individual deviants. Although the approach under New Labour was treatment led, quasi-compulsory and coercive drug treatment and testing were integral to sentencing. These kinds of coercive strategies, however, have been pushed somewhat to the sidelines now, as the coalition government favours a work-orientated approach to problematic drug use, with the 'recovery' agenda taking precedence. While the 'drugs–crime nexus' still informs policy, drug policy now focuses on reducing the number of drug-dependent benefit claimants and increasing the number of drug users in paid work.

Concluding observations and interpretations

This commentary and conclusion ends with brief additional observations about trends and interpretations, and on the Big Society. First, it can be seen from earlier chapters that one accompaniment of growing controls over behaviour has been an increasing exclusion or part-exclusion of people from specific services and forms of support. There have been massive implications from this at the grass roots, and numerous reports about the suffering induced by the withdrawal of finance or services (affecting not just vulnerable adults but also children in low-income families). Outcomes here – and the intensification of disciplinary practices themselves – reflect government's drive to reduce financial commitments to poor households, but also confirm that social control is not only about incentives, persuasion, therapies and coercion. For it can also involve punishment, stigma, indignity and penalty. Certainly, some people are being penalised by exclusions, disincentives or restrictions because they will not or cannot change their immediate situations or behaviours (or those of their children). The welfare state is no longer to be available as a form of shared social security for those who are 'in need' or 'at risk'. As Brown explained, due to links with 'deservingness', discourses of vulnerability 'subtly but pervasively serve wider policy mechanisms' that establish what is appropriate and 'correct' behaviour, and which 'subject people to sanctions should they fail to conform'.

Second, it can be argued that in policy environments dependency itself sometimes now seems to be assumed to be potentially reprehensible. Some of the very needs that once formed foundations for systematic debates about types, priorities and levels of provision may be cast as elements within a dependency culture linked with the supposed 'burden of welfare' carried by the state. Of course, such thinking is not universal in the politics of social policy domains, and there is still much policy and practice that focuses on specific needs and is genuinely supportive in intent. Nonetheless, some targets have become as much about reducing numbers covered by support systems as about trying to restrict unnecessary or inappropriate claims. Meanwhile, dependencies on state spending and other support and encouragement among better-off groups and businesses are often given surprisingly minimal scrutiny, and may generally be treated with greater approval than those among poor and vulnerable people. Interventions affecting low-income households have been varied, ranging from cuts and crude exclusions to programmes for 'work experience' that look rather like cheap forced labour exercises. Much has been made of the need for austerity strategies, yet it was not the poor who brought about the financial crash or the ensuing problems of the British economy.

Third, understanding and theorising social policy today requires recognition of the heightened significance of social control mechanisms, and of their systematic or patterned links with the complex social and economic differentiations that often characterise contemporary life. It is hoped that this collection may help contribute to future analytical work, by offering clues, hints or examples of what might be involved in a re-theorisation of welfare systems (taking account of contemporary conditions in a polity that may well have become less open to pluralistic influences, and increasingly responsive to demands for containment of the poor and vulnerable). As regards normative debates, the present editors believe (as indicated in Chapter One) that ethical or philosophical arguments over social control in social policy – complex and contested though these often seem – are frequently best explored against a backcloth that explicitly includes contexts in terms of social divisions and differences in power between social groups. For researchers, of course, there is a continuing need for empirical investigation and testing, to quantify and more precisely specify changes and conditions, and to verify or dismiss hypotheses about how people are living at the grass roots. The evidence base deserves more respect and in-depth attention than governments are generally prepared to give it, not least when policy impact is concerned.

A fourth point relates to the impact that enlarging social and economic exclusion through applying controls and restrictions may have on the capacity of households to engage fully as citizens, and to live lives that fulfil expectations that are very reasonable within a relatively wealthy society. Childhood poverty is especially disastrous, as is the restricting of disabled people's opportunities to enjoy genuinely independent living. As Chapter Two indicated, disabled people have been very much in the front line as retrenchment has taken hold, and have been subjected to stressful and often unjustifiable pressures, restrictions and disciplines. Given the importance of material circumstances for the ability of individuals to enjoy normal freedoms and participate in interactions and mutual support, it could be argued that the rise of economic liberalism and welfare restructuring have been accompanied by a very serious diminishing of day-to-day liberties linked to social security, resources and social rights. Rather than bringing greater freedoms as advocates claim, economic liberal discourses have underpinned a major downward shift in aspects of household empowerment that were once linked especially to possibilities for accessing common resources.

Fragmentation and exclusion: a not-so-big society

Early in this book some introductory comments were made on the Big Society, and a question was mentioned about the appropriateness of the term itself. That issue is returned to now. Even observers favourable towards Conservative Big Society aspirations might feel that outcomes have been disappointing. Any civic renaissance through transfers of power, resources and assets from the centre has remained muted against the backcloth of financial cuts, while there has been little evidence of a central share being taken by third sector and community bodies in controlling privatised assets and services. Indeed, some disadvantaged groups have lost 'voice' through decline of the channels or means of representation and intervention that helped protect them and provided advocacy, in both voluntary and public sectors. Meanwhile, penetration of public services by large and international companies strikes a highly discordant note with localist hopes (see for instance Harris, 2013b). Even the transfer of schools to independent providers apparently has been open to 'colonisation' by particularistic or private entrepreneurial interests (as it was under New Labour), and to development of chains and groups that curtail local choices and point to future private monopolies supported by government. One recent general review refers to the possibility that behind public sector reforms 'lurks the "Big Market"' (Morgan, 2012, p 478). Certainly, serious challenges for democracy have been raised by the limited scope for regulatory protection, participation, transparency, accountability and local ownership. It should be remembered that social controls are widespread facets of social and economic life, and often reflect patterns of power derived from control of resources; whether licensed or confirmed through law, inheritance, contract, custom or direct governmental commissioning of 'outsourced' services. In the new landscape of provision and client regulation, researchers need to monitor changes in participation, control of resources and ownership, along with shifts in practitioner environments and differentiation of opportunities among households. The picture may sometimes vary between England, Scotland, Wales and Northern Ireland, and comparative research remains vital (although investigation on that front lay beyond the scope of this book).

Central to this collection's relevance for understanding current Big Society outcomes are the findings about behaviourist trends, disciplinary practices and narrowing support for dependencies. Given the trends in social regulation, the 'not-so-big society' seems a more realistic term for what is being engineered. Not only have third sector and community organisations been unable to fill the growing gaps in support for vulnerable people (note Bawden, 2013), but societal institutions appear more fragmented, less empowering and less inclusive for those who are poor. Numerous children and adults are denied full and voluntaristic engagement opportunities across important facets of daily life. The disproportionate negative impact on women stands out (cf Walklate, 2012, p 496), alongside difficulties for disabled people. Overall, there has been growth in intrusive exercises of 'top-down' power over low-income households, facilitated by reliance on selectivist rather than rights-orientated avenues for delivering social and economic support. There is even a strengthened impetus from central government for spatial segregation, with new pressures on many of the tenants who receive support to move out of better-quality areas. Perhaps Big Society programmes might have taken more supportive forms if disconnected from economic liberalism (and there is something of a parallel on this with New Labour's supposed 'third way'; see Harrison, 2010). An alternative Big Society formulation might have prioritised a drive to embrace all groups and draw them voluntarily into social and political life by moderating inequalities of power, property, incomes, resources and participation. Such a path would have had resonances with descriptors such as 'big tent' (sometimes used in the United States to signify breadth of embrace for a political party or campaign) or 'broad church' (referring in Britain to an inclusive institution). Under the UK coalition government, however, Big Society visions have helped underpin divisive strategies, while images of localism and user control have faded in the face of the growing power of major corporations.

Notes

Chapter One

[1] An outstanding example of relevant in-depth research including engagement with practitioners is Dobson (2010).

[2] A recent press report seems to suggest that family relatives of government Minister Iain Duncan Smith have received over £1 million in public funding support for their farming business. Whether or not this is correct, it is amusing to read the observation that European Union contributions in such cases have been formally described as 'income support'. See Muir (2013).

[3] The idea of a *social division of social control* offers a potential tool or framework that fits alongside the social division of welfare thesis, potentially helping encompass complex patterns within social regulation. There may be parallels with insights from various other authors, such as Wacquant's 'centaur state', with its 'comely and caring visage toward the middle and upper classes' and 'fearsome and frowning mug toward the lower class' (Wacquant, 2009, pp 43, 312; but note also qualifications at p xix).

[4] To help exchange ideas, some of the contributors came together for a day workshop in June 2011 in Leeds. This was followed by a special issue of the journal *People, Place and Policy Online* (*PPPOnline*) in 2012, where initial ideas and material were published by four of the participants, prior to fuller development and closer linkage to trends under the coalition government in this collection (see Brown and Patrick, 2012). We would like to thank the editors of *PPPOnline* for their encouragement, and Peter Dwyer, John Flint, Judy Nixon and Emma Wincup for their invaluable participation as expert advisors in the workshop.

Chapter Two

[1] We are grateful for valuable comments from Kate Brown and Ruth Patrick on an earlier draft of this chapter.

[2] Chapter Twelve notes emergent themes around empowering communities in tackling anti-social behaviour, and indicates that new tools are in prospect at the time of writing. After the present chapter had been written, new law moved closer with the progress of the Anti-social Behaviour, Crime and Policing Bill 2013, which embraced a wide set of concerns, ranging from dangerous dogs to forced marriage, and from community and public spaces

protection to offences connected with riot. The promise seemed to be both for some continuity and for a substantial intensification of control.

Chapter Three

[1] For reasons of space, coverage focuses on the UK as a whole, but with the acknowledgement that distinctions in policy and practice are likely to exist within the various countries of the UK.

[2] The guidance addressed older people and disabled people under the same banner of 'vulnerable adults'.

[3] This followed the Bichard inquiry's investigation of the 2002 'Soham murders' in Cambridgeshire, where two school children (Holly Wells and Jessica Chapman) were killed by the caretaker of their school (Bichard, 2004).

[4] Young people on income support are teenage parents, teenagers living away from parents, and young people whose parents have died.

[5] Fiona's daughter was disabled and Fiona had repeatedly reported incidents of 'hate crimes' committed against members of the family to the police before killing both herself and her daughter (see IPCC, 2011).

[6] One example was the case *Ortiz v Westminster City Council* (1993), where a woman was deemed ineligible for 'priority need' status because it was ruled that her previous alcohol and drug use did not amount to her classification as 'vulnerable'.

[7] Pregnancy-related health advice is a useful illustrative example given by Lupton (1999).

Chapter Eleven

[1] It is not strictly accurate to speak in terms of UK drug policy. Although the main pieces of legislation regulating drugs apply to all four countries of the UK, the devolved administrations each have their own drug strategies. Consequently, this chapter focuses mainly on the situation as it stands in England.

[2] Thanks to Alex Stevens for pointing this out to me.

References

Abadie, A. and Gay, S. (2006) 'The impact of presumed consent legislation on cadaveric organ donation: a cross-country study', *Journal of Health Economics*, vol 25, no 4, pp 599-620.

ACMD (Advisory Council on the Misuse of Drugs) (1988) *AIDS and drug misuse*, London: Home Office.

ADSS (Association of Directors of Social Services) (2005) *Safeguarding adults: A national framework of standards for good practice and outcomes in adult protection work*, London: ADSS.

Alaszewski, A., Alaszewski, H., Manthorpe, J. and Ayer, S. (1998) *Assessing and managing risk in nursing education and practice: Supporting vulnerable people in the community*, London: English National Board for Nursing, Midwifery and Health Visiting.

Aldridge, H., Parekh, A., Macinnes, T. and Kenway, P. (2011) *Monitoring poverty and social exclusion 2011*, York: Joseph Rowntree Foundation.

Allen, C. (1999) 'Towards a comparative sociology of residence and disablement – Britain and Sweden in interventionist welfare regime perspective', *Housing, Theory and Society*, vol 16, no 2, pp 49-66.

Allen, G. (2011) *Early intervention: The next steps: An independent report to Her Majesty's Government*, London: Cabinet Office.

Amin, A. (2002) 'Ethnicity and the multicultural city: living with diversity', *Geography and Planning A*, vol 34, no 6, pp 959-80.

Amin, A. (2005) 'Local community on trial', *Economy and Society*, vol 34, no 4, pp 612-33.

Amir, A. and Lobel, O. (2009) *Stumble, predict, nudge: How behavioural economics informs law and policy*, Legal Studies Research Paper Series, Research Paper no 09-006, San Diego, CA: University of San Diego.

Anderson, I. (2011) 'Evidence, policy and guidance for practice: a critical reflection on the case of social housing landlords and antisocial behaviour in Scotland', *Evidence & Policy: A Journal of Research, Debate and Practice*, vol 7, no 1, pp 41-58.

Anon (2011) Dublin court cases, *The Guardian* [online], 7 October, www.guardian.co.uk/world/2011/oct/07/dublin-court-cases

Appleton, J.V. (1999) 'Assessing vulnerability in families', in J. McIntosh (ed) *Research issues in the community*, Basingstoke: Macmillan, pp 126-64.

Arendt, H. (1958) *The origins of totalitarianism* (2nd edn), New York, NY: Harcourt Brace Jovanovich.

Arnstein, S.R. (1969) 'A ladder of citizen participation', *Journal of the American Institute of Planners*, vol 35, no 4, pp 216-24.

Atkinson, R. and Blandy, S. (eds) (2005) Special issue on gated communities, *Housing Studies*, vol 20, no 2.

Atkinson, R. and Helms, G. (eds) (2007) *Securing an urban renaissance*, Bristol: The Policy Press.

Bagguley, P. and Mann, K. (1992) 'Idle thieving bastards: scholarly representations of the underclass', *Work, Employment & Society*, vol 6, no 1, pp 113-26.

Ball, S. (1994) *Education reform*, Milton Keynes: Open University Press.

Bankoff, G., Frerks, G. and Hilhorst, T. (eds) (2004) *Mapping vulnerability: Disasters, development and people*, London: Earthscan.

Barker, R. (2009) *Making sense of every child matters*, Bristol: The Policy Press.

Barlow, A., Duncan, S. and James, G. (2002) 'New Labour, the rationality mistake and family policy', in A. Carling, S. Duncan and R. Edwards (eds) *Analysing families: Morality and rationality in policy and practice*, London: Routledge, pp 110-28.

Barnes, C. (1990) *'Cabbage syndrome': The social construction of dependence*, London: The Falmer Press.

Barnes, C. (1997) *Older people's perception of direct payments and self-operated support systems* [online], www.leeds.ac.uk/disability-studies/archiveuk/Barnes/directpayments.pdf

Barnes, C. and Mercer, G. (1996) *Exploring the divide: Illness and disability*, Leeds: The Disability Press.

Barnes, C., Oliver, M. and Barton, L. (2002) *Disability studies today*, Cambridge: Polity Press.

Barnes, M. and Prior, D. (eds) (2009a) *Subversive citizens: Power, agency and resistance in public services*, Bristol: The Policy Press.

Barnes, M. and Prior, D. (2009b) 'Examining the idea of "subversion" in public services', in M. Barnes and D. Prior (eds) *Subversive citizens: Power, agency and resistance in public services*, Bristol: The Policy Press, pp 3-13.

Bauld, L., Hay, G., McKell, J. and Carroll, C. (2010) *Problem drug users' experience of employment and the benefit system* [online], London: Department for Work and Pensions, http://research.dwp.gov.uk/asd/asd5/rports2009-2010/rrep640.pdf

Bauld, L., McKell, J., Carroll, C., Hay, G. and Smith, K. (2012) 'Benefits and employment: how problem drug users experience welfare and routes into work', *Journal of Social Policy*, vol 41, no 4, pp 751-68.

Bauman, Z. (2000) *Liquid modernity*, Cambridge: Polity Press.

Bawden, A. (2013) 'We've got five years left, at best', *The Guardian*, Society, 24 July, p 32.

Beck, U. (1992) *Risk society: Towards a new modernity*, London: Sage Publications.

Beckett, A. (2006) *Citizenship and vulnerability: Disability and issues of social and political engagement*, Basingstoke: Palgrave Macmillan.

Benhabib, S. (2004) *The rights of others*, Cambridge: Cambridge University Press.

Bennett, F. (2012) 'Universal credit: overview and gender implications', in M. Kilkey, G. Ramia and K. Farnsworth (eds) *Social policy review 24: Analysis and debate in social policy*, Bristol: The Policy Press, pp 15-34.

Bennett, F. and Millar, J. (2005) 'Making work pay?', *Benefits*, vol 13, no 1, pp 28-34.

Bennett, T. and Holloway, K. (2005) *Understanding drugs, alcohol and crime*, Buckingham: Open University Press.

Bennett, T. and Holloway, K. (2009) 'The causal connection between drug misuse and crime', *British Journal of Criminology*, vol 49, no 3, pp 513-31.

Beresford, P. (2005) 'Theory and practice of user involvement in research: making the connection with public policy and practice', in L. Lowes and I. Hulatt (eds) *Involving service users in health and social care research*, London: Routledge, pp 6-17.

Beresford, P. (2011) 'Give social care the same priority as the NHS', *The Guardian*, 18 May, www.guardian.co.uk/society/joepublic/2011/may/18/social-care-same-priority-nhs

Beresford, P. (2012) 'From "vulnerable" to vanguard: challenging the coalition', in S. Davison and J. Rutherford (eds) *Welfare reform: The dread of things to come* [online], www.lwbooks.co.uk/ebooks/Welfare%20Reform%20(revise).pdf

Bhabha, J. (2004) 'Seeking asylum alone: treatment of separated and trafficked children in need of refugee protection', *International Migration*, vol 42, no 1, pp 141-8.

Bichard, M. (2004) *The Bichard inquiry report*, London: HMSO.

Bigo, D. (2008) 'Globalized (in)security: the field and the ban-opticon', in D. Bigo and A. Tsoukala (eds) *Terror, insecurity and liberty: Illiberal practices of liberal regimes after 9/11*, New York, NY: Routledge, pp 10-48.

Bilgel, F. (2012) 'The impact of presumed consent laws and institutions on deceased organ donation', *European Journal of Health Economics*, vol 13, no 1, pp 29-38.

Black, C. (2008) *Working for a healthier tomorrow*, London: The Stationery Office.

Blair, T. (1994) *Drugs: The need for action* [press release], London: Labour Party.

Blair, T. (1997) *Department of Social Security (1997)* [press release], 6 May.

Blair, T. (2001) *Speech by the Prime Minister at the Peel Institute* [online], 26 January, http://webarchive.nationalarchives.gov.uk/20061004085342/number10.gov.uk/page1577

Blake, S., Fradd, A. and Stringer, E. (2008) *Lost property: Tackling homelessness in the UK: A guide for donors and funders* [online], London: New Philanthropy Capital, http://socialwelfare.bl.uk/subject-areas/services-activity/housing-homelessness/newphilanthropycapital/142 177Lost-property-full.pdf

Bliss, N. and Lambert, B. (2012) *Tenant panels: Options for accountability* [online], http://nationaltenants.files.wordpress.com/2012/03/tenant-panels-options-for-accountability.pdf

Blond, P. (2011) 'Dave must take the red Tory turn', *The New Statesman* [online], 2 October, www.newstatesman.com/uk-politics/2011/10/society-social-economic

Blond, P. (2012) 'David Cameron has lost his chance to redefine the Tories', *The Guardian*, 3 October, www.guardian.co.uk/commentisfree/2012/oct/03/cameron-one-nation-u-turn-tory-tragedy

BMA (British Medical Association) (2007) *A rational way forward for the NHS in England*, London: BMA.

BMA (2012) *Building on progress: Where next for organ donation policy in the UK?*, London: BMA.

Bochel, H. and Defty, A. (2007) 'MPs' attitudes to welfare: a new consensus?', *Journal of Social Policy*, vol 36, no 1, pp 1-17.

Bochel, H. and Evans, A. (2007) *Making policy in theory and practice*, Bristol: The Policy Press.

Boff, A. (2012) *Silence on violence: Improving the safety of women: The policing of off-street sex work and sex trafficking in London*, London: Mayor's Office.

Bottoms, A. (1995) 'The philosophy and politics of punishment and sentencing', in C. Clarkson and R. Morgan (eds) *The politics of sentencing reform*, Oxford: Clarendon Press, pp 17-49.

Boutwell, B.B. and Beaver, K.M. (2010) 'The intergenerational transmission of low self-control', *Journal of Research in Crime and Delinquency*, vol 47, no 2, pp 174-209.

Bowpitt, G., Dwyer, P., Sundin, E. and Weinstein, M. (2011) *Comparing the priorities of multiply excluded homeless people and support agencies*, London: Economic and Social Research Council.

Bowring, F. (2000) 'Social exclusion: limitations of the debate', *Critical Social Policy*, vol 20, no 3, pp 307-30.

Bradley, Q. (2008) 'Capturing the castle: tenant governance in social housing companies', *Housing Studies*, vol 23, no 6, pp 879-97.

Branfield, F. and Beresford, P. (2006) *Making user involvement work: Supporting service users networking and knowledge*, York: Joseph Rowntree Foundation.

Breitkreuz, R.S., Williamson, D.L. and Raine, K.D. (2010) 'Dis-integrated policy: welfare-to-work participants' experiences of integrating paid work and unpaid family work', *Community, Work and Family*, vol 13, no 1, pp 33-69.

Brenner, N. and Theodore, N. (2002) 'Preface: from the "new localism" to the spaces of neoliberalism', *Antipode*, vol 34, no 3, pp 341-47.

Brent, J. (1997) 'Community without unity', in P. Hoggett (ed) *Contested communities*, Bristol: The Policy Press, pp 68-83.

Broadway and Resource Information Service (2006) *Accommodation for single homeless people in London: Supply and demand* [online], www.broadwaylondon.org/ResearchInformation/Research/main_content/Supplyanddemand.pdf

Brown, B.J. and Baker, S. (2012) *Responsible citizens: Individuals, health and policy under neoliberalism*, London: Anthem Press.

Brown, K. (2011) '"Vulnerability": handle with care', *Journal of Ethics and Social Welfare*, vol 5, no 3, pp 313-21.

Brown, K. (2012) 'Re-moralising "vulnerability"', *People, Place and Policy Online*, vol 6, no 1, pp 41-53.

Brown, K. (2013) *The concept of vulnerability and its use in the care and control of young people*, PhD thesis, University of Leeds.

Brown, K. and Patrick, R. (2012) 'Re-moralising or de-moralising? The coalition government's approach to "problematic" populations: editorial', *People, Place & Policy Online*, vol 6, no 1, pp 1-2.

Browne, J. (2012) *The impact of austerity measures on households with children*, London: Family and Parenting Institute.

Browne, J. and Levell, P. (2010) *The distributional effect of tax and benefit reforms to be introduced between June 2010 and April 2014: A revised assessment*, London: Institute for Fiscal Studies.

Bryson, A. (2003) 'From welfare to workfare', in J. Millar (ed) *Understanding social security: Issues for policy and practice*, Bristol: The Policy Press, pp 77-102.

Burnett, J., Carter, J., Evershed, J., Bell Kohli, M., Powell, C. and de Wilde, G. (2010) *State sponsored cruelty: Children in immigration detention*, London: Medical Justice.

Burney, E. (2005) *Making people behave: Anti-social behaviour, politics and policy* (1st edn), Cullompton: Willan.

Burney, E. (2009) *Making people behave: Anti-social behaviour, politics and policy* (2nd edn), Cullompton: Willan.

Butler, J. (2004) *Precarious life: The powers of mourning and violence*, London: Verso.

Butler, J. (2009) 'Performativity, precarity and sexual politics', lecture given at Universidad Complutense de Madrid, 8 June, *AIBR Revista de Anthropologia Iberomericana*, vol 4, no 3, pp i-xiii.

Butler, P. (2012) 'Cuts and lack of trust undermining Cameron's "big society" says study', *The Guardian*, 7 May, p 6.

Byrne, L. (2012) *A William Beveridge for this century's welfare state* [online], www.guardian.co.uk/commentisfree/2012/jan/02/beveridge-welfare-state-labour-revolution

Cabinet Office (1998) *Tackling drugs to build a better Britain*, London: Cabinet Office.

Cabinet Office (2010) *Britain: Building the Big Society*, London: Cabinet Office.

Cabinet Office Behavioural Insights Team (2011) *Behavioural Insights Team: Annual update 2010–2011*, London: Cabinet Office, www.cabinetoffice.gov.uk

Cameron, D. (2009a) Speech to the Conservative Party annual conference, 8 October, Manchester.

Cameron, D. (2009b) *The Big Society speech* [online], 10 November, www.conservatives.com/News/Speeches/2009/11/David_Cameron_The_Big_Society.aspx

Cameron, D. (2010a) *The big society speech* [online], 19 July, www.number10.gov.uk/news/big-society-speech/

Cameron, D. (2010b) *Our 'Big Society' plan speech* [online], 31 March, www.conservatives.com/News/Speeches/2010/03/David_Cameron_Our_Big_Society_plan.aspx

Cameron, D. (2011a) 'Human rights in my sights: I want to reclaim our society and restore people's pride in Britain', exclusive, *Sunday Express*, 21 August, pp 1, 4-5.

Cameron, D. (2011b) *The fight back after the riots* [speech], Oxfordshire, 15 August.

Cameron, D. (2011c) *PM's speech on the fightback after the riots* [online], 15 August, www.number10.gov.uk/news/pms-speech-on-the-fightback-after-the-riots/

Cameron, D. (2011d) *PM's speech on the Welfare Reform Bill* [online], 17 February, www.number10.gov.uk/news/pms-speech-on-welfare-reform-bill/

Cameron, D. (2012a) *Welfare speech* [online], 25 June, www.number10.gov.uk/news/welfare-speech/

Cameron, D. (2012b) *Prime Minister's speech to CBI*, 19 November, www.number10.gov.uk/news/speech-to-cbi.

Campbell, A. (1991) 'Dependency revisited: the limits of autonomy in medical ethics', in M. Brazier and M. Lobjoit (eds) *Protecting the vulnerable: Autonomy and consent in healthcare*, London: Routledge, pp 101-13.

Campbell, A. (2007) *The Blair years: Extracts from the Alistair Campbell diaries*, London: Hutchinson.

Campbell, A. and Martin, D. (2011) 'Every child matters: new ethical challenges arising in schools', in A. Campbell and P. Broadhead (eds) *Working with children and young people: Ethical debates and practices across disciplines and continents*, Oxford: Lang, pp 37-57.

Campbell, S., Baqueriza, M. and Ingram, J. (2009) *Last resort or first resort? Immigration detention of children in the UK*, London: The Children's Society and Bail for Immigration Detainees.

Carline, A. (2009) 'Ethics and vulnerability in street prostitution: an argument in favour of managed zones', *Crimes and Misdemeanours*, vol 3, no 1, pp 20-53.

Carline, A. (2011) 'Criminal justice, extreme pornography and prostitution: protecting women or promoting morality?', *Sexualities*, vol 14, no 3, pp 312-33.

Carter, P. and Peck, S. (2011) 'The unkindest cut ... homing in on res care', *Disability Now* [online], www.disabilitynow.org.uk/living/features/the-unkindest-cut-homing-in-on-res-care

Carter, T. and Beresford, P. (2000) *Age and change: Models of involvement for older people*, York: Joseph Rowntree Foundation.

Carvel, J. (2007) 'Care homes criticised for restraints on residents', *The Guardian*, 18 December 2007, www.theguardian.com/society/2007/dec/18/longtermcare.socialcare

Casey, L. (2012) *Listening to troubled families*, London: Department for Communities and Local Government.

Cassidy, S. (2012) 'More than 300,000 disabled people to have benefits cut says Esther McVey', *The Independent*, 13 December, www.independent.co.uk/news/uk/politics/more-than-300000-disabled-people-to-have-benefits-cut-says-esther-mcvey

Catalyst (2012) *Healthcare services sector* [online], www.catalystcf.co.uk/uploads/Catalyst_Healthcare_2012.pdf

Centre for Social Justice (2006) *Breakdown Britain executive summary* [online], www.centreforsocialjustice.org.uk/publications/breakdown-britain-executive-summary

Centre for Social Justice (2010) *Green Paper on the family*, London: Centre for Social Justice.

Chakrabarti, S. (2012) 'A facelift for old thinking', *The Guardian*, 23 May, p 28.

Chambers, R. (1989) 'Vulnerability, coping and policy', *Institute of Development Studies Bulletin*, vol 37, no 4, pp 33-40.

Children's Society (2011) *Almost 700 children detained in four months* [online], www.childrenssociety.org.uk/news-views/press-release/almost-700-children-detained-four-months

Chitty, C. (2011) 'The death of local democracy?', *Forum*, vol 53, no 3, pp 335-7.

Churchill, H. (2011) *Parental rights and responsibilities: Analysing policy and service user perspectives*, Bristol: The Policy Press.

Churchill, H. (2012) 'Family support and the coalition: retrenchment, refocusing and restructuring', in M. Kilkey, G. Ramia and K. Farnsworth (eds) *Social policy review 24: Analysis and debate in social policy*, Bristol: The Policy Press, pp 35-54.

Clapham, D. and Dix, J. with Griffiths, M. (1996) *Citizenship and housing: Shaping the debate*, Coventry: Chartered Institute of Housing.

Clarke, A. (1983) 'Prejudice, ignorance and panic! Popular politics in a land fit for scroungers', in M. Loney, D. Boswell and J. Clarke (eds) *Social policy and social welfare*, Milton Keynes: Open University Press, pp 255-69.

Clarke, J. (2005) 'New Labour's citizens: activated, empowered, responsibilised, abandoned?', *Critical Social Policy*, vol 25, no 4, pp 447-63.

Clarke, J. and Glendinning, C. (2002) 'Partnership and the remaking of welfare governance', in C. Glendinning, M. Powell and K. Rummery (eds) *Partnerships, New Labour and the governance of welfare*, Bristol: The Policy Press, pp 33-50.

Clarke, J., Gewirtz, S. and McLaughlin, E. (2000) *New managerialism, new welfare?*, London: Sage Publications.

Clayton, N. and Brinkley, I. (2011) *Welfare to what? Prospects and challenges for employment recovery*, London: The Work Foundation.

Clegg, N. (2010) *Nick Clegg declares end to child detention* [online], www.libdems.org.uk/speeches_detail.aspx?title=Nick_Clegg_confirms_end_to_child_detention_(full_speech)

Clegg, N. (2011) *Nick Clegg's speech to spring conference* [online], 13 March, www.libdems.org.uk/speeches_detail.aspx?title=Nick_Clegg%e2%80%99s_speech_to_Spring_Conference&pPK=9296205b-d75b-40b1-bbb1-72e74181473f

Cochrane, A. (1998) 'What sort of safety-net? Social security, income maintenance and the benefits system', in G. Hughes and G. Lewis (eds) *Unsettling welfare: The reconstruction of social policy*, London: Routledge, pp 291-331.

Cockburn, T. (1998) 'Children and citizenship in Britain: a case for a socially interdependent model of citizenship', *Childhood*, vol 5, no 1, pp 99-117.

Cohen, R. (1994) *Frontiers of identity: The British and the others*, London: Longman Publishing.

Cole, I. and Furbey, R. (1994) *The eclipse of council housing*, London: Routledge.

Conservative Party (2008) *Work for welfare: REAL welfare reform to make British poverty history*, London: Conservative Party.

Conservative Party (2010a) *A new welfare contract*, London: Conservative Party.

Conservative Party (2010b) *Conservative Party manifesto: Invitation to join the government of Britain* [online], www.conservatives.com/~/media/Files/Activist%20Centre/Press%20and%20Policy/Manifestos/Manifesto2010

Conservative Party (2012) *Where we stand: Schools* [online], www.conservatives.com/Policy/Where_we_stand/Schools.aspx

Co-operatives UK (2012) *The co-operative economy*, Manchester: Co-operatives UK, www.uk.coop/economy2012

Council of Europe (2012) 'International figures on donation and transplantation – 2011', *Newsletter Transplant* [online], www.ont.es/publicaciones/Documents/Newsletter2011.pdf

Craig, G. (2007) 'Community capacity-building: something old, something new?', *Critical Social Policy*, vol 27, no 3, pp 335-59.

Cramer, H. (2005) 'Informal and gendered practices in a homeless person's unit', *Housing Studies*, vol 20, no 5, pp 737-51.

Crawford, A. (2003) '"Contractual governance" of deviant behaviour', *Journal of Law and Society*, vol 30, no 4, pp 479-505.

Crawford, A. (2009) 'Governing through anti-social behaviour: regulatory challenges to criminal justice', *British Journal of Criminology*, vol 49, no 6, pp 810-31.

Crawley, H. (2010) *Chance or choice? Understanding why asylum seekers come to the UK*, London: Refugee Council.

Crawley, H. (2011) 'Asexual, apolitical beings': the interpretation of children's identities and experiences in the UK asylum system', *Journal of Ethnic and Migration Studies*, vol 37, no 8, pp 1171-84.

Crisp, R. (2008) 'Motivation, morals and justice: discourses of worklessness in the welfare reform Green Paper', *People, Place and Policy Online*, vol 2, no 3, pp 172-85.

Crisp, R., Batty, E., Cole, I. and Robinson, D. (2009) *Work and worklessness in deprived neighbourhoods: Policy assumptions and personal experiences*, York: Joseph Rowntree Foundation.

CSDH (Commission on Social Determinants of Health) (2008) *Closing the gap in a generation: Health equity through action on the social determinants of health*, Geneva: World Health Organization.

Culpitt, I. (1999) *Social policy and risk*, London: Sage Publications.

Cummings, C., Dyson, A. and Todd, L. (2011) *Beyond the school gates: Can full service and extended schools overcome disadvantage?*, Abingdon: Routledge.

Cunningham, H. (1995) *Children and childhood since 1500 in Western society*, London: Longman.

Cunningham, S. and Tomlinson, J. (2005) '"Starve them out": does every child really matter? A commentary on Section 9 of the Immigration and Asylum Act (Treatment of Claimants etc.) 2004', *Critical Social Policy*, vol 25, no 2, pp 253-75.

Daly, G. and Davis, H. (2002) 'Partnerships for local governance: citizens, communities and accountability', in C. Glendinning, M. Powell and K. Rummery (eds) *Partnerships, New Labour and the governance of welfare*, Bristol: The Policy Press, pp 97-112.

Daly, M. (2011) 'What adult worker model? A critical look at recent social policy reform in Europe from a gender and family perspective', *Social Politics*, vol 18, no 1, pp 1-23.

Daniel, B. (2010) 'Concepts of adversity, risk, vulnerability and resilience: a discussion in the context of the "Child Protection System"', *Social Policy and Society*, vol 9, no 2, pp 231-41.

Daniels, N. (2008) *Just health: Meeting health needs fairly*, Cambridge: Cambridge University Press.

Darling, J. (2009) 'Becoming bare life: asylum, hospitality, and the politics of encampment', *Environment and Planning D: Society and Space*, vol 27, no 4, pp 649-65.

Dartington, T., Miller, E.J. and Gwynne, G. (1981) *A life together*, London: Tavistock.

Davidson, K., Hunt, K. and Kitzinger, J. (2003) 'A blueprint for change?', *Sociology of Health and Illness*, vol 25, no 6, pp 532-55.

Davies, G. (2006) 'Patterning the geographies of organ transplantation: corporeality, generosity and justice', *Transactions of the Institute of British Geographers*, vol 31, no 3, pp 257-71.

Davies, J. (2005) 'Local governance and the dialectics of hierarchy, market and network', *Policy Studies*, vol 26, no 3/4, pp 311-35.

Day, G. (2006) *Community and everyday life*, Abingdon: Routledge.

Daycare Trust (2011) *Childcare costs survey 2011* [online], www.daycaretrust.org.uk/pages/summary-of-the-childcare-costs-survey-2011.html

DBC (Disability Benefits Consortium) (2011) *DLA mobility: Sorting the facts from the fiction* [online], www.disabilityalliance.org/dbcdla2.htm

DCLG (Department for Communities and Local Government) (2007) *NDC national evaluation: An overview of change data*, Research Report 33, London: DCLG.

DCLG (2008) *Creating strong, safe and prosperous communities: Statutory guidance* [online], www.communities.gov.uk/documents/localgovernment/pdf/885397.pdf

DCLG (2011a) *Website information on troubled families* [online], https://www.gov.uk/government/news/tackling-troubled-families

DCLG (2011b) *A plain English guide to the Localism Act* [online], https://www.gov.uk/government/uploads/system/uploads/attachment_data/file/5959/1896534.pdf

DCLG (2012a) *Policy helping troubled families turn their lives around* [online], https://www.gov.uk/government/policies/helping-troubled-families-turn-their-lives-around

DCLG (2012b) *Giving tenants control: Right to transfer and right to manage regulations: Summary of consultation responses* [online], www.communities.gov.uk/documents/housing/pdf/2179793.pdf

DCSF (Department for Children, Schools and Families) (2007) *Education (Parenting Contracts and Parenting Orders) (England) Regulations*, London: HMSO.

De Keseredy, W. (2011) *Contemporary critical criminology*, London: Routledge.

De Maeyer, J., Vanderplasschen, W., Camfield, L., Vanheule, S., Sabbe, B. and Broekaert, E. (2011) 'A good quality of life under the influence of methadone: a qualitative study among opiate dependent individuals', *International Journal of Nursing Studies*, vol 48, no 10, pp 1244-57.

Deacon, A. (2002) *Perspectives on welfare: Ideas, ideologies and policy debates*, Buckingham: Open University Press.

Deacon, A. and Patrick, R. (2011) 'A new welfare settlement? The coalition government and welfare-to-work', in H. Bochel (ed) *The Conservative Party and social policy*, Bristol: The Policy Press, pp 161-79.

Dean, H. (1999) 'Citizenship', in M. Powell (ed) *New Labour, new welfare state? The 'Third Way' in British social policy*, Bristol: The Policy Press, pp 213-33.

Dean, H. (2007) 'The ethics of welfare-to-work', *Policy & Politics*, vol 35, no 4, pp 573-90.

DfE (Department for Education) (2012a) *Early Interventions Grant FAQs* [online], www.education.gov.uk/childrenandyoungpeople/earlylearningandchildcare/delivery/funding/a0070357/eig-faqs

DfE (2012b) *Pupil Premium: What you need to know*, London: HMSO.

DfE (2012c) *Ensuring good behaviour in schools*, London: HMSO.

DfE (2012d) *Official statistics* [online], www.education.gov.uk/researchandstatistics/statistics/statistics-by-topic/schoolpupilcharacteristics

DfE (2012e) *Troops to teachers*, London: HMSO.

DfE (2012f) *Positive for youth: A new approach to cross-governmental policy for young people aged 13-19*, London: HMSO.

DfE, Department of Health and Home Office (2011) *Vetting and Barring Scheme remodelling review: Report and recommendations*, London: Home Office.

DfEE (Department for Education and Employment) (1997) *Excellence in cities*, London: DfEE.

DfEE (1998) *Local Sure Start programmes*, London: DfEE.

DfEE (1999) *Sure Start: A guide for trailblazers*, London: DfEE.

DfES (Department for Education and Skills) (2002) *Full service extended schools: Providing opportunities and services for all*, London: DfES.

DfES (2003) *Every child matters*, London: Cabinet Office.

DfES (2007) *Targeted youth support: A guide*, London: Cabinet Office.

DH (Department of Health) (1995) *Tackling drugs together*, London: DH.

DH (2000) *No secrets: Guidance on developing and implementing multi-agency policies and procedures to protect vulnerable adults from abuse*, London: Cabinet Office.

DH (2003) *Direct payments guidance: Community care, services for carers and children's services (direct payments) guidance England 2003* [online], www.dh.gov.uk/en/Publicationsandstatistics/Publications/PublicationsPolicyAndGuidance/DH_4096246

DH (2008) *Organs for transplants: A report from the organ donation taskforce*, London: DH.

DH (2010a) *A vision for adult social care: Capable communities and active citizens* [online], www.dh.gov.uk/prod_consum_dh/groups/dh_digitalassets/@dh/@en/@ps/documents/digitalasset/dh_121971.pdf

DH (2010b) *The NHS Constitution*, London: DH.

DH (2010c) *Review of the organ donor register: Report to the Secretary of State for Health*, London: DH.

DH (2012) *Report on the effect of the NHS Constitution*, London: DH.

Diamond, J. (2004) 'Local regeneration initiatives and capacity building: whose "capacity" and "building" for what?', *Community Development Journal*, vol 39, no 2, pp 177-89.

Dinham, A. (2005) 'Empowered or over-powered? The real experience of local participation in the UK's New Deal for Communities', *Community Development Journal*, vol 40, no 3, pp 301-12.

Disability Alliance (2010a) 'Triple-jeopardy in new government's welfare reform proposals puts disabled people at greater risk of poverty', press release, London: Disability Alliance, www.disabilityalliance.org/welreform2.htm

Disability Alliance (2010b) *Emergency budget* [online], www.disabilityalliance.org/emergency.htm

Disability Alliance (2011) *Incapacity benefits migration* [online], London: Disability Alliance, www.disabilityalliance.org/ibmigrate.htm

Dobson, R. (2010) *Discipline and support in housing and homelessness services*, doctoral thesis, University of Leeds.

Dobson, R. and McNeill, J. (2011) 'Review article: Homelessness and housing support services: rationales and policies under New Labour', *Social Policy and Society*, vol 10, no 4, pp 581-89.

Dodds, S. (2007) 'Depending on care: recognition of vulnerability and the social construction of care provision', *Bioethics*, vol 21, no 9, pp 500-10.

Dorling, K. and Hurrell, A. (2012) *Navigating the system: Advice provision for young refugees and migrants*, London: Coram Children's Legal Centre.

Drake, R. (1999) *Understanding disability policies*, Basingstoke: Macmillan.

Drake, R. (2000) 'Disabled people, New Labour, benefits and work', *Critical Social Policy*, vol 20, no 4, pp 421-39.

Driver, S. (2004) 'North Atlantic drift: welfare reform and the Third Way politics of New Labour and the New Democrats', in S. Hale, W. Leggett and L. Martell (eds) *The Third Way and beyond: Criticisms, futures, alternatives*, Manchester: University Press, pp 31-47.

DSS (Department of Social Security) (1998) *A new contract for welfare*, London: HMSO.

DSS (1999) *The changing welfare state: Opportunity for all: Tackling poverty and social exclusion*, London: HMSO.

Duke, K. (2006) 'Out of crime and into treatment? The criminalization of contemporary drug policy since Tackling Drugs Together', *Drugs: Education, Prevention and Policy*, vol 13, no 5, pp 409-15.

Duncan Smith, I. (2011) 'Reforming our pensions and welfare system speech' [online], 6 March, www.conservatives.com/News/Speeches/2011/03/Iain_Duncan_Smith_Reforming_our_pensions_and_welfare_system.aspx

Duncan Smith, I. (2012) Child poverty speech at Abbey Centre [online], 14 June, www.dwp.gov.uk/newsroom/ministers-speeches/2012/14-06-12a.shtml

Dunn, A. (2010) 'Welfare conditionality, inequality and unemployed people with alternative values', *Social Policy and Society*, vol 9, no 4, pp 461-73.

Dunn, M., Clare, I. and Holland, A. (2008) 'To empower or protect? Constructing the "vulnerable adult" in English law and public policy', *Legal Studies*, vol 28, no 2, pp 234-53.

Durose, C., France, J., Richardson, L. and Lupton, R. (2011) *Towards the 'Big Society': What role for neighbourhood working? Evidence from a comparative European study* [online], www.nwtwc.org.uk/uploads/ Neighbourhood_working_LR.pdf

DVLA (Driver and Vehicle Licensing Agency) (2006) *DVLA annual report and accounts 2006-2007*, London: HMSO.

DWP (Department for Work and Pensions) (2007) *Ready for work: Full employment in our generation*, Norwich: HMSO.

DWP (2008a) *Raising expectations and increasing support: Reforming welfare for the future*, Norwich: The Stationery Office.

DWP (2008b) *No-one written off: Reforming welfare to reward responsibility: Public consultation*, Norwich: The Stationery Office.

DWP (2010a) *Universal Credit: Welfare that works*, Cm 7957, London: HMSO, www.dwp.gov.uk/docs/universal-credit-full-document

DWP (2010b) *21st century welfare*, London: HMSO.

DWP (2011a) *The Work Programme*, London: DWP.

DWP (2011b) *Universal credit policy briefing note 11: Extending conditionality under universal credit to working claimants: Setting a new conditionality threshold* [online], www.dwp.gov.uk/docs/ucpbn-11-conditionality-threshold.pdf

DWP (2012a) *Welfare Reform Act 2012* [online], London: DWP, www. dwp.gov.uk/policy/welfare-reform/legislation-and-key-documents/ welfare-reform-act-2012/

DWP (2012b) *Explanatory memorandum for the social security advisory committee: Universal Credit regulations 2012*, Meeting of the Social Security Advisory Committee, 13 June, London: Department for Work and Pensions.

DWP (2012c) *Employment and Support Allowance* [online], London: DWP, www.dwp.gov.uk/policy/welfare-reform/employment-and-support/

DWP (2012d) 'Employment and Support Allowance – Incapacity Benefits reassessments: outcomes of work capability assessments', *Quarterly Official Statistical Bulletin*, 6 November, London: DWP.

DWP (2012e) *9 July 2012 – Grayling: First Work Programme data shows promising signs* [online], London: DWP, www.dwp.gov.uk/newsroom/ press-releases/2012/jul-2012/dwp075-12.shtml

DWP (2012f) *Benefit Cap (Housing Benefit) Regulations 2012: Impact assessment for the benefit cap* [online], www.dwp.gov.uk/adviser/ updates/benefit-cap

DWP (2012g) *Benefit cap factsheet* [online], www.dwp.gov.uk/adviser/updates/benefit-cap

DWP (2012h) *Income support lone parent regime: Official statistics February 2012* [online], http://statistics.dwp.gov.uk/asd/asd1/is/lone_parent_regime/index.php?page=lone_parent_regime_arc

Dwyer, P. (2000) *Welfare rights and responsibilities: Contesting social citizenship*, Bristol: The Policy Press.

Dwyer, P. (2004) 'Creeping conditionality in the UK: from welfare rights to conditional entitlements', *Canadian Journal of Sociology*, vol 29, no 2, pp 265-87.

Dwyer, P. (2008) 'The conditional welfare state', in M. Powell (ed) *Modernising the welfare state: The Blair legacy*, Bristol: The Policy Press, pp 199-218.

Dwyer, P. (2010) *Understanding social citizenship: Themes and perspectives for policy and practice* (2nd edn), Bristol: The Policy Press.

Dwyer, P. and Ellison, N. (2009) 'Work and welfare: the rights and responsibilities of unemployment in the UK', in M. Giugni (ed) *The politics of unemployment in Europe: Policy responses and collective action*, Farnham: Ashgate Publishing, pp 53-66.

Ebersohn, L. and Eloff, I. (2006) 'Identifying asset-based trends in sustainable programmes which support vulnerable children', *South African Journal of Education*, vol 26, no 3, 457-72.

Elias, N. and Scotson, J. (1994 [1965]) *The established and the outsiders* (2nd edn), London: Sage Publications.

Ellison, N. (2011) 'The Conservative Party and the "Big Society"', in C. Holden, M. Kilkey and G. Ramia (eds), *Social policy review 23: Analysis and debate in social policy*, Bristol: The Policy Press, pp 45-62.

Essex Coalition of Disabled People (2010) *Emergency budget announces potentially worrying changes to DLA* [online], www.ecdp.org.uk/home/2010/6/23/emergency-budget-announces-potentially-worrying-changes-to-d.html

Facer, K. (2011) *Learning futures: Education, technology and social change*, Abingdon: Routledge.

Farrall, S. and Hay, C. (2010) 'Not so tough on crime? Why weren't the Thatcher governments more radical in reforming the criminal justice system?', *British Journal of Criminology*, vol 50, no 4, pp 550-69.

Farrell, M., Ward, J., Mattick, R., Hall, W., Stimson, G., des Jarlais, D., Gossop, M. and Strang, J. (1995) 'Methadone maintenance treatment in opiate dependence: a review', *BMJ Fortnightly Review*, vol 309, no 6960, pp 997-1001.

Farrier, D. (2011) *Postcolonial asylum: Seeking sanctuary before the law*, Liverpool: Liverpool University Press.

Fawcett, B. (2009) 'Vulnerability: questioning the certainties in social work and health', *International Journal of Social Work*, vol 52, no 4, pp 473-84.

Feeley, M. and Simon, J. (2003) 'The new penology', in E. McLaughlin, J. Muncie and G. Hughes (eds) *Criminological perspectives: Essential readings*, London: Sage Publications, pp 434-46.

Fenton, A. (2010) *How will changes to Local Housing Allowance affect low-income tenants in private rented housing?*, Cambridge: Cambridge Centre for Housing and Planning Research.

Ferge, Z. (1997) 'The changed welfare paradigm: the individualization of the social', *Social Policy and Administration*, vol 31, no 1, pp 20-44.

Feucht, T.E. (1993) 'Prostitutes on crack cocaine: addiction, utility and marketplace economies', *Deviant Behaviour*, vol 14, no 2, pp 91-108.

Field, F. (2003) *Neighbours from hell: The politics of behaviour*, London: Politico's Publishing.

Field, F. (2010) *The foundation years: Preventing poor children becoming poor adults: The report of the Independent Review on Poverty and Life Chances*, London: HM Government.

Field, F. (2012) 'The foundation years: preventing poor children becoming poor adults', the annual Harold Wilson lecture, University of Huddersfield, 14 April.

Fielding, M. and Moss, P. (2011) *Radical education and the common school*, Abingdon: Routledge.

Finch, H., O'Connor, W., Millar, J., Hales, J., Shaw, A. and Roth, W. (1999) *The New Deal for Lone Parents: Learning from the prototype areas*, Leeds: HMSO.

Fineman, M. (2008) 'The vulnerable subject: anchoring equality in the human condition', *Yale Journal of Law and Feminism*, vol 20, no 1, pp 8-40.

Finkelstein, V. (1991) 'Disability: an administrative challenge? The health and welfare heritage', in M. Oliver (ed) *Social work: Disabled people and disabling environments*, London: Jessica Kingsley Publishers, pp 19-39.

Finn, D. (2011) 'Welfare to work after the recession: from the New Deals to the Work Programme', in C. Holden, M. Kilkey and G. Ramia (eds) *Social policy review 23: Analysis and debate in social policy*, Bristol: The Policy Press, pp 127-46.

Fletcher, D. (2008) 'Employment and disconnection: cultures of worklessness in neighbourhoods', in J. Flint and D. Robinson (eds) *Community cohesion in crisis?*, Bristol: The Policy Press, pp 99-117.

Flint, C. (2002) 'Social housing agencies and the governance of anti-social behaviour', *Housing Studies*, vol 17, no 4, pp 619-37.

Flint, C. (2008) Speech to the Fabian Society [online], 5 February, www.fabians.org.uk/events/speeches/flint-we-must-break-link-between-council-housing-and-worklessness

Flint, J. (2003) 'Housing and ethnopolitics: constructing identities of active consumption and responsible community', *Economy and Society*, vol 32, no 3, pp 611-29.

Flint, J. (2006a) 'Maintaining an arm's length? Housing, community governance and the management of "problematic" populations', *Housing Studies*, vol 21, no 2, pp 171-86.

Flint, J. (2006b) 'Housing and the new governance of conduct', in J. Flint (ed) *Housing, urban governance and anti-social behaviour: Perspectives, policy and practice*, Bristol: The Policy Press, pp 19-36.

Flint, J. (ed) (2006c) *Housing, urban governance and anti-social behaviour*, Bristol: The Policy Press.

Flint, J. (2009) 'Governing marginalised populations: the role of coercion, support and agency', *European Journal of Homelessness*, vol 3, no 4, pp 247-60.

Flint, J. (2012) 'The inspection house and neglected dynamics of governance: the case of domestic visits in family intervention projects', *Housing Studies*, vol 27, no 6, pp 822-38.

Flint, J. and Nixon, J. (2006) 'Governing neighbours: Anti-Social Behaviour Orders and new forms of regulating conduct in the UK', *Urban Studies*, vol 43, no 5/6, pp 939-55.

Flint, J. and Robinson, D. (eds) (2008) *Community cohesion in crisis?*, Bristol: The Policy Press.

Flint, J., Batty, E., Parr, S., Platts Fowler, D. and Nixon, J. (2011) *Evaluation of intensive intervention projects*, Sheffield: Sheffield Hallam University and Department for Education.

Fothergill, S. (2010) 'Welfare to work: time for a rethink', *People, Place and Policy Online*, vol 4, no 1, pp 3-5.

Fraser, N. and Gordon, L. (1994) '"Dependency" demystified: inscriptions of power in a keyword of the welfare state', *Social Politics*, vol 1, no 1, pp 4-31.

Freedland, M. and King, D. (2003) 'Contractual governance and illiberal contracts: some problems of contractualism as an instrument of behaviour management by agencies of government', *Cambridge Journal of Economics*, Commentary Section, vol 27, no 3, pp 465-77.

Freedland, M. and King, D. (2005) 'Client contractualism between the employment service and jobseekers in the United Kingdom', in E. Sol and M. Westerveld (eds) *Contractualism in employment services*, The Hague: Kluwer, pp 119-39.

Fremeaux, I. (2005) 'New Labour's appropriation of the concept of community: a critique', *Community Development Journal*, vol 40, no 3, pp 265-74.

Freud, D. (2007) *Reducing dependency, increasing opportunity: Options for the future of welfare-to-work: An independent report to the Department for Work and Pensions*, Leeds: HMSO.

Frost, A., Corker, S., Albanese, F. and Reynolds, L. (2009) *For whose benefit? A study monitoring the implementation of Local Housing Allowance*, London: Shelter.

Frost, N. and Stein, M. (1989) *The politics of child welfare: Inequality, power and change*, Hemel Hempstead: Harvester Wheatsheaf.

Furbey, R. (1999) 'Urban "regeneration": reflections on a metaphor', *Critical Social Policy*, vol 19, no 4, pp 419-45.

Furedi, F. (2007) *Invitation to terror: The expanding empire of the unknown*, London: Continuum.

Furedi, F. (2008) 'Fear and security: a vulnerability-led policy response', *Social Policy and Administration*, vol 42, no 6, pp 645-61.

Gallagher, P. (1982) 'Ideology and housing management', in J. English (ed) *The future of council housing*, London: Croom Helm, pp 132-53.

Gardiner, K. and Millar, J. (2006) 'How low-paid employees avoid poverty: an analysis by family type and household structure', *Journal of Social Policy*, vol 35, no 3, pp 351-69.

Garland, D. (2001) *The culture of control: Crime and social order in contemporary society*, Oxford: Oxford University Press.

Garrett, D. and Forrester, G. (2012) *Education policy unravelled*, London: Continuum.

Gentleman, A. (2011) 'Child detention has the government broken its promise to end it', *The Guardian* [online], 17 October, www.guardian.co.uk/uk/2011/oct/17/child-detention-government-broken-promise

Gentleman, A. (2012a) 'Off the streets and into profit', *The Guardian*, Society, 12 December, p 38.

Gentleman, A. (2012b) 'Third of Incapacity Benefit claimants ruled fit to work', *The Guardian*, 15 March, www.guardian.co.uk/society/2012/mar/15/third-of-incapacity-benefit-claimants-ineligible

Gerwitz, S., Ball, S. and Bowe, R. (1995) *Markets, choice and equality*, Buckingham: Open University Press.

Giddens, A. (1990) *The consequences of modernity*, Cambridge: Polity Press.

Giddens, A. (1998) *The Third Way: The renewal of social democracy*, Cambridge: Polity Press.

Gilbert, A. and Koser, K. (2006) 'Coming to the UK: what do asylum-seekers know about the UK before arrival?', *Journal of Ethnic and Migration Studies*, vol 32, no 7, pp 1209-25.

Gilbert, N. and Besharov, D. (2011) 'Welfare states amid economic turmoil: adjusting work-orientated policy', *Policy & Politics*, vol 39, no 3, pp 295-308.

Giles, C. (2010) Poorest areas to be hardest hit, *Financial Times* [online], 20 June, www.ft.com/cms/s/0/f906b3b4-7cad-11df-8b74-00144feabdc0.html#axzz2O645uDCM

Gillies, V. (2008) 'Childrearing, class and the new politics of parenting', *Sociology Compass*, vol 2, no 3, pp 1079-95.

Giner, C. (2007) 'The politics of childhood and asylum in the UK', *Children and Society*, vol 21, no 24, pp 249-260.

Gingerbread (2012) 'Statistics' [online], www.gingerbread.org.uk/content/365/Statistics

Giullari, S. and Shaw, M. (2005) 'Supporting or controlling ? New Labour's housing strategy for teenage parents', *Critical Social Policy*, vol 25, no 3, pp 402-14.

Godfrey, C., Eaton, G., McDougall, C. and Culyer, A. (2002) *The economic and social costs of class A drug use in England and Wales 2000*, London: Home Office.

Gold, T. (2013) 'Say hello to zero hours, kiss goodbye to workers' rights', *The Guardian*, Comment and debate, 15 April, p 26.

Goodin, R. (1985) *Protecting the vulnerable: A re-analysis of our social responsibilities*, London: University of Chicago Press.

Gove, M. (2009) 'Failing schools need leadership speech' [online], The Conservative Party Conference, Manchester, 7 October, www.conservatives.com/News/Speeches/2009/10/Michael_Gove_Failing_schools_need_new_leadership.aspx

Gove, M. (2010) 'Education: Questions and answer session', 15 November, London: Hansard.

Gove, M. (2011a) *New powers for teachers to restore discipline in schools* [online], www.education.gov.uk/inthenews/multimedia/a0076578/michael-gove-on-behaviour

Gove, M. (2011b) 'Statement to the House of Commons' [online], 28 March, London: Hansard, www.publications.parliament.uk/pa/cm201011/cmhansrd/cm110328/debtext/110328-0002.htm#11032822000002

Grabham, E. and Smith, J. (2010) 'From social security to individual responsibility (part two): writing off poor women's work in the Welfare Reform Act 2009', *Journal of Social Welfare and Family Law*, vol 32, no 1, pp 81-93.

Grant, E. and Wood, C. (2011) 'Disability benefits', in N. Yeates, T. Haux, R. Jawad and M. Kilkey (eds) *In defence of welfare: The impacts of the spending review*, London: Social Policy Association, pp 28-9.

Grant, R.W. (2012) *Strings attached: Untangling the ethics of incentives*, Princeton, NJ: Russell Sage Foundation and Princeton University Press.

Gray, N. and Mooney, G. (2011) 'Glasgow's new urban frontier: "civilizing" the population of Glasgow East', *City*, vol 15, no 1, pp 4-24.

Grayson, J. (2012a) 'Mobilising outrage: campaigning with asylum seekers against security industry giant G4S', *Open Democracy* [online], www.opendemocracy.net/ourkingdom/john-grayson/mobilising-outrage-campaigning-with-asylum seekers-against-security-industry

Grayson, J. (2012b) 'Yorkshire campaigners claim small victory over world's biggest security company G4S', *Open Democracy* [online], www.opendemocracy.net/ourkingdom/john-grayson/yorkshire-campaigners-claim-small-victory-over-world's-biggest-security-comp

Grayson, J. (2013) 'Opinion: below the radar – G4S asylum housing and housing professionals', www.24dash.com/news/housing/2013-03-22-Opinion-Below-the-radar-G4S

Gregg, P. (2008) *Realising potential: A vision for personalised conditionality and support: An independent report to the Department for Work and Pensions*, Norwich: The Stationery Office.

Grover, C. and Piggott, L. (2005) 'Disabled people, the reserve army of labour and welfare reform', *Disability and Society*, vol 20, no 7, pp 705-17.

Gunder, M. (2010) 'Planning as the ideology of (neo-liberal) space', *Planning Theory*, vol 9, no 4, pp 298-314.

Gungell, K. (2012) 'Schools must be made responsible for truancy even if parents are to blame', *The Daily Mail* [online], 30 March, www.dailymail.co.uk/debate/article-2122654/Schools-responsible-truancy-parents-blame.html

Gyngell, K. (2007) *Breakthrough Britain: Ending the costs of social breakdown: Volume 4: Addictions*, London: Conservative Party.

Hancock, L., Mooney, G. and Neal, S. (2012) 'Crisis social policy and the resilience of the concept of community', *Critical Social Policy*, vol 32, no 3, pp 343-64.

Hanley, L. (2007) *Estates: An intimate history*, London: Granta.

Harkness, S., Gregg, P. and Macmillan, L. (2012) *Poverty: The role of institutions, behaviours and culture*, York: Joseph Rowntree Foundation.

Harman, H. (1997) 'Harman highlights work as the best form of welfare', Department of Social Security press release, 6 May.

Harris, J. (2012) 'Back to the workhouse', *The Guardian*, 9 June, p 40.

Harris, J. (2013a) 'A timebomb waiting to go off', *The Guardian*, 26 January, pp 32-3.

Harris, J. (2013b) 'The biggest company you've never heard of', *The Guardian G2*, 30 July, pp 6-9.

Harris, J. and McElrath, K. (2012) 'Methadone as social control: institutionalized stigma and the prospect of recovery', *Qualitative Health Research*, vol 22, no 6, pp 810-24.

Harrison, M. (1995) *Housing, 'race', social policy and empowerment*, CRER Research in Ethnic Relations Series, Aldershot: Avebury.

Harrison, M. (2009) 'New contexts, new challenges: revisiting equal opportunities, particularism and ethnic relations', *People, Place & Policy Online*, vol 3, no 3.

Harrison, M. (2010) 'The new behaviourism, the "real Third Way", and housing futures: some ideas under development', paper presented to the HSA conference, York, April.

Harrison, M. and Sanders, T. (2006) 'Vulnerable people and the development of "regulatory therapy"', in A. Dearling, T. Newburn and P. Somerville (eds) *Supporting safer communities: Housing, crime and neighbourhoods*, Coventry: Chartered Institute of Housing, pp 155-68.

Harrison, M. with Davis, C. (2001) *Housing, social policy and difference: Disability, ethnicity, gender and housing*, Bristol: The Policy Press.

Harrison, M., Phillips, D., Chahal, K., Hunt, L. and Perry, J. (2005) *Housing, 'race' and community cohesion*, Coventry: Chartered Institute of Housing with Housing Studies Association.

Harrison, S. (2002) 'New Labour, modernization and the medical labour process', *Journal of Social Policy*, vol 31, no 3, pp 465-86.

Hasler, F. (2004) 'Disability, care and controlling services', in J. Swain, S. French, C. Barnes and C. Thomas (eds) *Disabling barriers – enabling environments* (2nd edn), London: Sage Publications, pp 226-32.

Hausman, D.M. and Welch, B. (2010) 'Debate: to nudge or not to nudge', *The Journal of Political Philosophy*, vol 18, no 1, pp 123-36.

Haux, T. (2010) *Activating lone parents: An evidence-based policy appraisal of the 2008 welfare-to-work reform in Britain*, Working Paper, Colchester: Institute for Economic and Social Research.

Hay, G. and Bauld, L. (2008) *Population estimates of problematic drug users in England who access DWP benefits: A feasibility study*, London: Department for Work and Pensions.

Hellowell, M. and Pollock, M. (2009) 'The private financing of NHS hospitals: politics, policy and practice', *Journal of Economic Affairs*, vol 29, no 1, pp 13-19.

Hemingway, L. (2011) *Disabled people and housing: Choices, opportunities and barriers*, Bristol: The Policy Press.

Henderson, J. and Karn, V. (1987) *Race, class and state housing: Inequality and the allocation of public housing in Britain*, Aldershot: Gower.

Hendrick, H. (1994) *Child welfare: England 1872–1989*, London: Routledge.

Hendrick, H. (2003) *Child welfare: Historical dimensions, contemporary debates*, Bristol: The Policy Press.

Henman, P. and Marston, G. (2008) 'The social division of welfare surveillance', *Journal of Social Policy*, vol 37, no 2, pp 187-205.

Herbert, N. (2013) 'This wink to developers won't fix the housing crisis', *The Guardian*, Comment and debate, 15 July.

Herbert, S. (2005) 'The trapdoor of community', *Annals of the Association of American Geographers*, vol 95, no 4, pp 850-65.

Hill, A. (2012) 'Safety net unravels as cuts hit the poor and vulnerable', *The Guardian*, 20 November, special report, *Breadline Britain*, pp 12-13.

Hills, J. (2007) *Ends and means: The future roles of social housing in England*, Report 34, London: Economic and Social Research Council.

Hills, J. (2008) *Policy briefing: The Hills review: Worklessness and social housing* [online], http://england.shelter.org.uk/__data/assets/pdf_file/0007/138580/Worklessness_and_social_housing_briefing.pdf

HM Government (1998) *Fairer, faster and firmer: A modern approach to immigation and asylum*, White Paper, Cm 4018, London: The Stationery Office.

HM Government (2009) *Pursue, Prevent, Protect, Prepare: The United Kingdom's strategy for countering international terrorism*, London, The Stationery Office.

HM Government (2010a) *Decentralisation and the Localism Bill: An essential guide*, London: Department for Communities and Local Government.

HM Government (2010b) *The coalition: Our programme for government*, London: Cabinet Office.

HM Government (2012) *Social justice: Transforming lives*, London: Department for Work and Pensions.

HM Treasury (2010a) *Budget 2010*, London: HMSO.

HM Treasury (2010b) *Spending review 2010*, London: HMSO.

Ho, D.E. (2012) 'Fudging the nudge: information disclosure and restaurant grading', *Yale Law Journal*, vol 122, no 3, pp 574-688.

Hodge, K. (2011) 'Disabled to be hit by spare room benefit cut', *The Guardian*, 26 May, www.guardian.co.uk/housing-network/2011/may/26/disabled-benefit-cut-first-time-buyers

Hodgkinson, S. and Tilley, N. (2011) 'Tackling anti-social behaviour: lessons from New Labour for the coalition government', *Criminology and Criminal Justice*, vol 11, no 4, pp 283-305.

Hodgson, A. and Spours, K. (2012) *Young people's participation, progression and transition to higher study and work: A London perspective*, London: Institute of Education.

Hodgson, P. and Canvin, K. (2005) 'Translating health policy into research practice', in L. Lowes and I. Hulatt (eds) *Involving service users in health and social care research*, Abingdon: Routledge, pp 48-65.

Hoggett, P. (ed) (1997) *Contested communities*, Bristol: The Policy Press.

Hollomotz, A. (2009) 'Beyond "vulnerability": an ecological model approach to conceptualizing risk of sexual violence against people with learning difficulties', *British Journal of Social Work*, vol 39, no 1, pp 99-112.

Hollomotz, A. (2011) *Learning difficulties and sexual vulnerability: A social approach*, London: Jessica Kingsley Publishers.

Holloway, K. and Bennett, T. (2004) *The results of the first two-years of the NEW-ADAM programme*, London: Home Office.

Home Affairs Committee (2002) *The government's drugs policy: Is it working?* [online], London: Home Office, www.publications.parliament.uk

Home Office (1998) *Guidance on statutory crime and disorder partnerships: Crime and Disorder Act*, London: Home Office.

Home Office (2003) *Respect and responsibility: Taking a stand against anti-social behaviour*, London: Home Office.

Home Office (2008) *Drugs: Protecting families and communities: The 2008–2018 drug strategy*, London: Home Office.

Home Office (2010a) *Drug strategy 2010: Reducing demand, restricting supply and building recovery: Supporting people to live a drug free life*, London: Home Office.

Home Office (2010b) *Policing in the 21st century: Reconnecting police and the people*, London: Home Office.

Home Office (2011) *More effective responses to anti-social behaviour*, London: Home Office.

Home Office (2012a) *Asylum – May–August 2012*, London: Home Office.

Home Office (2012b) *Putting victims first: More effective responses to anti-social behaviour*, London: Home Office.

Homes and Communities Agency (2012) *The regulatory framework for social housing in England from 2012*, London: Homes and Communities Agency.

Honneth, A. (1995) *The struggle for recognition: The moral grammar of social conflicts*, Cambridge: Polity Press.

Horton, T. and Reed, H. (2010) 'The distributional impact of the 2010 spending review', *Radical Statistics*, vol 103, pp 13-24.

Hough, M. (1995) *Drug misuse and the criminal justice system: A review of the literature*, London: Home Office.

Hough, M. (2011) 'Crime and criminal justice', in H. Bochel (ed) *The Conservative Party and social policy*, Bristol: The Policy Press, pp 215-28.

Housing Corporation (2007) *Housing associations tackling worklessness*, London: The National Affordable Homes Agency.

Housing Management Sub-Committee of the Central Housing Advisory Committee (1955, reprinted 1968) *Unsatisfactory tenants*, London: HMSO.

Hoyle, C. and Zedner, L. (2007) 'Victims, victimisation and criminal justice', in M. Maguire, R. Morgan and R. Reiner (eds) *The Oxford handbook of criminology* (4th edn), Oxford: Oxford University Press, pp 461-95.

Hughes, G. (1998) *Imagining welfare futures*, London: Routledge.

Hughes, R. and Anthony, N. (2006) 'Drugs, crime and criminal justice', in R. Hughes, R. Lart and P. Higate (eds) *Drugs: Policy and politics*, Maidenhead: Open University Press, pp 75-91.

Hunt, N. and Stevens, A. (2004) 'Whose harm? Harm reduction and the shift to coercion in UK drug policy', *Social Policy and Society*, vol 3, no 4, pp 333-42.

Hunt, P. (1981) 'Settling accounts with the parasite people: a critique of "A Life Apart" by E.J. Miller and O.V. Gwynne', *Disability Challenge* [online], London: UPIAS, http://disability-studies.leeds.ac.uk/files/library/UPIAS-Disability-Challenge1.pdf

Hynes, P. and Sales, R. (2010) 'New communities: asylum seekers and dispersal', in A. Bloch and J. Solomos (eds) *Race and ethnicity in the 21st century*, Basingstoke: Palgrave Macmillan, pp 39-61.

IFS (Institute for Fiscal Studies) (2011) *Universal Credit – A preliminary analysis* [online]. London: IFS, www.ifs.org.uk/publications/5417

Imrie, R. (2003) 'Housing quality and the provision of accessible homes', *Housing Studies*, vol 18, no 3, pp 387-408.

Imrie, R. and Raco, M. (2003) 'Community and the changing nature of urban policy', in R. Imrie and M. Raco (eds) *Urban renaissance? New Labour, community and urban policy*, Bristol: The Policy Press, pp 1-36.

Innes, M. (2003) *Understanding social control: Deviance, crime and social order*, Maidenhead: Open University Press.

IPCC (Independent Police Complaints Commission) (2011) *Report into the contact between Fiona Pilkington and Leicestershire Constabulary 2004-2007*, London: IPCC.

Jacobs, K. and Manzi, T. (2012) 'New localism, old retrenchment: the 'Big Society'. Housing policy and the politics of welfare reform', *Housing Theory and Society*, vol 29, no 1, pp 1-17.

James, A. and James, I. (2001) 'Tightening the net: children, community and control', *British Journal of Sociology*, vol 52, no 2, pp 211-28.

James, A. and Prout, A. (1997) *Constructing and reconstructing childhood: Contemporary issues in the sociological study of childhood*, London: Falmer.

Jenks, C. (2005) *Childhood* (2nd edn), London: Routledge.

Johnstone, C. and MacLeod, G. (2007) 'New Labour's "broken" neighbourhoods: liveability, disorder and discipline', in R. Atkinson and G. Helms (eds) *Securing an urban renaissance*, Bristol: The Policy Press, pp 75-89.

Jones, A. and Pleace, N. (2010) *A review of single homelessness in the UK 2000-2010*, York: University of York.

JRF (Joseph Rowntree Foundation) (2005) *Findings: Parental supervision: The views and experiences of young people and their parents*, York: JRF.

JRF (2011) *Findings: Transforming social care: Sustaining person-centred support*, York: JRF.

Kellner, P. (2012) 'A quiet revolution', *Prospect Magazine* [online], www.prospectmagazine.co.uk/magazine/a-quiet-revolution-britain-turns-against-welfare/

Kemshall, H. (2002) 'Key organizing principles of social welfare and the new risk-based welfare', in H. Kemshall (ed) *Risk, social policy and welfare*, Buckingham: Open University Press, pp 24-41.

Kendall, S., Johnson, A., Gulliver, C., Martin, K. and Kinder, K. (2004) *Evaluation of the Vulnerable Children Grant part I*, Nottingham: National Foundation for Educational Research.

Kerr, S. (2011) 'The Work Programme: massive boost for the "Big Society" or crumbs off the table?', *The Guardian*, 6 June, www.guardian.co.uk/voluntary-sector-network/2011/jun/06/work-programme-social-enterprise-involvement

Kintrea, K., Bannister, J. and Pickering, J. (2011) 'It's just an area – everybody represents it: exploring young people's territorial behaviour in British cities', in B. Goldson (ed) *Youth in crisis? 'Gangs', territoriality and violence*, London: Routledge, pp 55-71.

Kisby, B. (2010) 'The Big Society: power to the people?', *The Political Quarterly*, vol 81, no 4, pp 484-91.

Kittay, E.F. (1999a) 'Welfare, dependency and a public ethic of care', in G. Mink (ed) *Whose welfare?*, New York, NY: Cornell University Press, pp 189-213.

Kittay, E.F. (1999b) *Love's labor: Essays on women, equality and dependency*, New York, NY: Routledge.

Labour Party (2010) *The Labour Party manifesto 2010: A future fair for all* [online], www2.labour.org.uk/uploads/TheLabourPartyManifesto-2010.pdf

Laing, A., Hogg, G., Newhold, T. and Keeling, D. (2009) 'Differentiating consumers in professional services: information empowerment and the emergence of the fragmented consumer', in R. Simmons, M. Powell and I. Greener (eds) *The consumer in public services: Choice, values and difference*, Bristol: The Policy Press, pp 77-98.

Larner, W. and Craig, D. (2005) 'After neoliberalism: community activists and local partnerships in Aotearoa New Zealand', *Antipode*, vol 37, no 3, pp 402-24.

Law, I. (2007) 'Housing choice and racist hostility', *Better Housing Briefing Paper 4*, London: Race Equality Foundation.

Lawless, P. (2004) 'Locating and explaining area-based urban initiatives: New Deal for Communities in England', *Environment and Planning C: Government and Policy*, vol 22, no 3, pp 383-99.

Lawless, P (2007) 'Continuing dilemmas for area based urban regeneration: evidence from the New Deal for Communities Programme in England', *People, Place & Policy Online*, vol 1, no 1, pp 14-21

Lawton, K. (2009a) *Tackling in-work poverty* [online], London: Child Poverty Action Group, www.cpag.org.uk/content/tackling-work-poverty

Lawton, K. (2009b) *Nice work if you can get it: Achieving a sustainable solution to low pay and in work poverty*, London: Institute for Public Policy Research.

Lawton, K. (2010) *Spending review will weaken work incentives* [online], www.leftfootforward.org/2010/10/comprehensive-spending-review-will-weaken-work-incentives/

Levitas, R. (1998) *The inclusive society? Social exclusion and New Labour*, Basingstoke: Palgrave Macmillan.

Levy-Vroelent, C. (2010) 'Housing vulnerable groups: the development of a new public action sector', *International Journal of Housing Policy*, vol 10, no 4, pp 443-56.

Lewis, H. (2007) *Destitution in Leeds: The experiences of people seeking asylum and supporting agencies in Leeds* [online], York: Joseph Rowntree Charitable Trust, www.jrct.org.uk/text.asp?section=0001000200030006

Lewis, J. (2002) 'Individualisation, assumptions about the existence of an adult worker model and the shift towards contractualism', in A. Carling, S. Duncan and R. Edwards (eds) *Analysing families: Morality and rationality in policy and practice*, London: Routledge, pp 51-6.

Lexmond, J., Bazalgette, L. and Margo, J. (2011) *The home front*, London: Demos.

Lidstone, P. (1994) 'Rationing housing to the homeless applicant', *Housing Studies*, vol 9, no 4, pp 459-72.

Lister, R. (1999) 'Reforming welfare around the work ethic: new gendered and ethical perspectives on work and care', *Policy & Politics*, vol 27, no 2, pp 233-46.

Lister, R. (2001) '"Work for those who can, security for those who cannot": a Third Way in social security reform or fractured social citizenship?', in R. Edwards and J. Glover (eds) *Risk and citizenship: Key issues in welfare*, London: Routledge, pp 96-109.

Lister, R. (2003) *Citizenship: Feminist perspectives* (2nd edn), Basingstoke: Palgrave.

Lister, R. (2011) 'The age of responsibility: social policy and citizenship in the early 21st century', in C. Holden, M. Kilkey and G. Ramia (eds) *Social policy review 23: Analysis and debate in social policy*, Bristol: The Policy Press.

Lister, R. and Bennett, F. (2010) 'The new "champion of progressive ideals"? Cameron's Conservative Party: poverty, family policy and welfare reform', *Renewal*, vol 18, no 1/2, pp 84-109.

Lockwood, D. (1996) 'Civic integration and class formation', *British Journal of Sociology*, vol 47, no 3, pp 531-50.

López-Navidad, A. and Caballero, F. (2003) 'Extended criteria for organ acceptance: strategies for achieving organ safety and for increasing organ pool', *Clinical Transplantation*, vol 17, no 4, pp 308-24.

Luby, J. (2008) *Private access, public gain: The use of private rented sector access schemes to house single homeless people*, London: Crisis and the London Housing Foundation.

Lund, B. (1996) *Housing problems and housing policy*, London: Longman.

Lund, B. (2011) *Understanding housing policy*, Bristol: The Policy Press.

Lupton, D. (1999) *Risk*, London: Routledge.

MacBeath, G., Gray, J., Cullen, D., Frost, N., Stewart, D. and Swaffield, S. (2007) *Schools on the edge*, London: Sage Publications.

McCulloch, A. (2004) 'Localism and its neoliberal application: a case study of West Gate New Deal for Communities in Newcastle upon Tyne UK', *Capital and Class*, vol 83, pp 133-65.

McDowell, L. (2005) 'Love, money and gender divisions of labour: some critical reflections on welfare-to-work policies in the UK', *Journal of Economic Geography*, vol 5, no 3, pp 365-79.

McGhee, D. (2005) *Intolerant Britain: Hate, citizenship and difference*, Maidenhead: Open University Press.

MacGregor, S. (2000) 'Editorial: the drugs-crime nexus', *Drugs: Education, Prevention and Policy*, vol 7, no 4, pp 311-16.

Machin, S. and Vernoit, J. (2012) *Academy schools under Labour combated disadvantage and increased pupil achievement: The coalition's new policy may exacerbate existing inequalities*, London: London School of Economics.

McIntosh, J. and McKeganey, N. (2002) *Beating the dragon: The recovery from dependent drug use*, Harlow: Pearson.

McKee, K. (2009) 'The "responsible" tenant and the problem of apathy', *Social Policy and Society*, vol 8, no 1, pp 25-36.

Mackenzie, C. (2009) 'What is vulnerability', paper for the Vulnerability, Agency and Justice Conference, Sydney, August.

McLaughlin, K. (2012) *Surviving identity: Vulnerability and the psychology of recognition*, London: Routledge.

MacLeavy, J. (2009) '(Re)analysing community empowerment: rationalities and technologies of government in Bristol's New Deal for Communities', *Urban Studies*, vol 46, no 4, pp 849-75.

MacLeod, G. and Johnstone, C. (2012) 'Stretching urban renaissance: privatising space, civilising place, summoning community', *International Journal of Urban and Regional Research*, vol 36, no 1, pp 1-28.

McNeill, J. (2011) 'Employability pathways and perceptions of "work" amongst single homeless and vulnerably housed people', *Social Policy and Society*, vol 10, no 4, pp 571-80.

McSweeney, T., Hough, M. and Turnbull, P. (2007) 'Drugs and crime: exploring the links', in M. Simpson, T. Shildrick and R. MacDonald (eds) *Drugs in Britain: Supply, consumption and control*, Basingstoke: Macmillan.

McVeigh, K. and Taylor, M. (2010) 'Government climb-down on detention of children in immigration centres', *The Guardian* [online], 9 September, www.guardian.co.uk/uk/2010/sep/09/detention-children-immigration-centres

Maher, L. and Curtis, R. (1992) 'Women on the edge of crime: crack cocaine and the changing contexts of street-level sex work in New York City', *Crime, Law and Social Change*, vol 18, no 3, pp 269-99.

Malik, S. (2012a) 'Disabled people face unlimited unpaid work or cuts in benefit', *The Guardian* [online], 16 February, www.guardian.co.uk/society/2012/feb/16/disabled-unpaid-work-benefit-cuts

Malik, S. (2012b) 'Disabled benefits claimants face £71 a week fines for breaching work plan', *The Guardian*, 3 September, www.guardian.co.uk/society/2012/sep/03/disabled-benefits-claimants-fines-work

Malik, S. and Ball, J. (2012) 'Jobseekers face tougher unpaid work demands', *The Guardian*, 13 June, p 5.

Malik, S., Ball, J. and Davies, L. (2012) 'Jobseekers forced to clean private homes and offices for free', *The Guardian*, 25 February, p 6.

Mann, K. (1998) 'Lampost modernism: traditional and critical social policy?', *Critical Social Policy*, vol 18, no 54, pp 77-102.

Marsh, S. (2011) 'It's not 7,000, but 700,000 seriously ill people who'll lose their sickness benefit', *The Guardian*, 21 June, www.guardian.co.uk/commentisfree/2011/jun/21/losing-benefits-for-seriously-ill

Marshall, T.H. (1949) 'Citizenship and social class', in T.H. Marshall and T. Bottomore (eds) *Citizenship and social class*, London: Pluto Press.

Marsland, D. (2004) 'Social policy since 1979: a view from the right', in N. Ellison, L. Bauld and M. Powell (eds) *Social policy review 16*, Bristol: The Policy Press, pp 211-30.

Marteau, T., Ogilvie, D., Roland, M., Suhrcke, M. and Kelly, M. (2011) 'Judging nudging: can nudging improve population health?', *British Medical Journal*, vol 342, no 1, pp 263-5.

Martin, D. (2012) 'Schools and children and young people's services have successfully constructed local, holistic, multi-professional partnerships: but what next under the coalition government?', paper for the BERA Annual Conference, Manchester, 4 September.

Mead, L. (1997) *The new paternalism: Supervisory approaches to poverty*, Washington, DC: Brookings Institution Press.

Means, R. (1996) 'From "special needs" housing to independent living?', *Housing Studies*, vol 11, no 2, pp 207-31.

Miliband, E. (2011) *Responsibility in 21st century Britain: Speech at Coin Street neighbourhood centre* [online], 13 June, www.labour.org.uk/ed-miliband-speech-responsibility,2011-06-13

Millar, J. (2008) 'Making work pay, making tax credits work: an assessment with specific reference to lone-parent employment', *International Social Security Review*, vol 61, no 2, pp 21-38.

Millar, J. and Ridge, T. (2008) 'Relationships of care: working lone mothers, their children and employment sustainability', *Journal of Social Policy*, vol 38, no 1, pp 103-21.

Millie, A. (2007) 'Tackling anti-social behaviour and regenerating neighbourhoods', in R. Atkinson and G. Helms (eds) *Securing an urban renaissance: Crime, community and British urban policy*, Bristol: The Policy Press, pp 107-24.

Millie, A. (2010) 'Moral politics, moral decline and anti-social behaviour', *People, Place & Policy Online*, vol 4, no 1, pp 6-13.

Milne, S. (2012), 'G4S should make it easier to beat the privatisation racket', *The Guardian*, 18 July, p 26.

Milner, J. (2005) 'Disability and inclusive housing design: towards a life-course perspective', in P. Somerville with N. Springings (eds) *Housing and social policy: Contemporary themes and critical perspectives*, London: Routledge, pp 172-96.

Milner, J. and Madigan, R. (2004) 'Regulation and innovation: rethinking "inclusive" housing design', *Housing Studies*, vol 19, no 5, pp 727-44.

Ministry of Justice (2010) *Breaking the cycle: Effective punishment, rehabilitation and sentencing of offenders*, London: Ministry of Justice.

Ministry of Justice (2012) *Court statistics* [online], www.justice.gov.uk/statistics/courts-and-sentencing/judicial-quarterly

Mink, G. (1998) *Welfare's end* (revised edn), New York, NY: Cornell University Press.

Monaghan, M. (2012) 'The recent evolution of UK drug strategies: from maintenance to behaviour change?', *People, Place and Policy Online*, vol 6, no 1, pp 29-40.

Monaghan, M. and Wincup, E. (2013) 'Work and the journey to recovery: exploring the implications of welfare reform for methadone maintenance clients', *International Journal of Drug Policy* , vol 24, 6, pp 81-6.

Monbiot, G. (2011) 'This bastardised libertarianism makes "freedom" an instrument of oppression', *The Guardian*, Comment and debate, 20 December, p 27.

Moon, G. (2000) 'Risk and protection: The discourse of confinement in contemporary mental health policy', *Health and Place*, vol, 6, no 3, pp 239-50.

Mooney, G. and Fyfe, N. (2006) 'New Labour and community protests: the case of the Govanhill swimming pool campaign, Glasgow', *Local Economy*, vol 21, no 2, pp 136-50.

Moraes, B.N., Bacal, F., Teixeira, M., Fiorelli, A.I., Leite, P.L., Fiorelli, L.R., Stolf, N.A. and Bocchi, E.A. (2009) 'Behavior profile of family members of donors and non donors of organs', *Transplantation Proceedings*, vol 41, no 3, pp 799-801.

Morgan, R. (2012) 'Crime and justice in the "Big Society"', *Criminology and Criminal Justice*, vol 12, no 5, pp 463-81.

Morgan, S., Stephenson, M.T., Harrison, T.R., Afifi, W.A. and Long, S.D. (2008) 'Facts versus feelings: how rational is the decision to become an organ donor?', *Journal of Health Psychology*, vol 13, no 5, pp 644-58.

Morris, J. (1999) 'The meaning of independent living in the 3rd millennium', *The Disability Archive UK* [online], www.leeds.ac.uk/disability-studies/archiveuk/archframe.htm

Morris, K. (2012) 'Troubled families: vulnerable families' experiences of multiple service use', *Child & Family Social Work* [online], http://onlinelibrary.wiley.com/doi/10.1111/j.1365-2206.2011.00822.x/abstract

Morris, L. (2012a) 'Rights, recognition and judgement: reflections on the case of welfare and asylum', *British Journal of Politics and International Relations*, vol 14, no 1, pp 39-56.

Morris, L. (2012b) *Civic stratification and migrants rights* [online], http://podcasts.ox.ac.uk/series/centre-migration-policy-and-society-compas

Morris, S. (2012) 'Litter law enforcers raise liberty questions', *The Guardian*, Environment, 17 May, p 9.

Muir, H. (2013) 'Diary: will IDS speak out against "income support" for farmers? All kinds of people take public assistance from time to time', *The Guardian*, 30 May, www.theguardian.com/politics/2013/may/30/hugh-muir-diary-iain-duncan-smith

Mulcahy, H. (2004) '"Vulnerable family" as understood by public health nurses', *Community Practitioner*, vol 77, no 7, pp 257-60.

Murie, A. (2012a) 'The next blueprint for housing policy in England', *Housing Studies*, vol 27, no 7, pp 1031-47.

Murie, A. (2012b) 'Housing, the welfare state and the coalition government', in M. Kilkey, G. Ramia and K. Farnsworth (eds) *Social policy review 24: Analysis and debate in social policy 2012*, Bristol: The Policy Press, pp 55-76.

Muscular Dystrophy Campaign (2010) *Concerns raised over Prime Minister's remarks on social housing tenancies* [online], www.muscular-dystrophy.org/get_involved/campaigns/campaign_news/2575_concerns_raised_over_prime_ministers_remarks_on_social_housing_tenancies

National Audit Office (2012) *The introduction of the Work Programme*, London: Department for Work and Pensions.

National Centre for Social Research (2012) *Welfare, British social attitudes 29* [online], London: National Centre for Social Research, www.bsa-29.natcen.ac.uk/read-the-report/welfare/introduction.aspx

National Health Service Oxfordshire (2010) *Interim treatment threshold statement* [online], www.oxfordshirepct.nhs.uk/professional-resources/priority-setting/lavender-statements/documents/PS181Smokingandelectivesurgery.pdf

National Housing Federation (2012) *Discretionary housing payments – public consultation, August 2012* [online], www.dwp.gov.uk/docs/discretionary-housing-payments-consultation.pdf

National Treatment Agency (2009) *Breaking the link: The role of drug treatment in tackling crime*, London: National Treatment Agency for Substance Abuse.

National Treatment Agency (2012) *The role of residential rehab in an integrated treatment system* [online], www.nta.nhs.uk/uploads/roleofresi-rehab.pdf

NCIA (National Coalition for Independent Action) (2011) *Voluntary action under threat: What privitisation means for charities and community groups* [online], www.independentaction.net/wp-content/uploads/2011/06/NCIAprivatisation-paper2011.pdf

NEF (New Economics Foundation) (2004) *A well-being manifesto for a flourishing society*, London: NEF.

NEF (2005) *Behavioural economics: Seven principles for policy makers,* , London: NEF.

NEF (2012) *Everyday insecurity: Life at the end of the welfare state* [online], London: NEF, www.neweconomics.org/publications/everyday-insecurity

Neuberger, J. (2012) 'Rationing life-saving resources – how should allocation policies be assessed in solid organ transplantation', *Transplant International*, vol 25, no 1, pp 3-6.

Newman, I. (2011) 'Work as a route out of poverty: a critical evaluation of the UK welfare to work policy', *Policy Studies*, vol 32, no 2, pp 91-108.

Newman, J. (2000) 'Beyond the new public management? Modernising public services new management new welfare?', in J. Clarke, S. Gewirtz and E. McLaughlin (eds) *New managerialism, new welfare?* London: Sage Publications, pp 45-61.

NHS (National Health Service) (2010) *Social care and mental health indicators from the national indictor set – further analysis 2009-10* [online], www.ic.nhs.uk/webfiles/publications/009_Social_Care/socmhi09-10final/Provisional_Report_Social_Care_and_Mental_Health_Indicators_200910.pdf

Niner, P. (1989) *Homelessness in nine local authorities: Case studies of policy and practice*, London: HMSO.

Nixon, J. and Prior, D. (eds) (2010) 'Disciplining difference', themed section, *Social Policy and Society*, vol 9, no 1, pp 71-153.

Norman, J. (2010) *The Big Society*, Buckingham: University of Buckingham Press.

NRU (Neighbourhood Renewal Unit) (2005) *Research report 17: NDC 2001–2005 an interim evaluation*, London: HMSO.

Nutt, D., King, L.A. and Phillips, L.D. (2010) 'Drug harms in the UK: a multi criteria decision analysis', *The Lancet*, vol 376, no 9752, pp 1558-65.

Nutt, D., King, L.A., Saulsbury, W. and Blakemore, C. (2007) 'Development of a rational scale to assess the harm of drugs of potential misuse', *The Lancet*, vol 369, no 9566, pp 1046-53.

O'Hara, E. (2008) *Policy discussion paper: No place like home? Addressing issues of housing and migration*, London: Shelter.

ONS (Office for National Statistics) (2011) *Consumer price indices: August 2011* [online], www.ons.gov.uk/ons/rel/cpi/consumer-price-indices/august-2011/index.html

Oliver, B. and Pitt, B. (2011) *Working with children, young people and families*, Exeter: Learning Matters.

Oliver, M. (1983) *Social work with disabled people*, Basingstoke: Macmillan.

Oliver, M. (1990) 'The individual and social models of disability', paper presented at a Joint Workshop of the Living Options Group and the Research Unit of the Royal College of Physicians on people with established locomotor disabilities in hospitals, 23 July, *The Disability Archive UK*, http://leeds.ac.uk/disability-studies/archiveuk/archframe.htm

Oliver, M. (1991) *Social work: Disabled people and disabling environments*, London: Jessica Kingsley Publishers.

Orloff, A.S. (2006) 'From maternalism to "employment for all": state policies to promote women's employment across the affluent democracies', in J.D. Levy (ed) *The state after statism: New state activities in the age of liberalization*, Harvard, MA: Harvard University Press, pp 230-70.

Orton, M. (2009) 'Understanding the exercise of agency within structural inequality: the case of personal debt', *Social Policy and Society*, vol 8, no 4, pp 487-98.

Orton, M. and Rowlingson, K. (2007) 'A problem of riches: towards a new social policy research agenda on the distribution of economic resources', *Journal of Social Policy*, vol 36, no 1, pp 59-77.

Osborne, G. (2012a) *Autumn statement 2012 to the House of Commons by the Rt Hon George Osborne, MP, Chancellor of the Exchequer* [online], 5 December, www.hm-treasury.gov.uk/as2012_statement.htm

Osborne, G. (2012b) Speech to the Conservative Party conference [online], 8 October, www.cpc12.org.uk/Speeches/George_Osborne. aspx

Osborne, G. and Thaler, R. (2010) 'We can make you behave', *The Guardian*, 29 January, p 36.

OSW (Off the Streets and into Work) (2006) *The role of housing providers in enabling homeless people's employment success* [online], London: OSW and Centre for Economic and Social Inclusion, www.osw.org.uk/ librarydocs/Housing_and_Employment.pdf

Overell, S. (2011) 'Jobs are not enough: it's the quality of work that counts', *The Guardian* [online], 17 March, www.guardian.co.uk/ commentisfree/2011/mar/17/jobs-work-coalition-quality-of-life

Oxfam (2012) *The perfect storm: Economic stagnation, the rising cost of living, public spending cuts, and the impact on UK poverty*, Oxford: Oxfam.

Page, R.M. (2009) 'With love from me to you: the New Democrats, New Labour and the politics of "welfare" reform', *Benefits*, vol 17, no 2, pp 149-58.

Parley, F. (2011) 'What does vulnerability mean?', *British Journal of Learning Disabilities*, vol 39, no 4, pp 266-76.

Parton, N.B. (2007) 'Safeguarding children: a socio-historic analysis', in K. Wilson and A. James (eds) *The child protection handbook: The practitioner's guide to safeguarding children* (3rd edn), Philadelphia, PA: Elsevier, pp 9-30.

Passaro, J. (1996) *The unequal homeless: Men on the streets, women in their place*, London: Routledge.

Patrick, R. (2012) 'All in it together? Disabled people, the coalition and welfare to work', *Journal of Poverty and Social Justice*, vol 20, no 3, pp 307-22.

Pawson, H. (2011) *Welfare reform and social housing*, York: Housing Quality Network.

Pawson, H. and Wilcox, S. (2012) *UK housing review: 2012 briefing paper* [online], www.york.ac.uk/res/ukhr/ukhr1112/UKHRbriefing2012. pdf

Pawson, H., Bright, J., Engberg, L. and van Bortel, G. (2012) *Resident involvement in social housing in the UK and Europe* [online], www. hyde-housing.co.uk/client_files/Resident%20involvement%20in%20 the%20UK%20and%20Europe_A5_120117.pdf

Peacey, V. (2009) *Signing on and stepping up? Single parents' experience of welfare reform*, London: Gingerbread.

Pearson, C. (2000) 'Money talks? Competing discourses in the implementation of direct payments', *Critical Social Policy*, vol 20, no 4, pp 459-77.

Peck, J. (2001) 'Neoliberalising states: thin policies/hard outcomes', *Progress in Human Geography*, vol 25, no 3, pp 445-55.

Peck, J. and Tickell, A. (2002) 'Neoliberalizing space', *Antipode*, vol 34, no 3, pp 380-404.

Perera, S. and Mamode, N. (2011) 'South Asian patients awaiting organ transplantation in the UK', *Nephrology Dialysis and Transplantation*, vol 26, no 4, pp 1380-4.

Perkins, D. (2007) 'Improving employment participation for welfare recipients experiencing severe personal barriers', *Social Policy and Society*, vol 7, no 1, pp 13-26.

Phelps, L. (2010) 'The problem isn't Housing Benefit, it's the lack of social housing', *Roof*, vol 35, no 4, p 35.

Phillips, R. and Harper-Jones, G. (2003) 'Whatever next? Education policy and New Labour: the first four years, 1997–2001', *British Educational Research Journal*, vol 29, no 1, pp 125-32.

Phoenix, J. (2002) 'In the name of protection: youth prostitution policy reforms in England and Wales', *Critical Social Policy*, vol 2, no 2, pp 353-75.

Phoenix, J. (2012) 'Sex work, sexual exploitations and consumerism', in K. Carrington, M. Ball, E. O'Brien and J. Tauri (eds) *Crime, justice and social democracy: International perspectives*, Basingstoke: Palgrave Macmillan.

Phoenix, J. and Oerton, S. (2005) *Illicit and illegal: Sex, regulation and social control*, Cullumpton: Willan.

Picking, C. (2000) 'Working in partnership with disabled people: new perspectives for professionals within the social model of disability', in J. Cooper (ed) *Law, rights and disability*, London: Jessica Kingsley Publishers, pp 11-32.

Piggott, L. and Grover, C. (2009) 'Retrenching Incapacity Benefit: Employment Support Allowance and paid work', *Social Policy and Society*, vol 8, no 2, pp 159-70.

Pitts, J. (2011) 'Mercenary territory: are youth gangs really a problem?', in B. Goldson (ed) *Youth in crisis? 'Gangs', territoriality and violence*, London: Routledge, pp 161-82.

Pleace, N., Teller, N. and Quilgars, D. (2011) *Social housing allocation and homelessness: European Observatory on Homelessness comparative studies on homelessness*, Brussels: European Observatory on Homelessness.

Plsek, P.E. and Greenhalgh, T. (2001) 'The challenge of complexity in health care', *British Medical Journal*, vol 323, no 7313, pp 625-8.

Porter, D. (2011) *Health citizenship: Essays in social medicine and biomedical politics: Perspectives in medical humanities* [online]. San Francisco, CA: UC Medical Humanities Consortium, www.escholarship.org/uc/item/9ww2j8q1

Powell, M. (ed) (2002) *The Third Way in British social policy*, Bristol: The Policy Press.

Power, A. (2012) *The 'Big Society' and concentrated neighbourhood problems*, London: British Academy.

Power, A. and Tunstall, R. (1997) *Dangerous disorder: Riots and violent disturbances in thirteen areas of Britain, 1991-1992*, York: Joseph Rowntree Foundation.

Power, S. and Whitty, G. (1999) 'New Labour's education policy: First, Second or Third Way?', *Journal of Education Policy*, vol 14, no 5, pp 535-46.

Power, S. and Whitty, G. (2006) 'Education and the middle class: a complex but crucial case for the sociology of education', in H. Lauder, P. Brown, J. Dillaabough and A.H. Halsey (eds) *Education, globalization and social change*, Oxford: Oxford University Press, pp 446-53.

PPPOnline (People, Place & Policy Online) (2011) *Prospects for a Big Society*, P. Wells (ed), special issue, vol 5, no 2.

Prabhakar, R. (2010) 'Nudge, nudge, say no more', *The Guardian* [online], 9 March, www.guardianpublic.co.uk/nudge-beahavioural-economics-osborne-prabhakar

Prideaux, S. (2005) *Not so New Labour: A sociological critique of New Labour's policy and practice*, Bristol: The Policy Press.

Priestley, M. (1999) *Community care or independent living*, Cambridge: Polity Press.

Prior, D. (2005) 'Civil renewal and community safety: virtuous policy spiral or dynamic of exclusion?', *Social Policy and Society*, vol 4, no 4, pp 357-67.

Public Libraries News (2012) *Surrey chooses volunteers over paid staff at the same cost* [online], www.publiclibrariesnews.com/2012/07/surrey-chooses-volunteers-over-paid-staff-at-the-same-cost.html

Puffett, N. (2010) 'Early intervention grant represents 11% funding cut', *Children and Young People Now* [online], 13 December, www.cypnow.co.uk/cyp/news/1044636/early-intervention-grant-represents-funding-cut

Puttick, K. (2012) '"21st century welfare" and the wage-work-welfare bargain', *Industrial Law Journal*, vol 41, no 1, pp 122-31.

Raco, M. (2005) 'Sustainable development, rolled-out neoliberalism and sustainable communities', *Antipode*, vol 37, no 2, pp 324-47.

Raco, M. and Flint, J. (2001) 'Communities, places and institutional relations: assessing the role of area-based community representation in local governance', *Political Geography*, vol 20, no 5, pp 585-612.

Ramesh, R. (2012a) 'Only 3.5% of people referred to work programme find long-term jobs', *The Guardian* [online], 27 November, www.guardian.co.uk/politics/2012/nov/27/work-programme-long-term-jobs

Ramesh, R. (2012b) 'Iain Duncan Smith sets out new welfare agenda: blaming poverty on the poor', *The Guardian* [online], 14 June, www.guardian.co.uk/society/2012/jun/14/child-poverty-iain-duncan-smith

Ramesh, R. (2012c) 'Homeless families in B&B accommodation up by 44%', *The Guardian* [online], 17 September, www.guardian.co.uk/society/2012/sep/17/homeless-families-bed-and-breakfast

Randhawa, G. (2011) *Achieving equality in organ donation and transplantation in the UK: Challenges and solutions*, London: Race Equality Foundation [online], www.better-health.org.uk/briefings/achieving-equality-organ-donation-and-transplantation-uk-challenges-and-solutions

Ravetz, A. (2008) 'Is the government trying to abolish illness?', *New Statesman*, 5 May, vol 137, no 4895, pp 26-8.

Refugee Council (2011) *Asylum statistics 2011*, London: Refugee Council.

Reynolds, S. and Muggeridge, H. (2008) *Remote controls: How UK border controls are endangering the lives of refugees*, London: Refugee Council.

Richards, A. (2011) 'The problem with "radicalisation": the remit of "Prevent" and the need to refocus on terrorism in the UK', *International Affairs*, vol 87, no 1, pp 143-52.

Riddell, S., Edward, S., Weedon, E. and Ahlgren, L. (2010) *Disability, skills and employment: A review of recent statistics and literature on policy and initiatives*, Manchester: Equality and Human Rights Commission.

Ridge, T. (2007) 'It's a family affair: low income children's perspectives on maternal work', *Journal of Social Policy*, vol 36, no 3, pp 399-416.

Ridge, T. and Millar, J. (2011) 'Following families: working lone-mother families and their children', *Social Policy and Administration*, vol 45, no 1, pp 85-97.

Robinson, D. (2010) 'New immigrants and migrants in social housing in Britain: discursive themes and lived realities', *Policy & Politics*, vol 38, no 1, pp 57-77.

Robinson, D. (2012) 'Social housing in England: testing the logics of reform', *Urban Studies* [online], http://usj.sagepub.com/content/early/2012/10/12/0042098012462611

Rochdale Borough Safeguarding Children Board (2012) *Review of multi-agency responses to the sexual exploitation of children*, Rochdale: Rochdale Borough Safeguarding Children Board.

Roderick, P., Hollinshead, J., O'Donoghue, D., Matthews, B., Beard, C., Parker, S. and Snook, M. (2011) *Health inequalities and chronic kidney disease in adults* [online], www.kidneycare.nhs.uk/document.php?o=465

Rodger, J. (2008) *Anti-social behaviour and welfare in a de-civilised society*, Cullompton: Willan.

Rose, N. (1999) *Powers of freedom: Reframing political thought*, Cambridge: Cambridge University Press.

Rose, N. (2000) 'Community, citizenship and the Third Way', *American Behavioural Scientist*, vol 43, no 9, pp 1395-411.

Roudot-Thoraval, F., Romano, P., Spaak, F., Houssin, D. and Durand-Zaleski, I. (2003) 'Geographic disparities in access to organ transplant in France', *Transplantation*, vol 76, no 9, pp 1385-8.

Roulstone, A. (2000) 'Disability, dependency and the New Deal for Disabled People', *Disability and Society*, vol 15, no 3, pp 427-43.

Roulstone, A. (2011) 'Disabled people', in N. Yeates, T. Haux, R. Jawad and M. Kilkey (eds) *In defence of welfare: The impacts of the spending review*, London: Social Policy Association, pp 25-7.

Roulstone, A., Thomas, P. and Balderson, S. (2011) 'Between hate and vulnerability: unpacking the British criminal justice system's construction of disablist hate crime', *Disability and Society*, vol 26, no 3, pp 351-64.

RSA (Royal Society of Arts) (2010) *Connected communities: How social networks power and sustain the Big Society*, London: RSA.

Rudge C., Fuggle, S.V. and Burbidge, K.M. (2003) 'Geographic disparities in access to organ transplantation in the United Kingdom', *Transplantation*, vol 76, no 9, pp 1395-8.

Rudge C., Johnson, R.J., Fuggle, S.V. and Forsythe, J.L. (2007) 'Renal transplantation in the United Kingdom for patients from ethnic minorities', *Transplantation*, vol 83, no 9, pp 1169-73.

Rutter, J. and Latorre, M. (2009) *Social housing allocation and immigrant communities* [online], London: Equality and Human Rights Commission, www.equalityhumanrights.com/uploaded_files/ehrc_report_-_social_housing_allocation_and_immigrant_communities.pdf

Ryan, M. (1999) 'Penal policy-making towards the millennium: elites and populists; New Labour and the new criminology', *International Journal of the Sociology of Law*, vol 27, no 1, pp 1-22.

Sales, R. (2002) 'The deserving and the undeserving? Refugees, asylum seekers and welfare in Britain', *Critical Social Policy*, vol 22, no 3, pp 456-78.

Sambrook, C. (2013) 'Another G4S scandal: UK's privatised asylum housing market is falling apart', *OpenDemocracy*, 19 March, www.opendemocracy.net/ourkingdom/clare-sambrook

Sarewitz, D., Pielke, R. Jr and Keykhah, M. (2003) 'Vulnerability and risk: some thoughts from a political and policy perspective', *Risk Analysis*, vol 23, no 4, pp 805-10.

Saugeres, L. (2000) 'Of tidy gardens and clean houses: housing officers as agents of social control', *Geoforum*, vol 31 no 4, pp 587-99.

Schiller, A., de Sherbinin, A., Hsieh, W-H. and Pulsipher, A. (2001) 'The vulnerability of global cities to climate hazards', paper presented at the Open Meeting of the Human Dimensions of Global Environmental Change Research Community, Rio de Janeiro, October.

Schmidt, H. (2007) 'Patients' charters and health responsibilities', *British Medical Journal*, vol 335, no 7631, pp 1187-9.

Schmidt, H. (2009) 'Just health responsibility', *Journal of Medical Ethics*, vol 35, no 1, pp 21-6.

Schnellenbach, J. (2012) 'Nudges and norms: on the political economy of soft paternalism', *European Journal of Political Economy*, vol 28, no 2, pp 266-77.

Schuster, L. (2011) 'Dublin II and Eurodac: the (un)intended consequences?', *Gender, Place and Culture*, vol 18, no 3, pp 401-16.

Science and Technology Select Committee (2011) *Behaviour change report*, London: HMSO.

Scoular, J. and O'Neill, M. (2007) 'Regulating prostitution: social inclusion, responsibilization and the politics of prostitution reform', *British Journal of Criminology*, vol 47, pp 764-78.

Scraton, P. (ed) (1997) *Childhood in crisis*, London: UCL Press.

Seddon, T. (2006) 'Drugs, crime and social exclusion: social context and social theory in British drugs-crime research', *British Journal of Criminology*, vol 46, no 4, pp 680-703.

SEU (Social Exclusion Unit) (1998) *Bringing Britain together: A national strategy for neighbourhood renewal*, London: HMSO.

Shelter (2008a) *Immigration and housing* [online], http://england.shelter.org.uk/__data/assets/pdf_file/0009/132030/Factsheet_Immigration_and_housing.pdf

Shelter (2008b) *Worklessness and social housing: Policy briefing* [online], http://england.shelter.org.uk/__data/assets/pdf_file/0007/138580/Worklessness_and_social_housing_briefing.pdf

Shelter (2011) *Shelter response to CLG consultation: Implementing social housing reform: Directions to the Social Housing Regulator* [online], http://england.shelter.org.uk/__data/assets/pdf_file/0007/384577/09-11_CLG_directions_to_the_Social_Housing_Regulator.pdf

Shelter (2012a) *Who gets social housing?* [online], http://england.shelter.org.uk/campaigns/why_we_campaign/Improving_social_housing/who_gets_social_housing

Shelter (2012b) *Shelter response to Department for Communities and Local Government on high income social tenants: Pay to stay consultation paper* [online], http://england.shelter.org.uk/__data/assets/pdf_file/0009/585909/Shelter_response_to_DCLG_on_Pay_to_Stay_consultation_paper_-_September_2012.pdf

Shewan, D. and Dalgarno, P. (2005) 'Evidence for controlled heroin use? Low levels of negative health and social outcomes among non-treatment heroin users in Glasgow (Scotland)', *British Journal of Health Psychology*, vol 10, no 1, pp 33-48.

Shildrick, T. (2012) 'Low pay, no pay churning: the hidden story of work and worklessness', *Poverty*, vol 142, pp 6-9.

Shildrick, T., MacDonald, R., Webster, C. and Garthwaite, K. (2010) *The low pay, no pay cycle: Understanding recurrent poverty*, York: Joseph Rowntree Foundation.

Shoard, M. (1987) *This land is our land*, London: Paladin, Grafton Books.

Silverman, S. and Hajela, R. (2012) *Immigration detention in the UK*, Oxford: The Migration Observatory.

Siminoff, L.A. and Mercer, M.B. (2001) 'Public policy, public opinion, and consent for organ donation', *Cambridge Quarterly of Healthcare Ethics*, vol 10, no 4, pp 377-86.

Simmons, D. (2011) 'Universal Credit: universal panacea?', *Welfare Rights Bulletin 291*, vol 291, February.

Simon, B. (1960) *Studies in the history of education, 1780–1870*, London: Lawrence & Wishart.

Simon, C. and Ward, S. (2010) *Does every child matter? Understanding New Labour's social reform agenda*, Abingdon: Routledge.

Sinfield, A. (1978) 'Analyses in the social division of welfare', *Journal of Social Policy*, vol 7, no 2, pp 129-56.

Singh, D. (2012) *After the riots: The final report of the Riots, Communities and Victims Panel*, London: HMSO.

Singh, P. (2005) *No home, no job: Moving on from transitional spaces* [online], London: Off the Streets and into Work, www.equalworks.co.uk/resources/contentfiles/5638.pdf

Sirriyeh, A. (2010) 'Home journeys: im/mobilities in young refugee and asylum seeking women's negotiations of home', *Childhood*, vol 17, no 2, pp 197-211.

Sirriyeh, A. (2013a) *Inhabiting borders, routes home: Youth, gender, asylum*, Farnham: Ashgate.

Sirriyeh, A. (2013b) 'Burying asylum under the foundations of home', in N. Kapoor, J. Rhodes and V. Kalra (eds) *The state of race*, Basingstoke: Palgrave.

Skeggs, B. (2005) 'The making of class and gender through visualizing moral subject formation', *Sociology*, vol 39, no 5, pp 965-82.

Small, N. and Rhodes, P. (2000) *Too ill to talk? User involvement and palliative care*, London: Routledge.

Smith, K. (2012) 'Producing governable subjects: images of childhood old and new', *Childhood*, vol 19, no 1, pp 24-37.

Sointu, E. (2005) 'The rise of an ideal: tracing changing discourses of wellbeing', *Sociological Review*, vol 52, no 2, pp 255-74.

Sointu, E. (2006) 'Recognition and the creation of wellbeing', *Sociology*, vol 40, no 3, pp 493-510.

Somerville, P. (2005) 'Community governance and democracy', *Policy & Politics*, vol 33, no 1, pp 117-44.

South, N. (1999) 'Debating drugs and everyday life: normalization, prohibition and otherness', in N. South (ed) *Drugs: Cultures, controls and everyday life*, London: Sage Publications, pp 1-16.

Soysal, Y. (1994) *Limits of citizenship*, Chicago, IL: University of Chicago Press.

Spital, A. (1992) 'Mandated choice: the preferred solution to the organ shortage?', *Archives of Internal Medicine*, vol 152, no 12, pp 2421-4.

Squires, P. (2006) 'New Labour and the politics of antisocial behaviour', *Critical Social Policy*, vol 26, no 1, pp 144-68.

Squires, P. (ed) (2008) *ASBO nation: The criminalisation of nuisance*, Bristol: The Policy Press.

Standing, G. (2002) *Beyond the new paternalism: Basic security as equality*, London: Verso.

Standing, G. (2011a) 'Behavioural conditionality: why the nudges must be stopped – an opinion piece', *Journal of Poverty and Social Justice*, vol 19, no 1, pp 27-38.

Standing, G. (2011b) *The precariat: The new dangerous class*, London: Bloomsbury Academic.

Steiner, P. and Jacobs, A. (2008), 'Organ donation: an analytical typology', *Revue Française de Sociologie* [Supplement: An Annual English Selection], vol 49, pp 125-52.

Stepney, P., Lynch, R. and Jordan, B. (1999) 'Poverty, exclusion and New Labour', *Critical Social Policy*, vol 19, no 1, pp 109-27.

Stevens, A. (2007) 'When two dark figures collide: evidence and discourse on drug related crime', *Critical Social Policy*, vol 27, no 1, pp 77-99.

Stevens, A. (2011a) *Drugs, crime and public health: The political economy of drug policy*, London: Routledge.

Stevens, A. (2011b) 'Recovery through contradiction?', *Criminal Justice Matters*, vol 84, no 1, pp 20-1.

Stevens, A., Berto, D., Frick, U., Hunt, N., Kerschl, V., McSweeney, T., Oeuvray, K., Puppo, I., Santa Maria, A., Schaaf, S., Trinkl, B., Uchtenhagen, A. and Werdenich, W. (2006) 'The relationship between legal status, perceived pressure and motivation in treatment for drug dependence: results from a European study of quasi-compulsory treatment', *European Journal of Addiction Research*, vol 12, no 4, pp 197-209.

Stevens, A., Berto, D., Heckman, W., Kerschl, V., Oeuvray, K., Van Ooyen, M., Steffan, E. and Uchtenhagen, A. (2005) 'Quasi-compulsory treatment of drug dependent offenders: an international literature review', *Substance Use and Misuse*, vol 40, no 3, pp 269-83.

Stimson, G. (2000) 'Blair declares war: the unhealthy state of British drug policy', *International Journal of Drug Policy*, vol 11, no 4, pp 259-64.

Stone, J., Berrington, A. and Falkingham, J. (2011) 'The changing determinants of UK young adults' living arrangements', *Demographic Research*, vol 25, no 20, pp 629-66.

Stratton A. (2010) 'David Cameron aims to make happiness the new GDP', *The Guardian* [online], 15 November, www.guardian.co.uk/politics/2010/nov/14/david-cameron-wellbeing-inquiry

Sugden, R. (2009) 'On nudging: a review of Nudge: Improving Decisions about Health Wealth and Happiness by Richard H Thaler and Cass R Sunstein', *International Journal of the Economics of Business*, vol 16, no 3, pp 365-73.

Sumpter, S. (2011) 'The insidious government sources: betrayal of disabled people', *Disabled People Against Cuts (DPAC)*, 24 June, www.dpac.uk.net

Swyngedouw, E. (2005) 'Governance innovation and the citizen: the janus face of governance-beyond-the-state', *Urban Studies*, vol 42, no 11, pp 1991-2006.

Sykes, J.T. (1995) 'A second opinion', in D. Thursz, C. Nusberg and J. Prather (eds) *Empowering older people: An international approach*, London: Cassell, pp 7-50.

Tarr, A. and Finn, D. (2012) *Implementing Universal Credit: Will the reforms improve the service for users?*, York: Joseph Rowntree Foundation.

Taylor, D. (2011) 'Wellbeing and welfare: a psychosocial analysis of being well and doing well enough', *Journal of Social Policy*, vol 40, no 4, pp 777-94.

Taylor, M. (2003) *Public policy in the community*, Bristol: The Policy Press.

Taylor-Gooby, P. (2008) 'Assumptive worlds and images of agency: academic social policy in the twenty-first century?', *Social Policy and Society*, vol 7, no 3, pp 269-80.

Taylor-Gooby, P. (2011) 'The state and the economy', *The Guardian* [online], 15 March, www.guardian.co.uk/business/2011/mar/15/the-state-and-the-economy

Taylor-Gooby, P. and Stoker, G. (2010) 'The coalition programme: a new vision for Britain or politics as usual?', *The Political Quarterly*, vol 82, no 1, pp 4-15.

Thaler, R.H. and Sunstein, C.R. (2009) *Nudge: Improving decisions about health, wealth and happiness*, London: Penguin Books.

Thaler, R.H., Sunstein, C.R. and Balz, J.P. (2010) *Choice architecture*, SSRN Working Paper Series [online], http://papers.ssrn.com/sol3/papers.cfm?abstract_id=1583509&

Thatcher, M. (1993) *Margaret Thatcher: The Downing Street years, 1979-1990*, London: HarperCollins.

The Hardest Hit (2012) *The tipping point*, http://thehardesthit.wordpress.com

Theodore, N. (2007) 'New Labour at work: long term unemployment and the geography of opportunity', *Cambridge Journal of Economics*, vol 31, no 6, pp 927-39.

Titmuss, R.M. (1958) 'The social division of welfare: some reflections on the search for equity', in R. Titmuss (ed) *Essays on 'the welfare state'* (2nd edn), London: Allen & Unwin, pp 34-55.

Titmuss, R.M. (1967/2000) 'Universalism versus selection', in C. Pierson and F.G. Castles (eds) *The welfare state reader*, Cambridge: Polity Press, pp 40-8.

Titmuss, R.M. (1971) *The gift relationship: From human blood to social policy*, New York, NY: Random House.

Toynbee, P. (2010) 'This Conservative notion of a Universal Credit is a mirage', *The Guardian*, 5 October, p 29.

Toynbee, P. (2012) 'Families that want to work will suffer, not "scroungers"', *The Guardian*, 2 March, p 35.

Trades Union Congress (2008) *Hard work, hidden lives: The full report of the Commission on Vulnerable Employment* [online], London: TUC Commission on Vulnerable Employment, www.vulnerableworkers. org.uk/files/CoVE_full_report.pdf

Tsangarides, N. (2012) *The second torture: The immigration detention of torture survivors*, London: Medical Justice.

Tucker, J. (1966) *Honourable estates*, London: Gollancz.

Tunstall, R. (2011) *Social housing and social exclusion 2000-2011*, London: Centre for Analysis of Social Exclusion.

Turn2us (2012) *Read between the lines: Confronting the myths about the benefits system*, London: Elizabeth FinnCare, www.turn2us.org.uk/ pdf/Mythbusting.pdf

Turner, B. (2006) *Vulnerability and human rights*, Pennsylvania, PA: Pennsylvania State University Press.

Twivy, P. (2012) 'Why Cameron's Big Society failed', *The Guardian*, 14 November, p 40.

UKBA (UK Border Agency) (2010) *Review into ending the detention of children for immigration purposes*, London: Home Office.

UKDPC (UK Drug Policy Commission) (2008) *Working towards recovery: Getting problem drug users into jobs*, London: UKDPC.

UKDPC (2012) *Charting new waters: Delivering drug policy at a time of radical reform and financial austerity*, London: UKDP.

UPIAS (Union of the Physically Impaired Against Segregation) (1976) *Fundamental principles of disability*, London: UPIAS.

Van Ham, M. and Manley, D. (2012) *Segregation, choice based letting and social housing: How housing policy can affect the segregation process* [online], www.econstor.eu/bitstream/10419/58838/1/71551363X.pdf

Van Leiden, H.A., Jansen, N.E., Haase-Kromwijk, B.J. and Hoitsma, A.J. (2010) 'Higher refusal rates for organ donation among older potential donors in the Netherlands: impact of the donor register and relatives', *Transplantation*, vol 90, no 6, pp 677-82.

Vine, S. (2013) 'Our justice system is being turned into Profit plc', *The Guardian*, Comment and debate, 1 April, p 26.

Wacquant, L. (2008) *Urban outcasts: A comparative sociology of advanced marginality*, Cambridge: Polity Press.

Wacquant, L. (2009) *Punishing the poor: The neoliberal government of social insecurity*, Durham, NC and London: Duke University Press [English language edition].

Waddell, G. and Burton, K. (2006) *Is work good for your health and wellbeing? A review of the literature*, London: The Stationery Office.

Wade, J., Sirriyeh, A., Kohli, R. and Simmonds, J. (2012) *Fostering unaccompanied asylum seeking young people*, London: British Association of Adoption and Fostering.

Waiton, S. (2008) *The politics of anti-social behaviour: Amoral panics*, Abingdon: Routledge.

Walklate, S. (2012) 'Response 2: can the Big Society listen to gendered voices?', *Criminology and Criminal Justice*, vol 12, no 5, pp 495-9.

Wallace, A. (2007) '"We've had nothing for so long that we don't know what to ask for": New Deal for Communities and the regeneration of socially excluded terrain', *Social Policy and Society*, vol 6, no 1, pp 1-12.

Wallace, A. (2010a) *Remaking community? New Labour and the governance of poor neighbourhoods*, Farnham: Ashgate.

Wallace, A. (2010b) 'New neighbourhoods, new citizens? Challenging "community" as a framework for social and moral regeneration under New Labour in the UK', *International Journal for Urban and Regional Research*, vol 34, no 4, pp 805-19.

Warburton, H., Turnbull, P.J. and Hough, M. (2005) *Occasional and controlled heroin use: Not a problem?*, York: Joseph Rowntree Foundation.

Ward, C. (1974) *Tenants take over*, London: The Architectural Press.

Ward, D. (2000) 'Totem not token: groupwork as a vehicle for user participation', in H. Kemshell and R. Littlechild (eds) *User involvement and participation in social care: Research informing practice*, London: Jessica Kingsley Publishers, pp 45-64.

Ward, M. (2003) 'Entrepreneurial urbanism, state restructuring and civilising "new" East Manchester', *Area*, vol 35, no 2, pp 116-27.

Warner, J. (2008) 'Community care, risk and the shifting locus of danger and vulnerability in mental health', in A. Peterson and I. Wilkinson (eds) *Health, risk and vulnerability*, London: Routledge, pp 30-48.

Warnes, A.M., Crane, M. and Coward, S. (2010) 'Coping on marginal incomes when first re-housed: single homeless people in England', *European Journal of Homelessness*, vol 4, pp 65-87.

Warren, J. (2005) 'Disabled people, the state and employment: historical lessons and welfare policy', in A. Roulstone and C. Barnes (eds) *Working futures? Disabled people, policy and social inclusion*, Bristol: The Policy Press.

Watt, P. (2006) 'Respectability, roughness and "race": neighbourhood place images and the making of working-class social distinctions in London', *International Journal of Urban and Regional Research*, vol 30, no 4, pp 776-97.

Watt, P. and Wallace, A. (forthcoming) 'Why can't we have them [posh houses]? Housing redevelopment and community tensions in London and Salford', in A. Deboulet and C. Lelévrier (eds) *Rénovation urbaine en Europe: Quelles pratiques? Quels effets?*, Rennes, France: University of Rennes Press.

Watts, M.J. and Bohle, H.G. (1993) 'The space of vulnerability: the causal structure of hunger and famine', *Progress in Human Geography*, vol 17, no 1, pp 43-67.

Webster, C. (2007) 'Drug treatment', in M. Simpson, T. Shildrick and R. MacDonald (eds) *Drugs in Britain: Supply, consumption and control*, Basingstoke: Macmillan.

Wells, P. (2010) 'A nudge one way, a nudge the other: libertarian paternalism as political strategy', *People, Place & Policy Online*, vol 4, no 3, pp 111-18.

Welshman, J. (2013) '*Troubled Families': The lessons of history, 1880–2012*, History & Policy research paper, London: History & Policy, www.historyandpolicy.org/papers/policy-paper-136.html

Whelan, R. (ed) (1998) *Octavia Hill and the social housing debate: Essays and letters by Octavia Hill*, London: IEA Health and Welfare Unit.

Whitty, G. (2002) *Making sense of education policy*, London: Sage Publications.

Williams, F. (2012a) 'Care relations and public policy: social justice claims and social investment frames', *Families, Relationships and Societies*, vol 1, no 1, pp 101-17.

Williams, F. (2012b) Public lecture 'Transforming social policy: an international colloquium in honour of the work of Emeritus Professor Fiona Williams OBE', Leeds, 29 June.

Wilshaw, M. (2012) *The report of HM Chief Inspector of Education, Children's Services and Skills 2011–12*, London: HMSO.

Wincup, E. (2011) 'Carrots and sticks: problem drug users and welfare reform', *Criminal Justice Matters*, vol 84, no 1, pp 22-3.

Wincup, E. (2013) *Understanding crime and social policy*, Bristol: The Policy Press.

Wintour, P. (2011) '£5bn back-to-work scheme targets those on benefits', *The Guardian*, 1 April, p 13.

Wintour, P. (2012) 'Cameron backs plan to abolish social housing rent subsidy for high earners', *The Guardian* [online], 19 May, www.guardian.co.uk/society/2012/may/19/social-housing-income-cap-shapps

Wishart, G. (2003) 'The sexual abuse of people with learning difficulties: do we need a social model approach to vulnerability?', *The Journal of Adult Protection*, vol 5, no 3, pp 14-27.

Wolfenden, J. (1957) *Report of the Committee on Homosexual Offences and Prostitution*, London: HMSO.

Women's Budget Group (2010) *The impact on women of the coalition spending review 2010*, London: Women's Budget Group.

Wood, C. and Grant, E. (2011) *Tracking the lives of disabled families through the cuts … destination unknown*, London: Demos.

Wootton, B., assisted by Seal, V. and Chambers, R. (1959) *Social science and social pathology*, London: George Allen & Unwin.

Work and Pensions Committee (2011) *The role of Incapacity Benefit assessment in helping claimants into employment*, London: Work and Pensions Committee, www.parliament.uk/business/committees/a-z/commons-select/work-and-pensions-committee/publications/

Work and Pensions Committee (2012) *Universal Credit implementation: Meeting the needs of vulnerable claimants*, London: Work and Pensions Committee, www.parliament.uk/business/committees/a-z/commons-select/work-and-pensions-committee/publications/

Wright, S. (2009) 'Welfare to work', in J. Millar (ed) *Understanding social security: Issues for policy and practice* (2nd edn), Bristol: The Policy Press, pp 193-212.

Wright, S. (2012) 'Welfare-to-work, agency and personal responsibility', *Journal of Social Policy*, vol 41, no 2, pp 309-28.

Wrigley, T. (2007) 'Rethinking education in an era of globalisation', *Journal for Critical Education Policy Studies* [online], vol 5, no 2, www.jceps.com/print.php?articleID=95

Wyness, M. (2000) *Contesting childhood:* London: Falmer Press.

Yeung, K. (2012) 'Nudge as fudge', *The Modern Law Review*, vol 75, no 1, pp 122-48.

Young, J. (2004) 'Voodoo criminology and the numbers game', in J. Ferrell, K. Hayward, W. Morrison and M. Presdee (eds) *Cultural criminology unleashed*, London: Glass House Press, pp 13-28.

Young, K. and Kramer, J. (1978) *Strategy and conflict in metropolitan housing: Suburbia versus the Greater London Council 1965-75*, London: Heinemann.

Youth Justice Board (2006) *Asset*, London: Youth Justice Board.

Index